"Linda Marks writes with clarity and intelligence of the wounded capacity to love at the heart of the painful disconnection between men and women. This book offers a compelling and heartfelt invitation and pathway to healing this wound."
— Janet Surrey, PH.D.
Gender Relations Project, The Stone Center, Wellesley College

"This book beautifully evokes and then analyzes what Linda Marks calls 'the cultural heart wound' that pervades our common existence today. Linda gently draws us down from our detached mind-selves into the common longings of our lonely hearts, reveals to us the legacy of trauma and fear of the Other that makes it so difficult to fully connect in a spirit of love and compassion, and offers her wisdom as a therapist and as a person to help us heal each other to become fully embodied spiritual/sensual presences who can begin to fill the unnecessary cultural void that today everywhere separates us."
— Peter Gabel
President Emeritus and Director of the Institute for Spirituality and Politics, New College of California, Associate Editor of Tikkun magazine and Author, The Bank Teller and Other Essays on the Politics of Meaning

"Linda Marks expertly weaves together a coherent discourse on an age-old human drama and provides the reader with some extraordinarily valuable insights and tools for re-scripting this human drama. This book makes a very important contribution in serving as a guide for how to deal with one of the central issues for humanity's next evolutionary journey."
— Carroy U. Ferguson, PH.D.
Professor, University of Massachusetts-Boston Associate Editor, Journal of Humanistic Psychology

"In this courageous and insightful book, Linda Marks exposes how both males and females suffer unrecognized heart wounds as a by-product of assuming our proscribed gender roles. With expert guidance and many meaningful examples we are taken step by step to discover the path to our own wholeness and the road to understanding and supporting our partner's healing so that we may reclaim our most precious gift in life — loving, enduring relationships with those we truly love. This is an important book that is a must read for those in search of lasting happiness."
— Linda G. Russek, PH.D.
Co-Author, The Living Energy Universe President and Director, The Heart Science Foundation

"Whether your relationships are floundering or simply need fine-tuning and revitalization, **Healing the War Between the Genders** provides explanations and tools to help create more meaningful, fulfilling and intimate partnerships. Now I understand why my first marriage was often a battlefield and know how to enhance my current partnership into its fullest form — a soul-centered relationship. Linda Marks speaks not only from years of professional experience, but from her own heart — and it shows in this fine book."
— David Heitmiller
Author, Getting A Life

Other Books by Linda Marks:

LIVING WITH VISION:

RECLAIMING THE POWER OF THE HEART

THE EMOTIONAL-KINESTHETIC

PSYCHOTHERAPY STUDY GUIDE

Healing the War Between the Genders:

The Power of the

Soul-Centered Relationship

by Linda Marks

Healing the War Between the Genders: The Power of the Soul-Centered Relationship

Library of Congress Cataloging-in-Publication Data

Marks, Linda, 1958 -
    Healing the war between the genders: the power of the soul-centered
    relationship / by Linda Marks
— 1st ed.
        p. cm
    Bibliography: p.
    Includes index.
    ISBN 0-9744522-0-3
        1. Psychology 2. Interpersonal Relationships. I. Title.

Designer/Cover Illustration: Diane Menyuk, BlackCat Studio, Inc.
Printer: Booksjustbooks.com

Library of Congress Control Number: 2003111263

Requests for permission to use or make copies of any part of this work should
be sent to:
LSMHEART@aol.com or linda@healingheartpower.com or
3 Central Avenue, Newton, MA 02460

Published by HeartPower Press

For ordering information, go to http://www.heartpowerpress.com
or call 1-617-965-7846 or
write HeartPower Press,
3 Central Avenue, Newton, MA 02460.

First Edition

Dedication

J dedicate this book to my son Alexander,
and to all the children of his generation.

May those of us who are adults of all ages work together

to heal our individual and collective hearts

so that we may create a world that recognizes

the importance of soul-centered relating and

develops sustainable ways of living

rooted in the power of the heart.

Acknowledgements

It takes a village to write a book, and I am very grateful for the village that supported the evolution of this book over the two plus years it took from inception to completion. First to thank is my friend, colleague and soul-sister, Brenda Bush, who encouraged me to write a book about the cultural heart wound that afflicts us all, and in particular, the wound to the male heart. It was Brenda's spirit that gently sparked me to embark on the journey of book creation.

In the early days of the book's unfolding, Mark McDonough emerged as my "writer's muse," providing dialogue and feedback on the male and female heart wounds. Rick Charnes, Craig Moore and Jeff Weissglass were also important sounding boards and participants in the early days of this book. I am very grateful to Tracy MacNab for all the conversations we had exploring what I had written and where the book needed to go next. Chip Baggett, John Dore, Peter Gabel, Richard Grossman, Sparrow Hart, Doug High, Dan Kindlon, Heyoka Merrifield, and Lloyd Williams all had valuable contributions to my formulation of the male heart wound and its impact on men, women, children and our culture as a whole.

Deborah Taj Anapol, Randy Brown, Kevin Carty, Sam Cochran, Larry Cohen, Brian Crossman, Linda Cunningham, Robin Daiell, Molly Dwyer, Karen Engebretsen-Larash, Luke Entrup, Cuf Ferguson, Bob Francoeur, Megan Gleeson, Chellis Glendinning, Jerry Koch-Gonzalez, David Heitmiller, Tim Hodge, Loraine Hutchins, Yielbonzie Charles Johnson, Raven Kaldera, Will Keepins, Joseph Kramer, Miguel Liebovitz, Michael Meade, Rick Murphy, Michael Picucci, Bill Pounds, Stella Resnick, Lidia Rodrigues, Joel Rothschild, Nigel Russell, Brian Saper, Beth Sangree, Joanne Sewell, Peter Smith, Joe Snowdon, Annie Sprinkle, David Steinberg, and Joan Walker, to name just some of the many wonderful people who came forward to help shape this book, all contributed their reflections along the way.

Thanks to Stanley Knutson, Neal Katz, Tony Cifizzari and John Plugis. You have all been my teachers on this human journey.

Through a twist of fate, the book moved from its original focus on healing the male heart, to its current focus on healing the heart wounds in both men and women alike. My inner circle began to include women colleagues as well as men. Margaret Paul has been generous with feedback and support from the minute she became involved with this project. Kristi Boylan, Brenda Bush, Ani Colt, Susan Meeker-Lowry, Gina Ogden and Linda Russek all have contributed their editorial eyes to help refine the manuscript as well as their collegial love and wisdom.

A particular thanks to Carl Greisser, Char and Rich Tosi, and Bill Kauth from the Mankind Project, whose depth of experience and knowledge of the gender wars helped enrich many chapters in this book. Darkhawk, Luke Entrup, Jen Frisbee, Amy Hughes, Ludmilla Ivanovic, Peg Voss and Fia Wolf were some of the people who helped me create a context to explore healing the gender wars in the next generation.

Many men and women, some identified by name in the book, some who preferred to remain anonymous, came forward to volunteer for interviews for this book. To each of you who have contributed your thoughts, experiences and perspectives to this book, thank you.

I want to give thanks to my circle of colleagues at HeartPower Press, in particular, Diane Menyuk, whose graphic design skills shine from cover to cover and all pages in between. Matt Danielson helped me sort through the printer jungle to find Booksjustbooks.com, who printed this book.

I want to thank friends and acquaintances in the HAI Northeast Community, the Boston Area Sexuality and Spirituality Network, and Polyboston for providing stories and experiences of being a man, a woman and a human being in this culture. I want to thank my clients, students, and group participants for all the ways you have touched and inspired me as you have done your inner healing and evolving work.

A very special thanks to Carol Bedrosian and Spirit of Change magazine, where for many years I had a forum to express and develop my ideas and reach many people writing from the heart to the heart. A deep thank you to Stan Dale, founder of the Human Awareness Institute and its Love, Intimacy and Sexuality workshops, and Janet Dale, who runs the HAI organization. This incredible work has been my personal touchstone for fifteen years.

Thanks to my son, Alexander, for his patience all the times Mommy was writing letters and e-mails during Scooby Doo, Yu-gi-oh or PBS kids shows. Thanks to my long-term friends Nancy Ballantyne and Rosalind Roseinmann for compassionately tolerating my immersion in writer's cave for months and years on end. And a particular thanks to Bob DeIulio, my long-term coach, supervisor, therapist and soul-mentor for his steadfast presence in my life and work. Bob has been a real taproot for a significant portion of my adult life.

And finally, I want to honor some of the four-leggeds who have also supported my life, spirit and heart. Angelo, my first feral cat, was a great teacher and soul-mate until his death in 1998. Querida, a wise, elegant and peace-promoting red tabby, stood by my side from her birth in 1986 til her death as I was completing the last phases of this book in July 2003. Bandit, my friend Tony's Maine timber wolf, taught me much about the deep capacity of the heart and the healing power of love until his death in 1999. Jenny, my childhood brown tabby cat, developed my awareness of spiritual communication and the journey of the soul as she walked beside me from 1973 – 1986. And thanks to Golden, our English lab puppy, Toss, Buddha, Alexis and Angel, our four cats who watch over me and Alexander from day to day.

Thanks to you, the reader, for picking up this book and reading it. I hope you take with you some seeds of change and that you can pass them on to others in your life's travels.

Table of Contents

MALE FOREWORD

I love authors who challenge our long-held beliefs no matter what they may be. Linda Marks is one of those special people. She is about to challenge your long-held beliefs about what you think you know about yourself and other human beings. She will offer you the opportunity to try on a new pair of eyes that will see through even lead-lined garbage that has been ruining millions of lives since the beginning of time. As a matter of fact, be prepared to be gently turned inside-out in a very thrilling exploration of your mind, heart, body and soul.

The minute I read the first page of Linda's manuscript, "I was hooked." I hope the same will happen to you.

Did you even realize that there was a war going on between the genders?

Now I consider myself a fairly intelligent human being. After all, I even have a doctorate in human sexuality and I've been leading workshops on Love, Intimacy and Sexuality for the past 35 years. I even started the first psychologically-oriented telephone talk-back radio show. And guess what? I did not know that there was a war going on between the genders. Skirmishes, yes. Battles, yes. All out war, never. Thank you, Linda. I can now see and hear that war very clearly.

So, you see, what Linda is shining her spotlight of truth on pretty much equals what Louis Pasteur discovered with microbes and bacteria.

Microbes, bacteria and gender have been in our face, so to speak, since the beginning of time. We just haven't been able to see them without the proper tools and inquiry.

Now, that the "lens of the soul" has been given to us and the map charted, so we know where and what to look for, a new era is being born.

Welcome to the era of the heart and soul. Welcome to the era where the head is used in the service of heart and soul and not as a divider or conqueror.

Welcome to an era where we consider each person's gender identity uniquely theirs, where we never ostracize anyone because of their gender orientation or preference. Welcome to a world where everyone relates soul to soul. Welcome to the world of Linda Marks. Enjoy!

— *Stan Dale*
Foster City, CA July 2003

FEMALE FOREWORD

Linda and I met through the wonderful connecting world of e-mail. She was familiar with my Inner Bonding work and wanted to know if I would give her feedback on a book she was writing. I told her I would be happy to participate in and support her creative process, so every couple of weeks over a period of months, I received an e-mail from Linda with a chapter to review. It was through this process that I've discovered the soul and brilliance of Linda Marks.

I've been exploring and counseling in the realm of relationships for the past 35 years. I've read most of what others have written and one of the things I want you to know is that this book offers many new and powerful perspectives and concepts that will greatly deepen your understanding of the relationship challenge. Linda knows what she is talking about. It is evident that her deep understanding and knowledge comes, not only from her training as a therapist, but also from her own personal experience of relationships.

I often tell my clients that relationships are the Ph.D. of personal and spiritual growth. Relationships offer us our most profound arena for unearthing the unhealed wounds within. I have the experience over and over of working with people who thought they were "healed" only to discover layers of woundedness upon entering a new relationship. It is this deep woundedness that Linda addresses in this wonderful book. She not only beautifully articulates the cultural heart wounds that lead to gender wars, but also she shows us pathways to healing.

Linda helps us move out of operating just from our head — our intellectual understanding — and into collaboration between head and heart, which leads to understanding each other on the soul level. Obviously, the more we understand each other and ourselves, the easier time we will have in resolving the inevitable conflicts that arise in relationships. This book creates the sense of community we need to heal the male and female heart wounds that create such a distance and power struggles between us.

Power struggles — this is what characterizes most relationships. One partner pulls for time, attention, validation, sex — with demands, anger, niceness, tears, explanations — and the other partner withdraws and resists to avoid being controlled. The desire to be in control to feel safe battles with the desire to avoid being controlled to feel safe. Our fears of rejection and our fears of engulfment — stemming from the deep heart wounds that Linda describes so well — create the gender wars that characterize most relationships today — whether heterosexual or homosexual. Since we all have both male and female within, these wars can be part of any relationship.

It is time for us to move out of these power struggles and into compassion and true partnership with ourselves and each other. This cannot happen on the level of the intellect alone — it can only happen through partnership between our head, heart and soul. It is a spiritual journey.

Linda leads us through this journey toward the inner and relationship integration that is essential at this time in our evolutionary history. It is essential that we as women open with compassion to our own heart wounds as well as the heart wounds of the men with whom we share this planet. Linda beautifully shows us how to address the traumatized heart within all of us so that instead of acting out of fear and woundedness, we begin to act from consciousness, caring, compassion.

It is not an accident that you picked up this book. The fact that you are about to read it means that you are ready to move out of your old way of relating and into a new partnership — a partnership of the heart and soul with yourself and others. I wish you well on your journey to wholeness!

— *Margaret Paul, Ph.D.*
Lamy, New Mexico August 2003

Introduction

I never expected to be living the life I am living. Instead of having a lifelong bond to a wonderful husband as I imagined as a little girl, I'm divorced. As a babyboomer, growing up in the 1960's, the family I envisioned looked a lot like Father Knows Best and Leave It to Beaver. My reality consists of juggling many pieces as a single mother, who had her first child and probably last child at thirty-seven. I may be a stay-at-home mom, but this means I work from home and rent out part of the house I own so I can make ends meet working only 15 – 20 hours a week.

I had imagined my husband protecting me and supporting me, so I could develop my professional and artist interests on the side for balance and fulfillment. In reality, I have been the primary economic provider for my entire adult life, including during my marriage to my son's dad. While feeling fundamentally female, I have been forced to play both nurturer and provider roles. Maybe I am the husband I always imagined I would marry, as well as the wife I always wanted to be. I just thought there would be two of us, not one.

I gladly am the primary physical custodian of my son, although, in today's world a divorced mom like me is not assured this role. I make my son's lunch, buy his clothes, arrange his playdates, sign him up for extracurricular classes and lessons and organize doctors' appointments. I am also financially responsible for his school, camp, athletic and general life expenses. His dad sees him more than most divorced dads see their children. Yet, my ex-husband contributes only a small amount financially to my son's worldly expenses. I alone must save and invest for my son to go to college.

I have been creative in my work, which has allowed me a vital expression of my female essence while "making it in a man's world." I created my own method of body psychotherapy, as an innovator in my professional field. I ran a training program for therapists out of my home for nearly a decade prior to the birth of my son. I cut my practice in half once my son arrived, and booked clients around his nursing schedule for over three years, in spite of a separation and divorce. I probably make the lowest income of my fellow classmates from the Sloan School of Management's Class of 1982.

To sum it up, I live an unconventional, "out-of-the box" lifestyle, one that may be typical for today's cultural creatives. It is a lifestyle I have crafted out of necessity. I want to be my son's mom. And I have to be much more. Has this experience made me more gender fluid or gender integrated? Perhaps. I feel grounded and capable to weather the winds of life. I am equally comfortable baking homemade apple pies and doing public speaking. The only drawback is that I juggle more pieces than I would ever wish for, and wonder how the little girl who believed in family and marriage became both man and woman by necessity more than choice.

My little girl's heart still wishes for marriage and family with a partner for life. She wants to be feminine and receptive. She wants to be loved and cherished. She would really like the opportunity to be taken care of by an adult male peer, just to see what it feels like. While I have lived on the frontlines of the breakdown of gender roles, and have suffered the casualties of the war between the genders, deep down inside I have yearned for a simpler role and a less complex life.

I count my blessings. I have fulfilling work, a wonderful son, great friends and peace in my heart. I may be more fortunate than many, since God gave me a deep well of passion, creativity, resilience and strength of heart. It's just that my life hasn't turned out the way I had hoped it would be. In fact, I could never have imagined this life that has become mine.

I do have some peers whose lives fit the fantasy picture better than mine. Yet, most of my friends have also wrestled with balancing work and family, with trading off money and meaning, with being possessed by their possessions and having a simpler life. And of course, there are my friends for whom the fantasy doesn't apply at all. I have friends who are single by choice. I have friends who are single more through the progression of fate. I have friends who are gay, lesbian, bisexual or transgendered. I have friends for whom none of the gender, sexuality or relational boxes fit at all.

What does it mean to be a man? What does it mean to be a woman? These are not easy questions to answer anymore. When I lead "Healing the War Between the Genders" workshops, initially, men and women still brainstorm attributes of the traditional gender roles. But, it doesn't take long for gender role confusion to creep in, and suddenly what men have had to do is now what women have to do. And what women have traditionally done becomes an attribute for men.

Gender role confusion moves beyond women and men relating to each other. The war between the genders transcends heterosexual relationships. It also bleeds into relationships between women and women and men and men. A woman I have known for many years called me recently, despairing over the breakdown of her marriage to her female partner of ten years. The birth of the couple's second child became the catalyst for relational deconstruction.

My friend, Lila, had her son, Jeremy, four years ago. Following Jeremy's birth, Lila's partner, Martha, played more of the maternal femme role to Lila's career-focused working woman. While Lila is very maternal herself, she felt more comfortable moving and shaking in the professional world. Martha was happy to pitch in and care for baby Jeremy. Lila pumped breast milk and Martha delivered it to Jeremy.

Things unraveled when Martha had her daughter, Sarah. Martha had a long and difficult labor, and emerged quiet vulnerable and shaken. While prior to giving birth to Sarah, Martha was the first to chime in, "It really doesn't matter who gives birth to the baby. We are both the child's parents," after going through the labor experience, her sentiments changed. Now when career-focused Lila remained career-focused, and new mother Martha needed mothering and tender-loving care herself, a partnership that once worked eroded.

Martha felt abandoned as Lila failed to respond to Martha's post-delivery vulnerability with empathy, compassion and tender loving care. Lila loved Sarah, but also kept focused on her high-powered career. These two women, who had prided themselves on the way they had worked things out both in the world and on the homefront, became embittered enemies. Fighting, tension and resentment replaced what once was love.

As Martha moved out of the home she bought with Lila prior to the birth of both children, she took with her baby Sarah. She did not have the energy to deal with Jeremy, who was now "Lila's child." Lila was horrified that this woman who once said there was no difference who gave birth to a couple's children now saw a difference cast in stone. Sarah was "her" child. The custody and property battles these two women are painfully facing illustrate that the energy of the gender wars touches all.

As we individually and collectively struggle to integrate our inner male and our inner female, we enter new and uncharted territory. We are living at the threshold of a tremendous evolutionary leap for humankind, yet we may not recognize it. Our lives are fast paced. We are inundated with a glut of information. Yet, in the words of Wayne Dyer, we are also suffering from a spiritual deficiency. We are being asked to look at gender, sexuality, spirituality and all our relationships from a deeper place — through the lens of the soul.

We have lost the energy of relationship consciousness in what Terry Real calls an "anti-relational, vulnerability despising culture." We need to develop a new template for relatedness that allows us to restore the intimacy, connection, purpose, trust and meaning to our lives that we all crave deep down inside. We need this both for our health and happiness, and also for our survival. We have suffered many casualties, inner and outer, as the war between the genders has raged on.

Our understanding of gender is needing to change from socially prescribed roles we perform to part of our essence, our identity, our sense of soul. Men and women both have masculine and feminine parts of themselves. The energy of gender operates at a different level than just defining gender roles. For those of us who grew up with the safety of socially prescribed gender boxes, their deconstruction can be frightening. How do we come to know who we are? The new territory is uncharted. If we don't have a clear sense of our own identity, how on earth do we relate to others, be they members of another gender or our own?

This gender identity confusion, mostly unarticulated and undefined, provides some of the backdrop for the gender wars.

My son is growing up with first hand experience of the gender wars. Perhaps this is how it is for more children than not today. This breaks my heart. Alexander is one of those deep, wise, brilliant, caring, sensitive souls being born into the world today. His parents separated when he was 2 3/4, and have yet to make peace in their personal gender war struggle. When parents cannot find on-going peace treaties and move beyond the battle ground, their children feel the pain and pay a deep price. When his father and I struggle, I can feel the ache inside his young soul. I feel for my son's position. I work to remedy it to the very best of my ability every day. Yet, often I am in tears over the complexity of this landscape. Four years of divorce therapy have barely taken the edge off of the tension. I am trying to navigate a peaceful and respectful path with my ex-husband, putting my son's interests first at all times. It often seems so futile. There are no roadmaps or easy answers.

Why is it so hard? Sometimes the issues my ex-husband and I wrestle with feel bigger than we are. Are we caught in the breakdown of traditional gender roles? Is our fight a reflection of the collective angst between men and women trying to navigate their way?

I was raised to believe that a woman is supposed to provide a stable home base for her children, oversee their emotional, social and academic development, and offer food, clothing and nurturance as gestures of motherly love. When I provide consistent rituals and structures for my son's daily life, I feel I am expressing some of the best feminine qualities I have to offer. The very reality of a custody structure and split time between two parents eradicates much of what I hold dear. While I do my best with what we have, the kind of lifestyle I want to offer my son is dramatically compromised.

What does it mean to be female? What does it mean to be male? How do we reconcile our inner yearnings with a changing set of social gender role demands? We have been wounded in the battle of the head and the heart. Gender role confusion reigns as we live with the breakdown of traditional gender roles and many of the life structures we have built upon their foundation. We are cut off from one another, from the rhythms of the natural world, and our own bodies. We have become isolated entities — the islands that no man or woman should even become.

The images we see of men and women are constantly changing. While the news used to offer stories of deadbeat dads, the range of today's fatherly images are more diverse. Traditional gender roles polarize and women earn the daily bread. At-home dads tend the homefront. Several decades ago, the women's movement fought for equal rights in the workplace. Today, men and women seem to be engaged in a new kind of battle for gender equality on the homefront. Many men want more time with their children. Some fathers resent their children's mothers' sense of entitlement to the primary caregiving role.

Men and women seem to be trapped in the next cycle of anger and oppression. But as we fight one another, we miss the sociocultural level. In the heat of the battle, we often forget that today's men and women did not create the structures that don't serve us today. We fight with one another rather than join together to work for the common good.

HEALING THE WAR BETWEEN THE GENDERS shows us that at the center of our current struggle, is a cultural heart wound. We experience the wound in male and female forms. I discuss the cultural heart wound and its expression in male and female hearts in the first few chapters of this book. **HEALING THE WAR BETWEEN THE GENDERS** helps us to understand that this is a wound with a purpose, part of an evolutionary trajectory we are being called to follow. The heart takes its lead from a spiritual dimension. As we heal our male and female hearts, we can build many bridges, establishing peace within ourselves and also in the world at large.

When I wrote **LIVING WITH VISION: RECLAIMING THE POWER OF THE HEART** in 1988, I spoke of humanity's evolutionary call to grow from adolescence to adulthood. In our adolescence, which I call the "thinking phase," a key developmental task is differentiation. We search to discover who we are, separate from nature and different than other people. Our individual and collective efforts to grow through our emotional and spiritual adolescence are evidenced in the self-esteem, personal growth, holistic health and new age movements. Are we not intimately familiar in this culture of self-help, searching for meaningful work, a sense of purpose in life and self-love, with the seemingly unending task of finding out and becoming who we really are?

Ironically, any good effort carried to an extreme has its negative consequences. In our search for a sense of self, we have become disconnected from our sense of the rest of life. We have forgotten the essential experience of interrelatedness and interdependence. We are now being asked, if not demanded, to bring our awareness and actions into greater balance.

In **LIVING WITH VISION**, I write, "In our evolution as a species we are being forced to rediscover our own nature as well as the nature of life. In our separateness, we have forgotten or denied essential pieces of ourselves. We have lost touch with the feminine and so, have lost touch with our source of creative power. As a society, we are connected to our producer, doer, the masculine side of our nature and are uncomfortable with the flow of life, the receptive, the feminine side. The Earth, the darkness, the heart and the flow of life are all feminine aspects."

As we are called to mature, we are being asked to integrate our unique sense of self with a sense of connection to the natural world and the other beings around us. This "conscious/compassionate" phase of human development is one of partnership, healing and collaboration between the inner male and the inner female, head and heart, men and women, and humans and the natural world. As we mature emotionally and spiritually, the nature of human relationships is being asked to move to a higher level of consciousness as well. This is what I mean by the soul-centered relationship.

In our adolescence, our relationships were built at the personality level, founded on gender role performance, including the differentiation of essential life tasks along gender lines to assure our mutual survival. As we have moved along the evolutionary trajectory, relationships are being asked to take on more depth. But we have not yet become aware of what is involved in building and sustaining these soul-centered relationships. While we may WANT to have depth, intimacy and connection in a relationship, the road towards co-creating it includes a path through what I call, "the shadowlands." The shadowlands is a place where relationships often get stuck.

The hardest thing about being lost in the dark is when we neither realize we are lost nor recognize that it is dark out. We suspect something isn't quite as it should be, but we can't put our finger on what ails us or identify where to begin to tackle the problem. One could argue both that relationships as a whole in this culture are stuck in the shadowlands, and that the fact that this is indeed our experience remains unarticulated. We want to make soul connections, but we don't know how to make soul-centered relating a way of life.

HEALING THE WAR BETWEEN THE GENDERS is an intimate companion and a guide... Healing our male and female hearts is not a task we embark on alone. Just as it takes a village to raise a child, it also takes a village to heal a wounded heart. We fight in isolation without realizing some of our battles are common and not unique to the individuals struggling in the confines of their home. We lack social forums to talk about how we have been hurt by our own gender, the other gender and the gender war within. Our personal relationships have been the only forum for this gender struggle. Many have broken under this weight.

Whole sustainable partnerships between men and women (and women and women and men and men) begin with healing the gender war within ourselves. We need to learn to create safe, sacred spaces where we can speak and listen from the heart to truly understand what it is like to live inside male and female skin. As we compassionately grasp our differences and unearth our common human traits, we can rewrite the script of gender relations. We can learn to walk side by side as well as on our own, interdependently. We can be both free and connected. We can both savor the world and cherish our homes. We can be guides and participants as the human species matures, changing the nature of relationships as we evolve emotionally and spiritually

This book provides tools for both men and women, working together and alone, to create safe, respectful contexts for healing our hearts, and collaborating on new, mutually respectful ways of relating soul to soul. I have woven together concepts that will offer new ways of thinking with stories about real people wrestling with the issues each chapter addresses. I have included visual diagrams and charts to help communicate key ideas. I have provided exercises you can do to work with the content of each chapter. These exercises include meditations, journaling questions and discussion questions. You can work with the exercises on your own. You can also do them with a partner, or discuss them in a group.

This book is written as a guide and a roadmap to help men and women make sense out of chaos, and to create new ways of being that will guide us into the soul-centered relationships we yearn for and deserve. I hope you find it to be supportive, helpful and even healing. I hope it will help you heal the male and female heart wounds within your own heart. I hope it will help you create more depth, meaning and connection in your life and with those you love most.

More than anything, I write this book from my heart to your heart. I hope that by the time my son reaches adulthood, he will have a much wider spectrum of possibility both for being a man and for forming a deep lifelong bond with his partner of choice. With time, patience and the heart's wisdom, we can find our way through the shadowlands into a new level of spiritual partnership, intimacy, mutuality and sustainable love. A world based on soul-centered relationships is a world deeply rooted in everlasting love.

Chapter 1

THE TRAUMATIZED HEART

*"New definitions of mind-body medicine are recognizing
that all forms of organization on the psychological, physical
and biological levels actually are expressions of information.
The transformations between mind and body are called,
according to health psychology definitions, information
transduction. The heart, though as yet unrecognized
as such, seems to be the star performer and mediator
in the mind-body communication drama."*

— Dorothy Mandel
"Spirit and Matter of the Heart"

In many ways, we are just beginning to understand the true nature of the heart and its function in the body. During the past 20 years that I have practiced heart-centered, body-centered, spiritual psychotherapy I have found myself being asked, often by men with technical backgrounds, the infamous question, "What do you DO?" As I would answer, telling them that I work with the heart, I would often be greeted with, "The heart is a mechanical pump. It goes pump, pump. There is no emotional and spiritual life to the heart. That is all metaphor."

I knew in my gut that there was more to the heart than just the mechanical pump. I could tangibly demonstrate that there was an energetic component to working with touch, the body and the heart. Yet, for many years I did not have the scientific data or language to show people that what I knew and could do clinically was indeed scientifically grounded.

In my travels, I met colleagues who were illustrating through their work, that the heart was multi-dimensional, and did indeed have an emotional and spiritual life. Linda Russek's research in the early 1990's showed that the EKG of one person's heart could be measured in the EEG of another person's brain.[1]

Another colleague, cardiologist Bruno Cortese, spoke of how heart transplant recipients would often experience a literal change of heart. After a heart transplant, not only would their health condition be remedied, but also their personality would incorporate aspects of the personality of the person whose heart they had received. The Institute of Heart Math in California has gathered a wide body of research that speaks to the energetic and neurological dimensions of the heart. Indeed, we have a "heartbrain," in addition to our cerebral brain, and it is a powerful force in all of our human experience.

THE POWER OF THE HEART

The heart is the first organ to form in the body. It is the organizing factor for physical formation, including brain formation. The heart contains extensive brain-like neural matter and has recently been classified as a gland because it produces its own hormone. The heart not only puts out its own balancing and regulating hormones, but also instantaneously communicates electromagnetic and chemical information to the rest of the body and to other bodies near it.[2]

"The heart can act as an internal pharmacy-dispensing and communicating what is needed where and when. Its rhythm and pulse can entrain all of the body's rhythms and cycles into coherent harmony and communicate many other types of vital information as well."[3] Each person's EKG pattern is as unique as their fingerprint. The wave variations in each "heartprint" contain information about the different organ systems and rhythms in the body. When two people touch, the heartwave of one has been seen to register in the brainwave of the other.

Research by the Institute of Heart Math[4] has shown that the heart is the most powerful generator of electromagnetic energy in the human body:

❦   The heart's electrical field is about 60 times greater in amplitude than the electrical activity generated by the brain

❦   The magnetic field produced by the heart is more than 5000 times greater in strength than the field generated by the brain

❦   The electromagnetic energy of the heart not only envelops every cell of human body, but also extends out in all directions in the space around us

❦   Our cardiac field touches those within 8 - 10 feet of where we are positioned (and perhaps in more subtle ways at greater distances)

❦   One person's heart signal can affect another's brainwaves, and heart-brain synchronization can occur between two people when they interact

❦   Research conducted at the Institute of HeartMath suggests that the heart's field is an important carrier of information

Our mental and emotional state impacts the quality of contact we offer to another person. When we touch one another with safe, respectful, loving intention, both physically and emotionally, we call into play the full healing power of the heart. The greater the "coherence," a sense that life is comprehensible, manageable and meaningful, one develops, the more sensitive one becomes to the subtle electromagnetic signals communicated by those around them.

In my experience working with groups, the combined impact of the interaction of the electromagnetic fields of all the group members' hearts creates a powerful space in which individuals can do deeper healing work than one-on-one. As one group member goes deeper and gets closer to their core, the others in the group feel the energetic vibration of this person's "heart opening" and are touched by it — energetically as well as emotionally.

The power of the heart may extend beyond healing moments to our genetic make-up. Dorothy Mandel writes, "Genetically, cells adapt to what they perceive their environment to be. Because an event experienced in the midst of a heart response will be perceived and interpreted very differently than an event experienced in the midst of a stress response, the heart can also powerfully affect genetic expression."

LOVE, NEGLECT AND THE ABILITY TO TAKE IN LOVE

Linda Russek, Ph.D. from the Human Energy Systems Lab at the University of Arizona did research exploring the relationship between one's perception of parental love or neglect and health in later life. In the 1950's, a Mastery of Stress Study was conducted at Harvard University with its then all-male student population. The study looked at the ability to cope with stress and adapt over time. Linda Russek conducted 35-year and 42-year follow-up studies along with her colleague, Gary Schwartz, Ph.D.

Bio/psycho/social/spiritual interviews were conducted with study participants. The results were quite conclusive. At the 35-year mark, only 25% of participants with high positive reflections of parental love had illness in contrast to 87% of those with low perceptions of parental love. Results at the 42 year mark were similar. The study concluded that the perception of parental love is an independent risk factor in illness and one that may influence other risk factors. For instance, the perception of love was independent of family history of disease, the subject's smoking history, the death and/or divorce of parents and the divorce history of the subject himself.

What was equally important was what Linda discovered about the relationship between love and neglect and the ability to take in love. Linda and Gary were aware that the electromagnetic field of the heart was the strongest field in the human body and that you can literally measure one person's heartbeat in another person's brainwaves even when they are not touching. They studied "interpersonal heart-brain registration" with their research subjects. In simple language, how open were the participants to recognize and receive love?

Linda Russek comments, "We discovered that those people, now in mid-life, who perceived their parents as loving, just and fair when in college, were more open to loving energy and were more able to receive my energy. There was more of an energy registration of my electrocardiogram in their brain, because they were not defended against receiving my love. In contrast, those participants who came from backgrounds they perceived as neglectful were more defended against receiving love."

"All disease today has been identified as having a lowered heart rate variability association," notes Linda. "That refers to the beat change in heart rate, particularly as it increases and decreases with each breath. So, people with a high heart rate variability have beat-to-beat changes that increase with inspiration and decrease with expiration. This is considered healthier. In essence, these people are more engaged in and connected with life. The flexibility of the heart's variability is what is healthy. This directly relates to a person's emotional capacity for love. A healthy heart has a lot of space to feel and process whatever emotion is necessary to be alive and present — to flow through all experience."

People who have a lowered beat-to-beat ratio, which is connected to most diseases, are less engaged and connected to life. People whose hearts are ill are crippled and limited in their ability to respond to and take in what is offered in life. Before they die, they have a heart that beats like a clock — rigidly. This is very dangerous.

A person whose heart is rigid has less space to feel experience in any moment or to process and output emotional experience. Their experience of relating hits a wall. There is a limit to the degree that person fully engages emotionally with themselves or someone else. The pain and stress of hitting the wall can be life threatening. While perhaps this is a chicken and egg situation, there is certainly a correlation between heart disease and defenses against love.

ENCOUNTERING THE TRAUMATIZED HEART

When I was 16-years-old, a stranger tried to rape and murder me. I was walking home one night from my job at Fenway Park in Boston, having taken public transportation home. As I passed the Brigham's restaurant where I had my second job, a stranger jumped out from the shadows and tried to strangle me. I tried to fight him with my physical strength, but he was 6'2." I was just a 5'6" teenage girl, and no matter how physically fit I was, I was outmatched.

I tried to fight him with my mind, telling him the legal implications of what he was doing. That just made him mad. As he dragged me into an alley and started beating me, I realized I was powerless. I prayed to the God I was never raised to believe in to help me save my life.

God said to me, "If you are going to live, you must agree to what I have put you on this earth to do. You must follow the mission you know deep down in your heart. You must come out of your introverted closet, use what you know and speak." I said yes to God and chose my life. I realized this was a turning point for me, and the commitment I had just made was very powerful. A moment later, a little voice in my heart said, "Tell this man you forgive him."

Without a thought or understanding of what forgiveness meant, I opened my mouth and spoke from my heart with deep sincerity, "I forgive you." This rageful stranger stopped beating me for a moment, almost in shock, and burst into tears.

"I don't want to be doing this," were his first words. I lay there in the alley on my back, naked, present to the moment, and in shock myself. I remained emotionally present to this man, who only the moment before was the perpetrator of violence towards me. He began to pour out his life story. The floodgates opened, and what a story he had to tell!

He had raped and murdered other women. If he ever was caught, he would put a gun to his head and take his life, he told me. This man was so broken-hearted and powerless. In his rage, he seized me not as a person, but as an object for his aggression. In doing so, he could have taken my life. And here, by a twist of fate, I was holding a heart space for him to release his pain! My heart began to ask who the victim really was.

Just as he was done catharting, he seized his hand into a fist, as though he was going to start beating me again. My stomach tightened with a knot of anticipation. God was with me, and a car came down the alley. The man grabbed his pants and ran away.

My friend Brenda once shared with me an image she had seen in her mind's eye. She saw a traumatized little boy sitting at the control panel for a nuclear bomb. This little boy had been briefed fully on the meaning of pressing the button, and all the horrible consequences that would result from such an action. He had been told in minute detail why it was important never to push that button. But because of the deadness in his own body and heart, all the words were like raindrops, falling beyond him, of no consequence. So he pushed the button, blew up the world, and even then didn't really understand the magnitude of what he had done.

DEFENDED AGAINST LOVE: THE TECTONIC HEART

In my body-centered psychotherapy practice, I have seen that there are some people who have experienced such deep and profound trauma, that the heart literally cuts off, numbs out and freezes, becoming essentially dead in relational matters. The trauma can be emotional and/or physical. A person whose heart is traumatized can be cold, cruel and careless in relating — untouched and untouchable in any lasting way.

In the presence of a skilled and devoted lover, a person with a traumatized heart may experience an intimate moment briefly. But the moment is soon forgotten and not integrated into their experience. They have no relational memory of the person who touched them. The moment is just that — an isolated moment. They are essentially defended against real, healthy, sustained and sustaining love.

For most of my life, I believed love would heal all. Through experience, I have learned the painful lesson that love can only heal when it is felt for what it is. The traumatized heart is like an iron soldier, protected by a tectonic plate. This tectonic armor protects the soldier from the energetic experience of love. The risk of vulnerability, intimacy and connection is too high and, therefore, must never be undertaken. And so, this person lives in an altered state of consciousness, dissociated from their emotional body, and, most likely, dissociated from their soul.

Some men and women with wounded hearts can handle a measured amount of intimacy. Their heart wound and the tectonic plate protecting it doesn't emerge until a deeper intimacy develops. One man I knew was quite aware that deepening intimacy brought him closer to his wounded heart. He told me, "I don't let anyone get too close to me. It hurts too much." His strategy was to always date two women. By splitting his time and his emotional/sexual energy, he ensured that no one would really touch his heart.

I watched a painful drama unfold as he found himself involved with a woman who truly loved him for who he was, with whom he felt connected, and who treated him with great care and respect. While at times he admitted that he really liked the attention, and for moments could appreciate her love and care, over time he found himself distancing himself and pushing her away. When he finally broke up with her, he told her she had brought him more joy than he had ever experienced. However, with the joy also came his pain. As his heart opened, the very parts of himself that he had succeeded at keeping buried for so long surfaced. He decided he would rather give up his joy than face his pain.

This man, ultimately, could not receive and integrate real, unconditional love. I found myself wondering why some people don't recognize or respond to even the purest, most patient, loving gestures. Why do loving gestures feel like threats to people who live with severely traumatized hearts?

FAMILIAR IS SAFE

Rollin McCraty from the Institute of HeartMath offers scientific data that helps explain the neurophysiology of a person with a traumatized heart. Our fear of change, our resistance to new experience, is literally wired into our bodies.

"We can get cut off at the heart, but the loop starts in the perceptual mechanisms in the brain," says Rollin. The amygdala is the part of the brain where our emotional memories are stored — literal patterns, literal circuitry. The amygdala looks for associations and pattern matches. Certain emotional patterns become familiar and, therefore, comfortable, even if the emotional pattern is a maladaptation. We can become comfortable with being cut off from our feelings or being fearful of having emotional relationships. We can become comfortable living with anxiety or guilt simply because living with anxiety or guilt is familiar."

"In the case of the traumatized heart, for a person who has been hurt in the past, not being emotionally open has become the familiar pattern. When any new person appears, all external sensory input to the brain, including hearing, sight and touch, is compared to the familiar pattern stored in the amygdala and related circuitry. A change from the familiar pattern we are used to triggers an emotional response. The brain tries to make changes to get our internal experience back to the familiar. Returning to the stable baseline feels good If we are not able to return the pattern back to the stable baseline, then it results in anxiety, fear and often projections into the future," says Rollin.

This helps explain why a person offering healthy, present love to a person who has been emotionally traumatized is perceived as a threat rather than a comfort. The unfamiliar experience of the healthy, loving person disturbs the maladaptive status quo that has been established in the traumatized person's neural circuitry. And the traumatized person's circuitry seeks to remove the discomfort of the unfamiliar healthy, loving person, and return to the comfort of its maladaptive but familiar status quo. Rollin's model explains what happened to my male friend I described earlier to a "T".

LEARNING ABOUT THE FERAL HUMAN

Perhaps you have seen street cats that walk through alleys, make their rounds from neighbor to neighbor or live wild without the food, comfort and shelter of a home. They are called "feral cats," abandoned to the streets or born to animals who were already abandoned to the streets.

One of my greatest teachers about the traumatized heart and healing was a feral cat. His name was Angelo. He had been my friend and teacher for seven years when he died in 1998. Angelo first entered my life one spring day as I looked out the window and saw a big, macho-looking, mostly white cat with splotches of gray tabby markings, standing in my driveway. Emaciated, dirty and ill, Angelo arrived at my doorstep struggling to survive.

In actuality, Angelo did not arrive on my doorstep at all. My doorstep and all it symbolized was too scary for an animal worn in the cruel and neglectful ways of the human world. Feral cats are neglected, kicked, screamed at, and left to fend for themselves without food, shelter or protection. Perhaps you can see why it took many months for Angelo to actually "arrive" at my doorstep.

Building a strong enough relationship with Angelo so he could allow me to open the door of my house to him, and then he could choose freely to walk through the door and eventually stay, took much time, patience and commitment. The process of creating this safe, loving rapport with a hurt, sick and rightfully distrustful animal taught me more about being a good therapist than any other training or experience I ever had.

Angelo, the first of seven feral cats I had the privilege of working with, was the gatekeeper to important insights into the nature of trauma, and physical, emotional and spiritual resilience. I came to see that the feral cat is not the only animal who walks the streets of life. Many of my clients have responded to the metaphor of the feral cat. Indeed, many of us feel like feral humans, walking the emotional streets of life.

THE EMOTIONAL LANDSCAPE OF THE FERAL ANIMAL

Feral animals are quite remarkable. They are alone, often starving and injured and incredibly creative in spite of it all. Without medical care, the injured animal limps its way around the territory it calls its own. Homeless, the feral finds makeshift shelters — a garage, a shed, a crawl space under the foundation of a house. Unprotected, the feral animal is quite vulnerable to the elements and exposed to the cruelest conditions. The average feral cat's lifespan is only three years. The average house cat's lifespan is 13 – 20 years. Against all odds, the will to live and the quest to survive are strong forces in the feral soul.

The emotional costs of such a lifestyle are very clear. A feral cat lives hypervigilantly. Being alert at all times is a prerequisite for survival. Anticipating any potential threat, the feral animal does not let any signal go unnoticed. Even the most subtle cue that is impalpable to the average human being is cause for attention.

A profound lack of safety underlies the feral experience. So does a deep mistrust for human beings. After all, humans have abandoned these animals or their ancestors, and have left them to fend for themselves without the means to survive. They run from even the possibility of human contact — darting through a driveway faster than the human eye can fix on his/her presence. The feral animal chooses safety over nourishment or shelter. Even if it is snowing outside, and s/he is starving to death, a feral animal will not risk contact with a well-meaning person who wishes to bring him/her in from the cold.

SPIRITUAL TRAUMA AND THE LOSS OF RESILIENCE

Whether human or feline, the body and spirit have a limited capacity to respond to trauma. All our experience is recorded and held in the body. In this sense, the body is both an emotional and spiritual vessel, which like all vessels, has a limit to its holding capacity. When we experience pain and trauma, our bodies have a capacity to hold, work with and heal this experience. Once we stress ourselves beyond this capacity, we overload our emotional, spiritual and physical circuits and burn out. When the pain and trauma we experience is neverending, repeated incessantly, or just too big, we exceed and damage our holding capacity.

I have found that if a person lives through one traumatic experience, there may be a spiritual strengthening as s/he moves through the healing process. When trauma is not isolated but recurrent, sometimes in subtle and insidious ways the spirit can be broken and, with it, our capacity for resilience.

Marlene is a woman who worked with me many years ago. She knows both the experience of trauma as a strengthening, spiritual turning point, and trauma as a degenerative process that compromises the lifeforce. Now 45, Marlene reflects back on her experience of surviving from an attempted rape as a teenager. "It was really a turning point — a time the power of God really came into my life. I wasn't raised with any religious background, so God did not really exist in my experience. Surviving this attack was a spiritual gift. I emerged internally stronger and more able to focus on meaningful pursuits in my life. I can say I found God through surviving the attack."

Later in her life, her resilience was shattered. A relationship with an alcoholic husband who was emotionally abusive, endless legal battles over the custody of her two children, and the struggle to make ends meet as a single parent with little family support eroded her spirit. If a challenge becomes too great with an absence of emotional, spiritual and often practical support, the spirit can start to collapse.

NORMALIZING EMOTIONAL NEGLECT

As I will discuss in Chapter 2, individually and collectively, we are suffering from a cultural heart wound. The feral experience of both cats and people is just one of many byproducts of this cultural heart wound.

In her book **THE CONTINUUM CONCEPT**, author Jean Liedloff reflects that for all but the last several hundred to one thousand years of life on this planet, we have lived in a more collective tribal society. In such a society, babies are born with cellular expectations of connectedness and relatedness with self, others and all of life. As infants, we expect others to be present to us and care for our emotional, physical and spiritual needs. In the indigenous society Jean Liedloff studied, a village did indeed participate in the raising of each child. An abundance of presence, holding, touch and emotional connection were part of this way of life. Both children and adults were skilled at being with babies and younger children because they had experienced presence, holding and emotional connection themselves as they grew and matured. Each generation passed on this gift to the next.

As we have moved farther away from tribal, village and community-based societies and into fragmented, disconnected nuclear family units or broken nuclear families, the way we care for babies and children has changed. Babies and young children require tremendous presence, energy and both emotional and physical stamina. To fully attend to the needs of a baby, a young child or even an adult who is really in touch with his/her feelings requires a quality of heartspace. Heartspace is characterized by caring attention, with respect for the emotional and physical experience of self and other. It arises in a slow, emotionally present, in-the-moment lifestyle, possible in the indigenous village Jean Liedloff studied. Neither the pace of our culture nor the priority placed on work and material acquisition supports or allows for this quality of heartspace. When we lack time to slow down and just be, or to give primary focus to our relationships, emotional neglect is normalized from the very start of life.

To compound the situation, our culture as a whole is very uncomfortable with emotions and sensual experience. When children are emotionally sensitive, they are often negatively judged for it. They are told they are too intense, too needy or too much. Rarely do children or adults get positive feedback for being in touch with their emotions and having the capability to express them. We learn it is not safe to show vulnerability. We learn through experience that when we are vulnerable, we will be judged, humiliated, hurt or rejected. We learn to fear our emotions, not honor them. In school, we develop intellectual intelligence, rarely considering emotional or somatic intelligence. Children develop into adults who lead from the head, ignore the body and protect the heart. Is it a surprise that heart disease is such a major health problem in our culture?

THE NARCISSISTIC HEART WOUND

The wound to heart and psyche that gets called narcissism occurs when a child's vulnerable and developing core sense of self is not seen or reflected back by the adults around him/her. Each child is a unique individual with special gifts and personal challenges. The child's psyche is multi-layered and both simple and complex. For any one part of the child to develop, that part needs to be seen, heard, understood and valued. Children develop and integrate the many different parts of themselves through mirroring — the experience of having an adult bear witness to who they are at an essential level and reflect it back.

Recently, I was talking with the dad of one of my son's friends who is both an artist and an art teacher. Todd was commenting that all children have the capacity to be artists. The key is having someone who can reach in and meet the child on the level at which they experience the world. I watched him do this with his 2-year-old daughter, Roma. She would draw a few lines, and he would draw a few lines in response. He would ask her what she was drawing, and she would say the legs of a doggie. He would then draw some more legs of the doggie in a similar style to hers. I could see Roma smile with delight as her dad engaged in this multi-layered, not always verbal, communication dance. Her spirit was being nourished and validated by the quality of attention she was receiving from her dad.

My heart felt warm as I watched Todd and Roma play. I could see Todd mirroring Roma's essence and Roma basking in the attention of her dad. Children need safe contexts like this to explore and express their core sense of self. Children need adults who are grounded in their own souls so they have the emotional and psychic space to be receptive to the individual child at any moment. Too often, parents relate to children from their own unmet needs, the undeveloped parts of themselves or their impatience and exhaustion.

When a parent's own woundedness and unmet needs are the predominant force in relating to a child, the child's core sense of self can be lost, broken or undeveloped. This wound to the core sense of self is the root of the narcissism. Narcissism may include a simultaneous trauma to the core sense of self and neglect/deprivation of the core self. Healthy mirroring, much like Todd and Roma at play, reinforces a child's developing sense of self. Narcissistic mirroring breaks down the boundaries of the developing self. Overly focused on his/her personal agenda, and oblivious to the child's emotional and spiritual needs, a narcissistically wounded parent may simultaneously squish and starve a child's spirit. The child's developing self may be lost, overshadowed or never activated.

Looking at the conditions necessary for a seed to germinate provides a useful metaphor for understanding the developing self. A seed is full of potential. It contains all the raw ingredients needed to grow into the full embodiment of whatever plant it has descended from. Under the proper conditions, the seed is sparked to life. When the proper conditions are lacking, the seed may never sprout. It may remain dormant and decompose. It may also sprout and then shrivel and die.

Healthy mirroring allows for germination of soul and spirit. Narcissistic faux mirroring damages, if not destroys, the potential to germinate one's sense of self. It also damages our ability to put down roots that support our development, stunting our ability to fully engage in life This creates emotional birth defects which are physically unexpressed but set emotional limits. These emotional birth defects stunt our capacity to be fully human and program us for failure in some ways.

NARCISSISM AND THE TRAUMATIZED HEART

The narcissistic defense can be understood as a natural response to trauma. In this case, the trauma is an interpersonal violation of the boundaries of the self. For a child, these boundaries may be fragile to start with. The narcissism-generating trauma includes elements of deprivation and neglect The heart simultaneously starves from deprivation of essential contact and dies of toxicity as it is force-fed by the narcissistic caregiver. The child's emotional metabolism is compromised. S/he wires in emotional starvation and toxicity as a way of life. With the narcissistic heart wound, a child is unable to take in the good and release the bad.

Children who are physically or sexually abused routinely create a fantasy world to defend against an unliveable reality. For survival, they dissociate, splitting the core self into a collection of disconnected parts. We experience narcissistic wounding both as our spiritually empty culture cannot support our deepest needs and as our narcissistically wounded parents pass on their wounding to the next generation. Left unhealed, the map is set for a future trail of tears. Seeds of darkness are sown for the wounded, their mates and their offspring. This is the polar opposite of the experience of the children Jean Liedloff wrote about in **THE CONTINUUM CONCEPT.**

The Traumatized Heart	The Vital Heart
reduced coherence — loss of sense that life is comprehensible, manageable and meaningful	high coherence — experiences life as comprehensible, manageable and meaningful
defended against love	open to love
untouchable or less touchable — emotionally and physically	touchable — emotionally and physically
rigid	flexible
limited self-expression	free self-expression
afraid of intimacy	welcomes intimacy
isolated and disconnected	well connected
tense and hypervigilant	relaxed and at peace

HEALING THE TRAUMATIZED HEART

When I first started to build a relationship with Angelo, the feral cat mentioned earlier in this chapter, he would not stay in my driveway long enough to even notice the food I had started to put out for him. For many months I let him be, as he expressed his sense of terror and kept his distance. It was a long while before he felt safe enough to check out the food I had provided. And for a while Angelo could not eat the food if I were watching. He needed me to leave the food outside at the bottom of the stairs, go inside, close the door and give him his space.

At first, I never knew if Angelo actually got the food. Over time, as rapport and trust built, he would let me watch him from my kitchen window. I knew we had made progress in our relationship when I could move the food from the bottom of the staircase to the top. I both rejoiced and felt gratitude when he allowed me to open the door and be with him as he ate.

To offer healing to a being with a traumatized heart, involves:

1. *Creating safety.* This is the core building block on which all other pieces lie. To create safety, one needs both to respect the unique needs and pacing of an individual being, and to cultivate a sense of internal spaciousness. When one is internally spacious, one has both the time and psychic attention to just be with another and no agenda other than honoring the being as s/he is.

2. *Offering presence.* Being present with no strings attached is paramount. Any offerings — food, shelter, emotional support, or touch — need to be made without any attachment to how they are received. When I cared for Angelo, I was not looking for appreciation or a particular response. I cared for him as a pure act, complete in itself. Respecting another's free will is essential. Some beings will simply choose not to make contact or connect.

3. *Managing your own psychic energy.* This skill involves a sensitivity to both how physically close or distant you are to another, and how you stand in relationship to the other emotionally and spiritually. Sometimes a person needs your energy to be pulled back in order to have space and safety. At other times, the person may need to feel the strength of your commitment to them, while also feeling your non-attachment to outcomes. Managing psychic closeness and distance is an art form.

4. *Touch with permission.* A lot of groundwork may need to be laid before it is safe to touch a heart-wounded person. Even though Angelo was starved for touch, and ultimately needed safe touch to soften and heal, I needed to establish safety and trust at other levels first. As Angelo was ready and felt safer with me, he would come closer. My first touch was greeted with a swat. In time, Angelo sought me out. For the longest time, I made sure to ask permission, making sure he was open to my touch. After a couple of years of this dance, Angelo chose to sleep on top of my heart every night!

5. *Being very patient.* Building safety and trust with Angelo took many baby steps slowly over time. Not every step seemed to be making progress. In retrospect, I am sure every patient, loving gesture was

worthwhile. The more spacious we can be in our own hearts, the more easily we can be patient with another.

BASIC HUMAN NEEDS

Without recognizing our basic human needs, it is easy to overlook them. Without understanding the cultural heart wound, or the way it manifests in our own lives and hearts, we cannot invest the emotional and spiritual energy needed to heal. It is essential we find safe spaces to heal our wounded hearts and become more aware of our most basic needs. If we have not had our most intimate needs met over the course of our lives, we will both perpetuate the pattern we have suffered from and be unable to provide a new road map for self and for others. Writing this book is one step I am taking to help develop a new road map.

In 1990, my colleague Brian Schulz and I developed a list of six basic human needs. Each one is pretty simple. Yet, most of us live our lives without receiving our recommended daily allowances of most of them:

1. The need for abundant, nurturing, non-sexual touch and holding.

2. The need for full expression of emotions and a listener who responds to this expression with warmth, understanding and respect.

3. The need for play and pleasure.

4. The need for satisfying and creative work.

5. The need for a satisfying and uninhibited sexual life with a loved and loving partner.

6. The need for immersion in and contact with the natural environment.

ESSENTIAL QUESTIONS:

1. Have you had experiences that have made you aware of the power of the heart?

2. Can you relate to the image of the feral human?

3. Have you ever tried to love someone with a traumatized heart? If so, what was the experience like?

4. In what ways has your heart been wounded? What do you need for your heart to heal?

5. Do you think men's and women's hearts are wounded in similar or different ways? What is similar and what is different about male and female heart wounds?

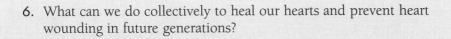

6. What can we do collectively to heal our hearts and prevent heart wounding in future generations?

MEDITATION: Basic Human Needs

Take a moment to find a comfortable place to do this meditation, whether it be sitting or lying down. When you find the comfortable place, close your eyes and begin to take a few deep breaths. As you inhale, feel your body very slowly melt and relax. Take a moment to see if you are comfortable or you need to adjust your position in any way to be more comfortable.

Whenever you feel ready, allow your focus to be with your heart, noticing where you feel your heart as you hear the word "heart." If it helps to put your hand on your heart to help focus there, you are welcome to do so. Take a moment to notice how your heart is feeling physically and emotionally. Is it full? Is it empty? Is it heavy? Is it light? Is it separate? Connected? Take a moment to let yourself become a little more familiar with whatever is happening in your heart now.

Whenever you feel ready, take a moment to look at where you are in your life with regard to abundant, nurturing non-sexual touch and holding. How comfortable are you with non-sexual touch? How available is it for you? On a scale from 1 to 10, where 1 is lacking and 10 is abundant, what number would you choose to describe the availability of non-sexual nurturing touch?

And whenever you feel ready, allow your focus to move to your emotional expression. How comfortable are you expressing your deepest feelings? Are there people in your life who can really hear and respect your heart? Do you seek out listeners for your emotional experience or do you keep your experience to yourself? On a scale from 1 to 10 where 1 is lacking and 10 is abundant, what number would you choose to describe the availability of emotional expression to a caring listener?

And whenever you feel ready, allow your focus to move to play and pleasure. How freely do you allow yourself to enjoy play and pleasure? What are your favorite ways to play? What brings you pleasure? Are there ways you keep yourself from enjoying play and pleasure? On a scale from

1 to 10, where 1 is lacking and 10 is abundant, what number would you choose to describe the amount of play and pleasure in your life?

And whenever you feel ready, allow your focus to move to your work. How satisfying and creative is it? Does your work feel fulfilling and meaningful? Can you express your spirit through your work? On a scale from 1 to 10, where 1 is lacking and 10 is abundant, what number would you choose to describe how creative and satisfying your work is?

And whenever you feel ready, allow your focus to move to your sexual expression. How comfortable are you expressing your sexuality with a loved partner? How freely can you express yourself sexually? Do you have any inhibitions? How fully can you enjoy your sexuality? On a scale from 1 to 10, where 1 is lacking and 10 is abundant, what number would you choose to describe your sexual expression?

And whenever you feel ready, allow your focus to move to your relationship with the natural world. How much time do you give yourself to be in nature, to feel a connection with the natural world? Are there particular activities you enjoy or places you like to go to feel connected with the natural world? On a scale from 1 to 10, where 1 is lacking and 10 is abundant, what number would you choose to describe your sense of connection with the natural world?

And whenever you feel ready, at your own pace, you can mark your answers on the following chart. You may want to write notes in your journal too, about how well you feel you are meeting your basic human needs, and what steps you might want to take to meet them more fully.

NON-SEXUAL NURTURING TOUCH

1	2	3	4	5	6	7	8	9	10
Lacking									Abundant

EMOTIONAL EXPRESSION TO A CARING LISTENER

1	2	3	4	5	6	7	8	9	10
Lacking									Abundant

PLAY AND PLEASURE									
1	2	3	4	5	6	7	8	9	10
Lacking									Abundant

CREATIVE AND SATISFYING WORK									
1	2	3	4	5	6	7	8	9	10
Lacking									Abundant

SEXUAL EXPRESSION WITH A LOVED PARTNER									
1	2	3	4	5	6	7	8	9	10
Lacking									Abundant

CONTACT WITH NATURE									
1	2	3	4	5	6	7	8	9	10
Lacking									Abundant

Notes:

1. See *"Interpersonal Heart-Brain Registration and the Perception of Parental Love: A 42-Year Follow-Up of the Harvard Mastery of Stress Study,"* by Linda G. Russek and Gary E. Schwartz, Subtle Energies, 1994.

2, 3. From *"Spirit and Matter of the Heart"* by Dorothy Mandel, Grace Millennium, Winter 2001.

4. The research done by the **HeartMath Institute** is available on **www.heartmath.org**

Chapter 2

THE WAR BETWEEN THE GENDERS

*"Today, the world is so small and so interdependent that the
concept of war has become anachronistic, an outmoded approach...
Unfortunately, although we are in the 21st century, we still have
not been able to get rid of the habit of our older generations...
the belief or confidence that we can solve our problems with arms.
It is because of this notion that the world continues to
be dogged with all kinds of problems."*

— His Holiness the Dalai Lama
*Shared at the Great Prayer Festival
March 11, 2003 in Dharamsala*

The Dalai Lama's words above are very poignant to me. In so many ways, the concept of war is truly anachronistic, not only for nations, but also for individual people and for relationships between people. In spite of this knowledge, so often our reactions and behavior remain rooted in archaic, triggered ways of being. This applies to intimate relationships whether the partners be a man and a woman, two women or two men. There is a gap between our potential for relating and how we actually behave.

In order to understand where we are, where we are going, and how to grow into what we wish to be, it is helpful to realize that the war between the genders is a symptom of an evolutionary transition we are in the midst of. In this chapter, I will discuss the energy of war and the cultural heart wound that is so prevalent in our current experience, and develop an evolutionary framework to help understand the war between the genders.

THE ENERGY OF WAR

War is based on a dualistic way of thinking, where in a conflict, there must be a winner and a loser, one who is right and one who is wrong, one who gains the power and one who loses it. My colleague Chip Baggett reflected, "When I think of war, I think of an enemy whose self-interests are in conflict with my own with such intensity that one of us must overcome the other in order to have our interests met." In our relational struggles, as in international relations, we can feel so separate, so polarized, so removed from one another, that we do experience this energy of war.

The energy of war makes me think of experiments with magnets I used to do as a child.When people feel a sense of alignment and connectedness, they are very much like magnets experiencing the force of attraction. They are pulled together with a focus and a strength. They unite and become one. They become almost inseparable. When two magnets experience the force of repulsion, however, there is an equally strong and opposite experience. The two magnets push apart from one another with an intensity that is unstoppable. As a child, no matter how hard I tried to get the magnets to come together when they were positioned in the repulsion configuration, I always failed. I could not overcome the force pulling them apart, keeping them separate.

THE UNRAVELING OF GENDER AS WE KNEW IT

I was born in late November 1958, at the tail end of the baby boom generation. Roles for men and women were black and white and crystal clear. Dad went to work. Mom stayed at home. My parents fit into the societally prescribed model in many ways, but without the squeaky clean signs of family perfection I watched on TV.

I felt the tension of the war between the genders in my parents' relationship. My father worked for the government. While he was a steady provider, he was often angry and irritable at home. At times he seemed to be a workaholic, absorbed with his job. When my father retired and I attended the retirement party, I discovered that I had never met the man those at work were bidding farewell. He had two personalities. At work, he was powerful, respected and effective in his job. At home, with children, a wife and all that came with it, his inner demons let loose. The societally defined male gender role served my father well. His emotional shortcomings were more visible in the shadows of our home.

My mother was at home with me and my brother when we were very young. She tried to find part-time work once we entered school. She suffered from depression and had trouble finding jobs that really worked for her. She often felt frustrated, displaced and hopeless about ever finding a meaningful way to connect with the world. The traditional female gender role provided both a way to participate in the world and a safe escape from the professional and economic pressures the world relegated to men.

Neither one of my parents seemed very happy in their gender boxes. On the one hand, they could pride themselves at successfully playing their external gender roles. But they were always fighting with one another, seemingly never at peace. Their power struggles were a struggle of painful powerlessness. Their language reeked of blame and dissatisfaction. Their internal landscapes appeared to be barren and empty. My little girl's heart was deeply saddened by this model of an adult male-female relationship. Often, I was outright terrified as their yelling and screaming escalated, feeling unsafe and that things were out of control. My parents threatened divorce in fights, but lacked the gumption or conviction to follow through.

Neither one of my parents had the tools for emotional and spiritual growth and healing. Perhaps they felt locked in their gender boxes and the social structures built on this commonly understood foundation. The framework of personal growth and evolution did not exist. In those days, therapy carried a huge stigma. It was something only "crazy" people did. One's problems and struggles were kept quiet to the outside world. Our culture carried an emotional code of silence, unspoken, but commonly upheld. The shades were pulled down at night so the neighbors could not see the shadows that lurked next door.

Over the past several decades, our sense of gender has changed dramatically. As just one example, in my parent's generation, the "provider" and "homekeeper" roles were divided clearly along gender lines. Today, that line has blurred or in some cases, been erased. The mother of my son's best friend is the primary breadwinner in the family, while his dad has been the primary parent at home. In many families, both parents work, and daycare or afterschool programs take over the "at home parent" role. Many people in the baby boom generation have experienced a reverse polarization of gender roles. I know men who have focused on developing their feminine side to the point of losing touch with their masculine side. I know women who have developed their masculine side to the point that their responses, behaviors and actions are more masculine than some men.

While our ultimate goal is integration, evolution follows a spiral pathway, swinging from one extreme to the other before coming to rest in the center. As we move along this spiral path, we can feel more modern and enlightened and experience increased freedom in the greater fluidity of our gender roles. Too, there is an added complexity and confusion about what it means to be a man and what it means to be a woman. How do we individually and jointly provide the qualities and functions once assigned to a particular gender?

In the "Healing the War Between the Genders" workshops and groups I lead, I ask participants the questions, "What does it mean to be a man?" and "What does it mean to be a woman?" the conversation usually starts with the stereotypical traits from my parents' generation. However, it doesn't take long for a deeper level of dialogue to break through. Suddenly, the traits and qualities assigned to one gender list get put on the other gender list. Confusion begins to set in, as does a thick tension, often unspoken. There are strong emotions just under the surface waiting to emerge.

While some of the people who have participated in these workshops and groups dislike the term "war between the genders," many recognize that in intimate relationships we can simulate the behavior of the two repelling magnets, experiencing the intensity and energy of war. "Sometimes the whole thing seems so much bigger than me and anyone else I am involved with," reflected one woman. "I don't know how to avoid it or how to change it. I get exhausted even thinking about it." A man in one workshop reflected, "I just don't know how to build a lasting relationship with a woman. The rules have changed, and no one gave me the rulebook!"

The war between the genders is fueled by the struggle to find a new sense of identity in a rapidly changing world as the tools and models that served us in the previous time unravel. We have entered into uncharted territory without a roadmap. Both men and women need new frameworks, language, tools and skills as we move forward into our next evolutionary phase.

Polarization of Male and Female Gender Traits

Male Traits	Female Traits
better at spatial relations	better at relating
the surgeon	the nurse and healer
action	process
solar	lunar
penis	vagina
intellect	heart
self-confidence	modesty
assertive	receptive
dominant	submissive
provider	homekeeper
physicality	emotionality
protector	protected
tough/hard	vulnerable/soft
abuser	victim
angry	bitchy
builder	vessel
visioner	birther
silent	verbal
self-contained	expressive
priest	priestess
linear/rational	intuitive
lustful	good girls don't
power	beauty
questioning	deep wisdom

OUR EVOLUTIONARY TRANSITION

We are at a poignant and precarious phase in human evolution, transitioning between an old way of living, thinking and being... and a new one evolving. Our old way of living, thinking and being originated two to three thousand years ago when our developmental task as a species was to separate and individuate, differentiating ourselves from nature and one another. Some of my colleagues consider this point in history the beginning of what we now call the "patriarchal era." In my first book, **LIVING WITH VISION: RECLAIMING THE POWER OF THE HEART**, I called this stage the "thinking phase."

The new stage we are entering is what I called "the conscious/compassionate phase." In this phase, our evolutionary task is synthesis and integration. As conscious/compassionate people, we can both have a well developed individual sense of self AND a sense of interconnection with nature and other people. The new ways of living, thinking and being that come with the conscious/ compassionate phase are available to us in some ways, but still developing.

The earliest developmental phase in my model I called the "primal phase," the infancy of the human species. I want to note that this model is not a scientific one, but one I have created to offer a backdrop in which we can understand where we have come from, along with where we are going and where we are now. I feel it is valuable at least as a metaphor or a mythology. The chart below sum-marizes the three phases I presented in **LIVING WITH VISION**, along with distinguishing characteristics.

Our Evolution From Primal People to Conscious/Compassionate People[1]			
	Where We Have Come From:	Where We Have Been:	Where We Are Going:
Our Developmental Stage	Primal people: newborn children Nature is parent.	Thinking people: adolescents God is parent.	Conscious/compassionate people: emotionally and spiritually mature adults Both parent and child.
Our Sense of Identity	Part of nature — something larger than self. Separate personal identity not yet defined.	Separate from nature and different than other people. Differentiation.	Part of nature while maintaining a unique sense of self. Reconnection and integration.
Our Relationship with Nature	Nature has power over humans. Nature in control.	Strive to have power over nature. Humans in control.	Co-creators with nature in our evolution. Creative power is part of our nature, the power of nature works through us.
Our Concept of God	Nature as creator and provider — an outside power — source of all, which humans are vulneable to.	God in our image — an outside power who judges, rationalizes, and determines what is "right."	God as a life force, a creative power residing inside and working through every human being.
Our Relationship with Our Bodies	At the mercy of the Mind is used to keep body alive.	Mind over matter. Body as subject of the mind.	Partnership of mind and body. Each a source of wisdom
Prevailing Energy	Feminine energy predominates.	Masculine energy predominates.	Moving toward the balance of both masculine and feminine energies.

Since we are now making the transition from the thinking phase to the conscious/compassionate phase, I want to paint a picture of the current transition, and how it relates to the war between the genders.

THE AWKWARDNESS OF THE "IN BETWEEN PHASE"

For the first year of my son's life, I attended a weekly "mothers and babies" group at our local YMCA. Over time, I watched infants transform from tiny, still, fragile beings to larger, moving, active ones. I noticed the "in between" phases in the babies' development These were the times when a child had mentally grasped that crawling or walking was their next developmental target, but their actual body and nervous system hadn't quite caught up with what they were mentally prepared to do. Mentally, a baby had a conceptual map of where s/he was going. But his/her wiring could not execute this new understanding until it developed further. In the transition phase between one stage of development and the next, the baby was clumsy. S/he would fall flat on his/her face or belly. S/he would be unsteady on his/her feet. S/he would try and try and try again, working until exhaustion, efforting to move from one side of the room to another.

The image of the growing babies in the mothers and babies group resonates for me with the Dalai Lama's observation of where we are in relationship to the concept of war. We are in an "in between" phase of emotional and spiritual evolution. We have developed some of the understanding and tools to move beyond war. This more evolved part of us knows that win-win is a preferable outcome to win-lose. This same part realizes that life consists of continuums with shades of gray beyond black and white. When we get "triggered," we become mired in interpersonal conflicts. Often the issue we are fighting over is not the deeper issue at the heart of the matter. Yet our triggered responses of blaming, withdrawing, disconnecting or "othering" our supposed loved one emerge and often prevail. We are clumsy as we transition from old, familiar "personality-based relating" to new and still uncharted "soul-centered relating."

Today as my son was having a playdate with one of his friends, the boy's dad told me about the way they handled conflict between kids at the school where he had taught. This school, whose philosophy is based in emotional intelligence and triune brain theory, understood that anger is rooted in hurts and wants. So, when two kids were angry, my son's friends' dad had learned to ask them, "How is it you are hurting? What is it you are wanting?" It did not take long for the layer of anger to melt and a much deeper conversation to become possible.

The teachers in this school had developed tools to get underneath the personality and defenses of the children and speak to their souls. As the teachers did this, the children learned a language to navigate their most deeply felt inner terrain. I was moved, in particular, because this was such a rare situation. It is far more common just to separate fighting children and tell them to cool off. What a difference when their teachers were looking through the lens of soul-centered relating, rather than the more familiar personality-based relating.

It is just this kind of skillful presence and facilitation that helps a growing person develop the emotional capacity to evolve and mature. When this presence and facilitation is lacking, a child may emotionally and mentally beat his/her head against a wall, unable to come up with answers, alternatives or behaviors that could take him/her out of the dark. All change involves growing pains. However, the pain of constructive growth feels very different than the pain of hitting one's heart or head against the wall!

THE SHADOWLANDS

In my parents' generation, while pulling down the shades may have shielded the neighbors from dark visions, it did not make the pain of the fights or their underlying causes go away. My parents felt relief from the privacy afforded by their shades. I felt an inner turbulence. Avoiding dark issues by pushing them away only strengthened them. Facing the darkness was the only way I knew how to dissolve the shadows and find safety and peace. By getting underneath anger to reveal hurts and wants, my son's friend's dad helped kids learn how to navigate the shadowlands.

The shadowlands is a place that all emotionally intimate relationships inevitably hit and that most of us wish to avoid or make go away. As safety and trust develop, our defenses start to melt away. I define the shadowlands as those places in our emotional and relational landscape that are uncharted, vulnerable, and often wounded or undeveloped. Past wounds surface to be healed. Undeveloped parts of ourselves emerge for growth. Differences we never realized existed become crucial.

Individually and collectively, our relationships are stuck in the shadowlands. Few of us have ever been told that entering the shadowlands is a necessary and even important phase in the development of an intimate, sustainable, healthy relationship. So, we lack the understanding, tools and language to navigate this emotionally complex terrain. We experience fear and discomfort, and often fight against one another in due course.

Because we have not been educated about the importance, value and power of our emotional landscape, we are afraid of our feelings, especially deep and strong ones. So many people I have worked with have said, "I can't show my vulnerability. I'll only be hurt," "What good does it do to get angry? It doesn't change anything." or "I don't want to feel pain. I'd rather feel numb." I remember one man I worked with who felt he didn't even have a choice when it came to experiencing difficult feelings. "I'm on automatic," he laughed. "When the scary stuff comes, I automatically go somewhere else!"

Our fear of the darkside and our inability to feel pain, anger, vulnerability, and also joy, are symptoms of a cultural heart wound that we must heal to move from personality-based to soul-centered relationships. I discuss this in more detail in Chapter 6, The Lonely Couple.

THE CULTURAL HEART WOUND

Human evolution follows the path of a spiral. The same spiral path also applies to social change. There is a time and place for energy to swing from one extreme to another and to come to rest at any point on the continuum. If we have difficulty letting go of what has been and moving on to what is next, a sense of imbalance develops. We can feel this individually and collectively.

In the "primal phase" of human evolution, when people were closely connected with nature and less differentiated from it, feminine energy was the guiding force. Feminine values of heart, being, relationship and interconnection were central to this time in our development as a species. As we evolved into the "thinking phase," we entered a new era where masculine energy predominated. Masculine energy was a necessary balance and counterpoint to help us develop and differentiate in this evolutionary stage. Our current political structures, notions of power and allocation of resources, work structures and even what we call "traditional" gender roles are rooted in the masculine energy of the thinking phase.

As men, women and society evolve towards the next phase of development, the "conscious/compassionate" phase, our social, cultural and economic institutions have not yet changed sufficiently to meet our emerging needs. For this reason, the predominant political, social, and economic institutions and practices can feel oppressive to both men and women today. A lot of the anger I see directed at the "patriarchy," by women in particular, reflects the need for our old institutions to change with the times and for new, more congruent models to emerge.

As we feel the effects of reaching the extreme polarity of masculine energy, we can experience the denial and rejection of the feminine qualities of heart, being, relationship and interconnection. We have driven the feminine underground, and, in doing so, have created a state of imbalance. Author Terry Real speaks of our "anti-relational, vulnerability-despising culture." We energize the linear brain separate from and unrelated to heart energy. We fixate on intellect without including emotional intelligence. We value doing over being. We choose production over relationality.

We are left feeling the effects of a **cultural heart wound**, a painful reality that has mental, emotional, physical and spiritual impact. Symptoms include:

- ✂ *a lack of emotional safety.* This contributes to an inability to be vulnerable with self or other, to speak or even know one's deepest truth or to be emotionally authentic.

- ✂ *mental and physical illness.* Anxiety, depression, narcissism and the laundry list of addictions we use to numb ourselves from emotional and spiritual pain are present in epidemic proportions. Heart disease and high blood pressure are common ailments.

- ✂ *disconnection.* We have lost our sense of connection with the natural world and our own nature. We are disconnected from our bodies, our hearts and our souls, from others, from the collective and from the divine.

- ✂ *powerlessness and battles for power.* We seek dominance, instead of mutual understanding. The war between the genders and the gender war within are just two such battles.

- ✂ *a widespread sense of alienation.* People ask endlessly, "Where do I fit? and "What is my purpose?"

The cultural heart wound touches both male and female hearts. Men learn it is not okay to cry, be vulnerable, scared or express their feelings, and are sentenced to a life of emotional imprisonment. As women are taught to nurture, serve and forgive without considering their own needs, they become imprisoned with powerlessness. Raw and tentative with wounded hearts, men and women struggle in relationships, be they opposite or same gender-based. They lack both the tools necessary to relate intimately, authentically and powerfully and the roadmap outlining the new territory of soul-centered relating.

Another part of the cultural heart wound is a loss of connection with a sense of something greater than oneself, with the spirit of life. Molly Dwyer reflects, "We are taught through this culture to be narcissistic and self-indulgent. This is a form of violence." We have lost our sense of responsibility to the collective as well as self. Western culture has been enamored with individuality and the rights of the individual. Dwyer continues, "We fear anything with a community base to it."

The Cultural Heart Wound

❤ anti-relational, vulnerability-despising culture

❤ disconnection of human beings from our fundamental energy sources: earth, soul, relationships, community and God/higher power

❤ depression, anxiety, addictions and narcissism in epidemic proportions

❤ violence, oppression and domination — destruction of earth and living beings

❤ a culture of untouchables

❤ breakdown between the genders

❤ political, economic and social structures based on the false power of separation

❤ widespread alienation (where do I fit? where do I belong?)

❤ false conditioning and artificial social roles

❤ elaborate systems for self-protection

❤ polarizations of head and heart, self-interest and collective needs, rich and poor, models for personal growth and social change, money and meaning and sexuality and spirituality

BATTLEFIELD ON THE HOMEFRONT

The war between the genders gets played out in the workplace, but even more powerfully on the homefront. Will Keepins, who leads Gender Reconciliation workshops with Molly Dwyer, acknowledges that gender injustice and imbalance is a longstanding affliction in human society. "It tends to get processed in intimate relationships because it is not processed anywhere else. Our culture has no forum for dealing with this in the collective. This problem is like a gigantic mountain of injustice that is so huge we take it for granted." Individual relationships break under the weight of this collective shadow.

Molly Dwyer reflects, "For most people, the most startling, painful and revealing lessons of their lives come through intimate relationships. I went through a marriage that ended in emotionally violent dynamics that surprised me about myself and my partner. Why are personal relationships so difficult? Why do they fail so often? What was I carrying that were cultural phenomena and what was in myself?"

I counsel couples who are successful managing work relationships and who are able to have lasting friendships, who hit the skids when it comes to their primary partnership. "We both have good communication skills," reflected Barry. "Why do they go to the wind when we try to relate to one another?"

Research by John Gottman, Ph.D., author of **THE SEVEN PRINCIPLES FOR MAKING MARRIAGE WORK**, finds that it is often emotional distance — not conflict — that determines whether a relationship will flourish or begin to disintegrate. Neither men nor women know how to co-create truth-telling intimacy or the safe context that allows them to be vulnerable. As we try to protect our wounded male and female hearts, we may feel more comfort in the distance of fighting than the frightening intimacy of connecting.

Men and women have different tools of war, but the result is equally painful and isolating. Women use words as their weapon of choice. Men use their fists or their silent withdrawal. These are just different ways of expressing and responding to pain. Unfortunately, both genders fail to recognize or respond to the pain that underlies the harsh words, the fists or the silence. They lack the model my son's friend's dad brought to the children at school. Sadly, men and women both objectify the pain of their partner, leading to the experience of "othering" their loved one.

Both men and women feel isolated and lonely, wanting to connect deeply, for their souls to meet. Several decades ago, we clung to each other out of our woundedness, hoping that one-half plus one-half would equal a whole. In time, this mode of relating got a bad rap, and was labeled "codependence." We learned to put tectonic plates over our hearts so that others could not hurt us. While this put a damper on codependence, it didn't heal our wounded hearts.

Molly Dwyer acknowledges that both genders yearn to bring forward a spiritual capacity that runs deeper than emotions or sexuality alone. "The dynamic is larger than can be confronted on a psychological or sociological basis. It is a spiritual dilemma. We need to work with larger forces. We won't solve it through human ingenuity, through political processes, through psychological efforts. We see it as something bigger than just a human dilemma or a human dilemma that is so large that it needs a larger force to address it."

CONFLICT'S INVITATION

Danaan Parry, a wonderful colleague of mine I met in 1986 at the Findhorn Community in Sweden, made a statement that has always stayed with me. Conflict, Danaan would assert, provides an invitation to true intimacy. Danaan offered a vision and tools to help us make war, in the words of the Dalai Lama, "anachronistic." Danaan, who died in 1996 and was known around the world for his work in conflict resolution, looked at conflict not only from the personality-based perspective, but also from the deeper soul-centered perspective. Conflict invites, if not demands, that we dig deeper in ourselves and with one another. Conflict asks that we remove the veils that separate us and join in the heartfelt connection residing deeper down without our human core.

As I write this book, war is happening not only between the genders but between nations. As each day's headlines speak of developments in this war whose very necessity is questionable, I think of Danaan and his words. War between people, between governments, between nations, seems to be one of the most profound enactments of conflict human beings are capable of. Yet, what seems to be lost in the choreography of war is the vision of conflict as a force of integration and connection. We seem to lock onto conflict as the ground for violence, the way to vie for power, and the justification for destruction of the other, if necessary, to move forward one's individual goals. It's as though our primitive wiring for survival of the fittest has been triggered, and only he who dominates survives.

This primitive wiring is part of the bedrock of the structures, institutions and ways of being that comprise our world today. When the stakes get high enough and the threat gets great enough, we revert to this wiring as the basis of our actions. We create battles in which countless people are wounded and die. As we stand at the brink of the next phase of human evolution, our personal, relational and societal wars are an invitation to dig deeper and move beyond our models that no longer work. We are being asked to come together, to find a way to meet at the human core. We are being asked to recognize that war IS an anachronism.

For the past 15 years, I have participated in workshops about Love, Intimacy and Sexuality led by the Human Awareness Institute (HAI). One of the rituals I loved in HAI workshops is an exercise called "Hand on Heart." In this exercise, everyone in the workshop stands in two concentric circles, the innermost one facing out and the outermost circle facing in. The circles rotate and pivot, so that every person in the workshop gradually encounters every other person in the workshop, and has a chance to connect with them face to face, eye to eye, hand to hand and heart to heart. What initially appears to be a group of strangers melts and unfolds into a heartful circle of compatriots. If only we could stand in a circle, facing our purported enemies, and open our hearts to one another. How world politics would change!

And to be able to do this with our partners, friends and loved ones! We are so terrified of removing our veils, facing the risk and vulnerability of intimacy. We need to learn to build a climate of safety and trust if we are to make conflict an opportunity and dig down deep beneath the roots of the gender wars. We need to heal our wounded hearts, to balance our sense of separation with a dose of integration and to restore a sense of wisdom, relatedness and power. In this way, the gender wars offer a profound opportunity for healing, intimacy and growth. May we become both skilled and brave enough to safely stand before one another, to remove our veils and restore the connection possible in the meeting of two human hearts.

ESSENTIAL QUESTIONS: *Questions for reflection and discussion:*

1. What parts of your thinking and behavior seem rooted in the "thinking phase?"

2. What parts of your thinking and behavior seem rooted in the "conscious/compassionate phase?"

3. What are ways you get triggered in intimate relationships? How do you behave when you are triggered? What do you do? What do you say?

4. What can you do to go deeper and work through shadow pieces that emerge in yourself and with a partner?

5. When you get angry, what do you really want or need?

6. What do you need most from an intimate partner? What do you need most from yourself?

7. What do you have the hardest time providing to an intimate partner? What do you have the hardest time giving yourself?

8. What do men and women need to develop to really understand what it is like to live inside one another's skin?

MEDITATION: Your Gender Identity: *Being a Man, Being a Woman*

Take a moment to get comfortable, sitting up or lying down. Close your eyes, as long as that is comfortable, and take a few deep breaths. As you inhale, feel the support your seat or the floor provides for your shoulders, back, tailbone, legs and feet. As you inhale, let your body be supported. As you exhale, very slowly and gently allow your body to be supported by the chair or the floor.

Whenever you feel ready, allow your focus to move to your heart, noticing where you feel your heart when I say the word heart. If it helps to place your hand on your heart to help focus there, you are welcome to do so. Whenever you feel ready, take a moment to notice how your heart is feeling physically and emotionally right now. Is it full? Is it empty? Is it heavy? Is it light? Is it separate? Connected? Take a moment to let yourself become a little more familiar with whatever is happening in your heart now.

And whenever you feel ready, take a moment to look back to your childhood and see how you learned about what it meant to be a man or a woman. What kinds of role models did you have? How did your parents demonstrate what maleness and femaleness meant? What did you learn about love between men and women? Women and women? Men and men? Did you witness your parents caught in the gender wars? If so, in what ways? What kinds of other role models did you have for male and female behavior? What kinds of messages did you get from the community you were part of — from other kids, and from other adults in your life? What messages felt helpful? What messages felt limiting? What was your inner experience of maleness or femaleness? On what beliefs, images, values and experiences did you build your own sense of gender identity?

Taking whatever time you need to be with whatever you are sensing, thinking, feeling, at your own pace, very slowly and gently, take a deep breath and bring your focus into the room. You are welcome to take notes from your experience with the meditation. You can then share your thoughts and feelings with a partner, other loved one or group, if you like.

Notes:

1. From **LIVING WITH VISION: RECLAIMING THE POWER OF THE HEART** by Linda Marks (Knowledge Systems, Inc, 1989)

2. From *"Save Your Relationship"* by Susan Johnson, Ph.D. in Psychology Today, April 2003.

Chapter 3

Honoring the Male Heart

"Like Ulysses, a man's calling is always to duty,
never to what might be emotionally fulfilling for him.
This need for men to not feel is so universal,
that it has become, basically, our definition
of what it is to be a man."

— Daphne Rose Kingma

It has been more than 35 years since Paul Simon wrote his hit song, "I Am A Rock." While the past several decades have brought a lot of change in how we view men and women, and how individual men and women view themselves, the image of "man as rock" still lingers in the shadows and remains central in the emotional lives of many men. It was the socially-accepted standard as baby boomers grew up, modeled by their parents. This image is central to the male heart wound that men today are both suffering and healing.

As the mother of a now seven-year-old son, I have found young boys to be vulnerable, emotionally expressive and loving. When my son went off to preschool at age three, I remember how pure, open and emotionally sensitive he was. Early in his preschool experience, he came home one day shocked and broken-spirited. He and several of his other three-year-old male friends had been bullied by the four-year-old boys on the playground. The four-year-old boys had wielded their power verbally and physically. They had called the younger boys names and had punched my son and his friends before the teachers intervened and brought the violent episode to a close.

My still innocent son didn't understand why the older boys had to be so mean. "Why did they hurt us, Mommy?" he asked mournfully. My eyes filled with tears as I watched this veil of innocence be removed from my son's pure heart. His arm hurt where he had been punched. It made no sense to his little boy's heart why the older boys had to hurt him and his friends. They had done nothing to merit the attack. Even in a well-run school with teachers skilled at conflict resolution, it took only a few minutes for the three-year-old boys to learn a painful lesson about power and domination from the older boys. The socially generated wounding to the male heart was already taking place.

"Hiding in my room, safe within my womb, I touch no one and no one touches me...." as Paul Simon writes, many men protect their wounded hearts, shielded in their armor, protected by the safety of their intellect. This armor keeps men from feeling the soul-deep pain that accompanies disconnection from self, others and nature, and from expressing the pain and grief that accompanies this loss. As their hearts are wounded, many men in our culture are sentenced to a life of emotional imprisonment. This is a silent life sentence, never spoken, never talked about. And these men are expected to be stoic and bear their cross. They are expected to do their duty and find strength in their armor.

Sadly, the honor, loyalty and goodness inherent in the male psyche gets contorted as men do their best to conform to society's misdirected standards. It takes tremendous courage for a man to know his own soul in light of the cultural pull away from introspection for men. This is the way it was as the baby boom generation came into adulthood. Longstanding institutions die slowly and hard. Even those men working to heal their hearts and consciously change are faced with the power of the way it was for so long.

THE MALE HEART WOUND

A concise way to generalize about the male heart wound is that men in this culture lack a sense of essential self. This is true for some women, too, especially as gender roles have unraveled and both genders feel displaced. As more women have achieved professional status in the workplace, women experience the symptoms of the male heart wound as well as men. There are also unique ways our culture wounds male and female hearts. In Chapter 4, I speak specifically to the wounding of the female heart. Here I focus on the male heart wound, recognizing that what I am describing may apply to more than just men.

Physical, sensitive, and intuitive by nature, men in our culture have been cut off from their power both individually and collectively. They have been cut off from their emotional experience, their bodies and their souls. Since the heart is the gateway to the soul, when men's hearts are wounded they become cut off from their souls. They lose touch with their inner wisdom, intuition and body knowing. The male heart wound renders men voiceless. This heart wound has developed over many generations, as men have lost their sense of space and place. I speak to the loss of space and place later in this chapter.

Voltaire once said the mirror is an utterly wasteful and useless invention because the only way to see yourself is in the reflection of someone else's eyes. It is not surprising that so many men and women suffer from the narcissistic heart wound I discussed in Chapter 1. When a child's vulnerable and developing core self is not seen or reflected back by the adults around him, the wound to heart and psyche that gets called "narcissism" occurs.

Psychologist and writer Richard Grossman comments, "To avoid the narcissistic heart wound, a child has to be valuable to their parents from day one. This means being valued for the basic core self you are, not values determined by the parents."

For example, one man Richard Grossman worked with told him, "'My parents trained me to be an Olympic swimming champion, but when I looked inside, I felt totally empty.' What needs to be valued is an inherent part of the child's natural self. Parents have to find a way to see this inherent part of the child and value it. When boys don't receive this, they have many ways of responding to try to establish the fact that they have value in spite of what their parents think." This is true for all children, not only boys.

"A big way men try to feel worthwhile is in the workplace with workaholism. Work is a way to say, 'I'm a worthwhile person.' The harder you work, the more you'll be worth, both financially and emotionally. " Men overwork to fill the emptiness they would feel inside if they could dare to take off their armor. Deep down inside, many men experience a void."

As career achievement has become a central force in more women's lives, they too turn to work for self-worth and social standing. Workaholism can be as significant a problem for women as for men. Some career-focused women have become "masculinized." These "masculinized women" have highly developed their male side, while neglecting or disconnecting from the feminine within. These women experience and display characteristics of the male heart wound, including a resistance to deep introspection and feeling. Like their male colleagues, they protect themselves from feeling an inner void.

"Another way some men try to find worth when it is lacking is in the inability to settle into one relationship. When a man has someone who values him, the value diminishes over time. He takes it for granted. At the beginning, when a new person says, 'I like you,' he feels self-worth." His life becomes a string of conquests, moving on and on again in pursuit of that initially fulfilling, but never sustainable, sense of self-worth, comments Grossman."

Again, with more "gender equality" expected on both the home front and the work front, women may feel less compelled to settle into one primary partnership for the rest of their lives, too. Men and women run the risk of missing each other emotionally, as they both look continually for greener pastures that offer short-term validation without long-term rootedness.

"Alcohol and drug addiction offer more of a palliative solution. It removes the pain of the core sense of worthlessness. However, it does not change the sense of having no value. This core sense of worthlessness becomes encoded in our synapses. It is learned and developed in pathways within us. This kind of encoding comes not from one single trauma, but from a constant background message that is received. The primary caregiver delivers this message in its most lethal form", acknowledges Grossman.

In Chapter 2 I described the cultural heart wound and presented the symptoms we experience in the wounding of our collective heart. I also mentioned that the cultural heart wound contributes to the wounding of both male and female hearts. Here are some of the symptoms of the male heart wound.

Symptoms of the Male Heart Wound

💙 disconnection from feelings, intuition and body

💙 lost, broken and/or undeveloped sense of self

💙 emotional truncation and numbness

💙 denial of desire and needs

💙 defended against vulnerability

💙 untouched and untouchable

💙 voicelessness

💙 isolation and aloneness

💙 compartmentalization

💙 doing valued over being

💙 putting duty ahead of emotional fulfillment

💙 lack of safety being authentic as a man

MOLDING THE UNEMOTIONAL MAN

In **THE MEN WE NEVER KNEW**, Daphne Rose Kingma writes that "obviously male children feel and feel deeply, but eventually socialization takes care of all of that...the feeling boy is gradually molded into the unemotional man." Our culture destroys sensitivity in men. It annihilates the male emotionally, sexually, spiritually and creatively.

"Men have been taught that in order to hold the world together, to make political, economic or social decisions, they have to ignore their emotions because the intervention of feelings could make mincemeat of their choices," says Kingma. "They have been encouraged not only to NOT have feelings, but have also been specifically instructed to shove down whatever random tendrils of feelings should, from time to time, manage to crop up."

I have watched this happen even with young boys. Many teachers fail to understand the nature of "boy energy," which can feel wilder and less controlled than "girl energy." When I taught my son's first grade Unitarian Universalist Sunday school class, I gave the kids an assignment to first assemble a series of puzzles and then make some of their own. The group had an equal number of boys and girls. Immediately, the class split into two teams. The boys chose to work together on one side of the room. The girls chose to work together on the other side of the room.

The boys jumped into action, climbing on the tables, joking as they exchanged puzzle pieces, and made a contest of the assignment. "I'm going to get done first!" prodded one team of boys to another. Even with their high energy level, they remained task focused and quickly assembled each of the puzzles. The girls, quietly congregated over one puzzle, and watched as one or two deft teammates actually manipulated the pieces to see if they would fit.Their pace was much slower and laid back than the pace of the boys.

A parent of one of the girls walked into the room, bringing her late arriving daughter to class, and was taken aback. The energy of the two groups was dramatically different. The girls were pretty quiet and self-contained. The boys were exuberant and spirited. "How can you stand this!" exclaimed the sincere parent to me. While the boy energy was intense, it was positive and productive. I realized I was allowing the boys to be boys, and the girls to be girls. I had been in many a classroom where the boys would be punished, yelled at, separated and scorned for this very output of exuberant energy.

As these kids moved on to the task of making their own puzzles, the boys got a little bit more out of control. They started drawing bathroom pictures and puncturing the pieces of paper they were drawing on — seeking my attention as I spent more time on the girls' side of the table. One of the girls had discovered it was easier to make a puzzle if I drew puzzle pieces on a square and she only had to draw an image over the pieces and color them in. Several other girls lined up asking me to do the same for them.

I found myself trying to both set limits, like "no bathroom language in the classroom, please," and "keep your hands on your own project — don't puncture your neighbor's project" while also allowing the boys to express themselves and have fun with their puzzles. I found myself being both patient and clear.

For the most part, the boys responded and towed this line. Sometimes,there is a fine line between containing boy energy and squashing it.

THE EMOTIONAL BURDEN OF BEING MALE

Male identity is based on suppressing the male heart and the wounded male heart. Kingma notes that we have enculturated beliefs that men "by nature are willing to carry and inflict pain that is required for civilization to advance. Whether it's in the form of laying railroad tracks or fighting a war, we have always assumed that men have a special capacity for bearing pain in silence." As men sacrifice their hearts and their lives, we have collectively been taught to assume men will not be affected by what the male role requires of them.

Many women complain that the men in their lives are like big children. With traditional gender roles, men have asked women to be their hearts, just as women have asked men to provide for their survival in the world. Men as a result, have not been given the support or social context to mature emotionally. Many men have not realized they need to do their emotional work. Women have felt responsible for doing all the emotional work for a couple. This does not work. The results include resentments, barriers to intimacy, and inadequate skills for communication.

Tim Hodge, a 44-year-old father of three children commented, "I'm really successful at my job in the computer industry. Now, I have a big house and I have to keep it up. Guys get stuck. Everyone thinks that is what you are supposed to do. We have to be responsible and take care of everyone else. And nobody's taking care of me. Lots of things I need in my life are missing. No one is worrying about that."

Author Terry Real describes "toxic masculinity — the legacies of drinking, womanizing, depression and fury" which has swept through a whole generation of men. Without having developed a grounded core sense of self, men truly are lost, and have treated themselves in disconnected ways far more self-destructively than women. They have been taught to put duty ahead of emotional fulfillment, to work until they burn out, and to keep going in the face of pain. A 58-year-old man I spoke with reflected, "Men wait for social security and death, not really caring which comes first."

With the advent of working women and a displacement of some of the traditional feminine ways of living, this toxic masculinity is now shared by both genders. Statistics on alcoholism and heart disease indicate women are catching up quickly with men. As more women suffer from the male heart wound, they demonstrate the same kinds of disconnection and self-destructive behavior as men.

The Personal Price Paid for Being a Man

♥ not allowed to be, rest or feel

♥ carries unexpressed pain in body

♥ disconnected from own heart and soul

♥ not supported to emotionally mature

♥ serves others at expense of himself

♥ stamps out deepest dreams to do his duty

♥ works beyond his own physical and emotional limits

♥ seeks comfort through addictive behavior (alcohol, drugs, sex, work)

♥ cannot not look deeply at who he is

LOSS OF SPACE, PLACE AND TRADITIONAL ROLE

My colleague, writer and psychologist Chellis Glendinning, lives in Chimayo, NM, a village of people closer to their indigenous roots than we experience in the cities and towns where so many of us live. Chimayo is a land-based community. It is Chicano. The people have a disparate background. They are partially from Spain, including Moorish. They are partially from Mexico. They intermarried with native people.

When they arrived, they lived in Chimayo the same way the indigenous people were living. They grew corn. They hunted elk, deer and wild turkey. They fished. They grew squash, beans and chile. This indigenous life brings with it a sense of space and place. That way still exists AND it is being destroyed.

In 1848, the U.S. won the Mexican-American war and took over half of what was at that time Mexico. Prior to the Mexican-American war, both men and women had clear gender roles. With each traditional role came a sense of space and place. As I listened to Chellis describe both gender roles, I sensed they were rich with spiritual identity and meaning. The women's place in this community was in the village. Women owned homes, the small domestic animals and the gardens. This was their space. The men's job was to go into la sierra — the forest, the common land. This land provided a space and a place for men to be, to work and to feel their spiritual rootedness as men.

Although the U.S. promised it would honor the system the land-based people had been living with, over the years this became a broken promise.The U.S. took away the men's hunting land, which wounded them deeply. The men were cut off from their sense of space and place. The women weren't cut off the same way. They still had the land and houses in the village.

Glendinning reflects, "The male heart wound is evident in this community. Some men have compensated by developing the hard shell of narcissism. They have lost their relational qualities and abilities. It is the men who have become the heroin dealers. The county I live is in #1 in the country for drug overdose deaths. It is an everyday part of life here — the wounding of men."

"The wounding is so evident to us all. It goes back to the loss of the ability to fulfill their psychological role as hunters." In the pre-1848 Chimayo, men's social function was integrated with their spiritual life. When their sense of space and place was taken away, both their spirits and their sense of male identity were broken.

THE MALE SPIRIT

"There is an essential warrior energy in a young male that needs to be acknowledged, seen for what it is, blessed and guided by elder members," says therapist and men's group leader John Dore. "Each man's sacred duty is to become his own king. A young man moves through initiation processes that inculcate a sacred masculinity." Contemporary society fails to provide opportunities for this kind of personal maturation and spiritual growth.

Both men and women have learned to become the social role assigned to their gender without an inner life. From this vantage point, the social functions we fulfill define our identities. Going to work in the corporate world is the modern translation for male hunting. However, the connections to nature, family and the collective have been lost in the translation. Modern day work for many is long hours without spiritual meaning.

David Gilmore, an anthropologist, wrote a book, **MANHOOD IN THE MAKING: CULTURAL CONCEPTS OF MASCULINITY**. This book on male development identifies three functions for men: the three P's. According to Gilmore's research, a man is to procreate, protect and provide. These social functions place a lot of pressure on men. Because our culture has taught men to look outward to define their identity and gender role, serving these functions has often been at the expense of a man's inner life rather than an expression of it.

LIVING INSIDE MALE SKIN

Many of the men I interviewed felt no one cared how they really felt. "Women don't take men's pain seriously," reflected one man. "My wife seems to dismiss it or just cannot hear it. Have both men and women gotten so used to men being tough that we don't know what to do when a man expresses his pain?" Men need their emotional turn. We need to learn how to listen, so we can learn to understand what it is like to live inside male skin.

Terry Real notes that few people have spoken to men's actual experience, including men's experience of pain. "For a generation, feminists have held men responsible for privileged, insensitive and, at times, offensive behavior. But most feminists have not spoken of men's subjective experience of pain. Psychologists and those in the men's movement, by contrast, have begun to look at the cultural gauntlet through which our sons must pass, and the damage it does to them. But in all their empathy, they rarely acknowledge the power men wield. One camp speaks to the violence men do, the other of the violence done to them. If men and women are to learn how to preserve the natural state of love and respect each deserves, both aspects of masculinity must be addressed — the wounding and the wound."

It is hard to grow into manhood from the inside out. Real acknowledges for boys who step out of the box of the highly constricting rules expected to become a man, there is a double bind. When men push against the invisible, yet societally upheld boundaries of maleness, the consequence is psychological and often physical, brutality. If men surrender to these societal forces, the consequence is emotional truncation, numbness and isolation. If a boy tries to be who he is at a most essential level, he will be "killed" or have to kill himself to survive.

IF YOU DON'T FEEL, YOU DON'T HAVE TO DEAL

Men live with a challenging paradox. The culture we have created and are evolving from was created by male power. Yet, the very way it provides men power also undermines their power. This is particularly true when it comes to the wounding of the male heart. Our society offers pathways to professional and financial success and personal power, wounding the male heart as a rite of passage.

Our society provides secondary gains for men with wounded hearts. Power and wealth are two great anesthetics for the male heart wound. Power and wealth get men the social trappings, including pretty women and all the toys that allow men to avoid the emptiness in their own hearts. "When I am feeling powerful, I have no pain," commented a man I interviewed. Men's identity and social standing are founded on externally-based power, which can be garnered and can also be taken away. The power that comes from inner rootedness, heart power, is what is undermined and ignored.

If a man is functional and successful in the world, he is rewarded. Unless he loses a job, a primary relationship ends or some other tragedy shakes up his far-removed inner life, he can find contentment focusing on externals, on worldly accomplishments. That his essential self is undeveloped, fragile, broken or lost is of little consequence. His elaborately built psychic/emotional defense system draws power and attention towards him and keeps pain at bay. His core self is undesirable and inaccessible. For this reason, the collapse of his external anchors can throw a man into a profound identity crisis, marked by excruciating psychic pain.

Michael Meade identifies two manifestations of the heart wound. In the case of the first, the narcissistic heart wound, a man is too well-defended to be touched from the inside or the outside. The second manifestation is numbness or depression, where the heart is too distant to be reached. In either case, Meade says, "the wound is carrying an albeit unvoiced and unseen genius which is necessary for healing that wound. The word genius goes back to an African word that means 'the spirit that is there.' What is the unspoken voice of the wound? The wound can readily be seen as an injured mouth trying to find its voice, language and words."

"We all have this demon of anxiety and depression that eats around the edges and wants to eat us up," reflects Mark McDonough, an entrepreneur and explorer of the male heart wound. "We throw different bones at it: power, sex, alcohol, workaholism, entertainment. There are so many ways to keep that demon from eating you up. Nobody wants to sit with the monster. It's too horrendous."

Many men are afraid to feel. If they did, what they would uncover might question and erode the foundation and the structures on which they have built their identities and their lives. "Because of the nature of the male heart wound, many men are closed to considering that the male heart wound exists," notes Art Matthis, a father of three boys in the Chicago area. "A characteristic of the male heart wound is the denial of the existence of the male heart wound."

Daphne Rose Kingma says, "Because they've suppressed their feelings for so long, men are unconsciously terrified of what might occur if they did experience their feelings.... men fear they won't be able to move from the feeling state back into the rational state" which provides a safe and productive ground to stand on and act from. Many men experience the split between head and heart. They have often not experienced that emotional process leads to resolution. The discomfort and time required to reach resolution in an emotional process may seem unbearable. So, many men routinely deny and rearrange feelings to defend against and suppress anything they don't want to see about themselves. While this keeps pain away, it also keeps real love out.

FEAR AND THE MALE HEART WOUND

At the very center of the male heart wound is a core of fear. Emotional violence is a common result of fear of vulnerability, fear of being exposed, fear of emotions. A scared man with a wounded heart holds on to control for dear life. Doug High comments, "A man thinks if I am afraid, I am going to defend myself. I'm going to strike out at the demons and I'm going to go after them." Instead of going inward to face the fear or reaching out for comfort and support, the scared and wounded male heart shuts off and strikes out. In doing so, the man may actually seriously injure himself emotionally as well as hurt the ones he loves.

When the dark side remains unacknowledged, we pay a high price. Unfortunately, we lack both role models of men who courageously face their shadow head on, and community settings where we can gather to support one another's passage through the shadowlands. We have enculturated a denial of the dark side. Unitarian Minister Yielbonzie Charles Johnson comments that George Bush gives us a model that says,"Forget the shadow. Just get on with it." He used to do cocaine. Now he is past it. We all know that when you suppress the shadow rather than embrace it, at a deep level you can never get on with it. In the Western world, we starve both for rituals and for a community context in which to do our shadow work.

North Carolina psychologist and writer Chip Baggett found that the desire to get beyond pain was what motivated many people to enter therapy Yet, he discovered over and over again that it was not the pain that debilitated people in the long run, but the fear which was entwined with it. "I had found that people have an enormous capacity to experience sorrow at its deepest and all the related feelings which are part of grief. These experiences do not harm us when entered into fully but transform us. But most people didn't trust this fact."

"It was as though every person had some unnamed limit to the amount of feeling he or she believed could be tolerated without being utterly shattered. Everyone seemed to have some bottom line of pain beyond which lurked an uncharted wilderness of vague or imagined horrors: will this pain ever end and will I be able to withstand it? where will it lead me? will I go crazy? will I wither and die? will I kill? will I lose all that I hold dear? will I be forever loveless? will God forsake me? Of course these fears are not intrinsic to the present loss but of the imagined pain of the future. Yet because of these fears, most people resist the intensity of such losses. So, rather than completely entering each experience as it arises moment by moment, allowing it to envelop our whole being, we try to suppress, avoid or otherwise move away from it. But in doing so, we are unable to achieve the deep peaceful balance at the center of our emotional truth...a center which can only be found by standing straight up in the present moment."

"The consequence then is that we each create a journey of incomplete moments. And since we cannot make peace with what we don't allow ourselves to experience, we accumulate a lifetime of unhealed wounds. The longer we avoid the experience, the deeper it is lodged in fear, and in time, like the child imagined monster in the closet, the fear grows bigger than life. So, we keep a vigilant guard outside the closet. Although we may temporarily avoid the immediacy of the crisis, we become chronically imprisoned by our fear, disconnected from our heart, and less open and vulnerable to life along the way."

People will do ANYTHING to avoid the dark side, the black hole. Embracing the shadow is painful, often excruciating. When we are in it, it can feel boundless and endless. Yet, as the Virginia Woolf character in the movie "The Hours" said repeatedly, "we must look life straight in the eye." The cycle of death and renewal we pass through at different times in life is an essential part of the creative process. Each passage through the black hole contributes to building a strong and unshakeable sense of self.

THE MALE HEART WOUND IN RELATIONSHIP

While both men and women need love, Daphne Rose Kingma acknowledges that "it is exactly at the point where love, the feeling, intersects relationship, the reality, that men have so many problems. Indeed, it is the very relationships that have made women despair of ever having a real experience of intimacy with men that the true dimension of men's suffering is ultimately revealed. For it is in relationship, the very essence of which is to be a sanctuary for the nurturing and exchange of feelings, that men, by virtue precisely of what it is to be a man, are most deprived. In the province of feeling, men are called upon to serve and not to feel, to perform and not to reveal, to behave like heroes and not mere human beings." Women contribute to the struggle for intimacy as well, as they ask men to go forth and conquer the world, and then are amazed when they cannot take their armor off at home.

Art Matthis notes, "Men live with a tension between a deep desire to connect and some strong social training that as a man you shouldn't have to. While all human beings have a natural need to be in community, men have been taught they need to function as rugged individualists. The male identity gets split apart between an organic human need and a social convention."

Terry Real writes that studies demonstrate that young children are innately connection-seeking, naturally sensitive readers of others' emotions, inherently compassionate and honest. "Intimacy is our natural state as a species, our birthright....neither boys nor girls are allowed to maintain healthy relatedness for long. Instead of cultivating intimacy, turning nascent aptitudes into mature skills, we teach boys and girls, in complementary ways, to bury their deepest selves, to stop speaking, or attending to, the truth, to hold in mistrust, or even in disdain, the state of closeness we all, by our natures, most crave."

"Men are seeking a full relationship of their own heart in relationship with women," reflects Chip Baggett. "They become so emotionally dependent because they confuse where the experience they feel in their hearts is coming from."

Now 49, Chip spoke of a relationship he had with a woman while in his 20's. "I felt as though I had found the home from which I had long been estranged; a deep, fulfilling satisfaction of completeness, which before that point I had not even known existed." Because he did not recognize this experience was centered within his own heart, he credited the woman as the source.

"So, as she invited me into the deep and passionate woundedness of her heart, I found myself more and more drawn to her. I was more open and receptive to becoming one with her than I had ever experienced with another human being. Before long, merging with her became all that mattered. In her presence I was full. Away from her I was empty. Before I realized it, I had fallen desperately in need with her in order to experience my own fulfillment."

"The increasing intensity of my need dissolved any remaining vestige of emotional self-sufficiency as the solid ground of my inner being collapsed beneath me. Without realizing it, my feelings became an implicit demand that she make me whole, that she be my emotional savior. And in the face of her own desperate need, out of which she was turning to me, my desperation became like a voracious sea in which she was drowning." Well over a year after their break up, when they were able to talk to one another and make sense of what they had been through his friend said, "My rock turned to sand and I had to sweep you out the door."

As Chip came home to his own heart, he discovered everything he had felt when he was in love with another person, "the openness, the passion, the feminine, the masculine, the peace, the fullness of the moment, the joy" were all a part of who he already was. "It was simply the nature of my heart to feel such unbounded depth and fullness." But he, like many of us, had not been taught that this is the nature of our own hearts. We are taught to look outside to a specific circumstance, activity or relationship to feel these feelings.

So, rather than developing direct access to our own hearts, we live in a perpetual search for "an other" to be in love with. We hold back our hearts from others who might wish to give and receive love, as we save the open-hearted quality for "the one." What Chip is describing is true for both men and women. Our heart-wounded state is a fertile ground for incomplete, codependent, unsustainable relationships.

As I mentioned earlier in the chapter, traditional gender roles invite men and women to make an emotional deal with each other. Men ask women to be their hearts. In exchange, women ask men to go out and gather resources from the world. Neither gender can fully mature with such a deal. Men lack the context to emotionally mature. Women professionally and economically remain little girls.

The New Male Manifesto

from Knights Without Armor by Aaron R. Kipnis, Ph.D.
published by Jeremy P. Tarcher, Inc.

Men are beautiful. Masculinity is life-affirming and life-supporting. Male sexuality generates life. The male body needs and deserves to be nurtured and protected.

A man's value is not measured by what he produces. We are not merely our professions. We need to be loved for who we are. We make money to support life. Our real challenge, and the adventure that makes life full, is making soul.

Men are not flawed by nature. We become destructive when our masculinity is damaged. Violence springs from desperation and fear rather than from authentic manhood.

A man doesn't have to live up to any narrow, societal image of manhood. There are many ancient images of men as healers, protectors, lovers, and partners with women, men, and nature. This is how we are in our depths: celebrators of life, ethical and strong.

Men do not need to become more like women in order to reconnect with soul. Women can help by giving men room to change, grow, and rediscover masculine depth. Women support men's healing by seeking out and affirming the good in them.

Masculinity does not require the denial of deep feeling. Men have the right to express all their feelings. In our society this takes courage and the support of others. We start to die when we are afraid to say or act upon what we feel.

Men are not only competitors. Men are also brothers. It is natural for us to cooperate and support each other. We find strength and healing through telling the truth to one another — man to man.

Men deserve the same rights as women for custody of children, economic support, government aid, education, health care, and protection from abuse. Fathers are equal to mothers in ability to raise children. Fatherhood is honorable.

Men and women can be equal partners. As men learn to treat women more fairly they also want women to work toward a vision of partnership that does not require men to become less than who they authentically are.

Sometimes we have the right to be wrong, irresponsible, unpredictable, silly, inconsistent, afraid, indecisive, experimental, insecure, visionary, lustful, lazy, fat, bald, old, playful, fierce, irreverent, magical, wild, impractical, unconventional, and other things we're not supposed to be in a culture that circumscribes our lives with rigid roles.

We can see the signs of the paradigm shift in the ways women have fought for economic opportunity over the past few decades and have had to take responsibility for their survival in the world. Likewise, men are being asked to take responsibility for their emotional lives and develop skills to foster relationality. The evolution of both genders is changing the playing field for what is expected and provided in relationship. As men and women come to recognize their wounded hearts and seek healing pathways, they are more likely to meet as peers rather than broken little girls seeking protective daddies and broken little boys seeking nurturing mommies.

HEALING THE MALE HEART WOUND

Healing the male heart wound requires a multi-tiered approach. At the individual level, men first need to feel safe enough to acknowledge their heart wounding, feel the impact of this wounding and seek healing pathways. This is as in 12-step programs, the first step is to recognize that there is a problem. Until the heart wound is acknowledged, healing cannot begin.

Some healing work is very personal, involving introspection and self-care. Other parts of healing cannot be done alone but need to be done in the company of other men or in a mixed gender circle where men and women come together for healing. *The following are important pieces in the healing process.*

1. **Radically shifting how we live.**

   Sacred artist Heyoka Merrifield feels healing the male heart wound requires a radical shift in how we live. "Men need to make space in their lives for more than their work. Many men can't imagine this since work is the only space in their life where they feel in control. Many men live with broken relationships and feel inadequate in the relational realm."

   Heyoka feels the healing process needs to become a way of life. "You have to radically change just about every area of your life. This includes what your priorities are, how you eat, how you exercise, having time for daily meditation, your habits and how you live your daily life."

2. **Making it safer to be a man.**

   Many men I have interviewed feel as a society we need to make it safer to be a man. Men need to feel effective in making things happen and need to be supported in making their dreams real. A man's actions are the expression of his heart. Men need to be appreciated for what they do.

   A 42-year-old father of three children noted, "Collectively, we need to understand the pressure society puts on men. We are breakable, and we have learned to hide it."

3. **Listening to the male heart's voice: caring about what it is like to live inside male skin.**

One man I interviewed lamented, "It is hard for me to find people to talk with about my real concerns. My male friends don't talk about their feelings. I feel like I am in a double bind with the women in my life. They complain if I am silent, yet they don't like it when I tell it like it is."

Men need safe spaces to find their voice and be heard by caring, compassionate listeners. This includes both other men and women. I had no idea how healing some of the interviews I conducted for this book would be for the men who were speaking with me. As I provided a safe, respectful place for men to express their truth, I was deeply touched by what was shared. As the men I interviewed felt cared about and heard, many a tear was shed. I realized the process of asking and listening to the male heart voice was itself part of healing the war between the genders. As men are able to express their heart's voice, they reclaim their emotional power.

In addition to being listened to compassionately by women, a man may also need to learn to listen to himself, and to speak and listen with other men. As a man is able to listen to his own heart's voice, he becomes more facile at listening to others.

4. **Making it safer to reach out to others and seek help.**

Sadly, men often need a personal crisis, usually achieved through failure, serious illness or the collapse of a key relationship or important hope to find the impetus to go inward and do introspective work. We need to make it okay for men to be in therapy and to reach out to others for help and support. Letting others matter and letting others in close in an on-going way is essential for heart healing and long-term emotional well-being.

There is no quick fix, and those who seek a magic bullet or pill will find disappointment. Good therapy establishes a safe, steady, emotionally intimate relationship where a man can take off his armor and express his true heart. Therapists need to learn to balance confrontation with empathy, and individual men need to endure taking responsibility for their own actions and their own impact on others in their lives. Men need to become patient and have faith in the value of long-term healing work.

5. **Gathering together with other men.**

"How can a boy grow up to be a man if he doesn't know what it means?" asks Sparrow Hart, leader of the Mythic Warrior Training.

Boys and men need both role models and coaches to help them develop a mature male identity. Men need to be put in a place where they can learn to love other men and receive love from other men. A peer group can support each man's development physically, emotionally, as a member of a community and as a unique soul. Likewise, older men need to mentor younger men and children.

6. **Developing a language of gender equality.**
   The words "healing" and "male heart wound" may be language that men cannot or will not wish to hear. These words may be considered "women's language." Finding a language that can be heard by the male psyche is critical to healing the male heart wound. One man I interviewed commented, "When men hear words like 'healing' and 'male heart wound,' they run for the hills! They think 'you want to HEAL me?!' 'You think I am not whole? You think I'm not good enough, I'm not okay?' This is very threatening and hard for men to hear and absorb."Healing the male heart wound will be easier if we develop a language that is acceptable to both men and women. This new language needs to reflect compassion for each gender's unique strengths and challenges. A language of growth, creating, building a full life and even nurturing might be acceptable to both genders.

7. **Redefining male power.**

   Men's retreat leader Sparrow Hart asks, "How can we redefine what we call male power and see that there is really a vulnerability and even an oppression behind it? One of the fundamental things men learn is that they are disposable. A boy walks on the outside of the road with a girl on the inside. It's not as great a tragedy if he gets killed. Men get the message that their lives don't count. To have a conversation with a man about self-care is almost an affront."

8. **Creating ceremony and sacred rituals in daily life.**
   "Without ceremony, we are not whole human beings," acknowledges Heyoka Merrifield. "Our spirituality is locked up in the brain. We need ceremony to get it down into the body." Meditation, ceremony and sacred rituals allow us to attune to nature, the life force and our own highest self. Living from this place of attunement inspires us to follow a higher road, and invites a deeper consideration of what our responsibilities are as human beings to self, other and the natural world.

ESSENTIAL QUESTIONS:

1. How have you come to define what it means to be a man?
2. As a man, what are the deepest values on which you have built your identity?
3. Do you recognize the symptoms of the male heart wound?
   In what ways is your heart wounded?
4. What do you do with your fear, pain, vulnerability and anger?
5. What would it mean to take care of yourself? What are barriers to self-care (internal and external)?
6. How comfortable are you at acknowledging your deepest feelings?
   To yourself? To others? To a primary partner? To women? To men?
7. How does your heart woundedness impact your relationships?
   With a partner? With other men? With women? With children?

MEDITATION: *Listening to the Male Heart*

This is an exercise that can be done alone, with a partner, in a group of men or in a mixed gender group. First, close your eyes and experience the meditation. Then journal your thoughts and feelings once the meditation is done. Once you have journaled your thoughts and feelings:

❦ With a partner, create a safe space of heartful listening, where it is safe to speak what is true within your heart.

❦ In a group of men, take turns speaking and listening heartfully as each man shares his experience.

❦ In a mixed gender group, give space for each man to speak, as both men and women listen heartfully.

Once all men have spoken in either kind of group, discuss what it felt like to listen to what the men had to say as they spoke. What feelings, thoughts and questions did it raise in your heart and mind?

Take a moment to do this meditation, whether it be sitting or lying down. When you find a comfortable place, close your eyes and begin to take a few deep breaths. As you inhale, feels your chest and belly fill with air. As you exhale, allow your chest and belly to very slowly and gently melt and relax. Take a moment to see if you are comfortable....or if you need to adjust your position in any way to be more comfortable.

Whenever you feel ready, allow your focus to be with your heart, noticing where you feel your heart when I say the word "heart." If it helps to put your hand on your heart to help focus there, you are welcome to do so. Take a moment to notice how your heart is feeling physically and emotionally. Is it full? Is it empty? Is it heavy? Is it light? Is it separate? Connected? Take a moment to let yourself become a little more familiar with whatever is happening in your heart now.

Whenever you feel ready, take a moment to reflect on the state of your male heart... Does it feel accessible? Distant? Does it feel safe? Cautious?

If you were to invite it to speak, would words come easily? With great struggle? Not at all? See what your heart needs to feel safe and welcome right now.

And whether your heart feels distant or accessible, expressive or quiet, take a moment to ask your heart the following questions. Know that the questions are as important as having answers...and it is okay not to have clear or immediate answers. Just give yourself the space and permission to inquire, to ask.

What are you most proud of as a man? What is hardest for you? What have been your greatest victories? And what have you sacrificed for these victories? What do you feel is off limits to you as a man? How safe is it to have dreams? To go after your dreams? How well do you know the yearnings of your heart?

What is hardest about relating to other men? to women? What is easiest to women? What do you wish other men understood about your experience? What do you wish women understood about your experience? If someone was to really understand what it was like to live inside your skin, what would you they need to know? What is most important for someone to understand about you for you to feel they really know you?

Take whatever time and space you need to be with your heart, to be with whatever you are sensing, thinking, feeling...And whenever you feel ready, honoring your heart and the space you have given yourself to reflect, very slowly and gently take a deep breath, and beginning to bring your focus back into the room. Whenever you feel ready, you can very slowly and gently open your eyes and begin to make notes from this meditation.

Chapter 4

HEARING THE FEMALE HEART

*"The feminine character, and the ideal of femininity
of which it is modeled, are products of
masculine society."*

— Theodor Adorno

At the very root of the cultural heart wound I described in Chapter 1, is the suppression of the feminine, and a primary source of feminine power, the heart. While we can trace women's social progress over the past several generations, to understand the depth and intensity of the female heart wound, we need to look back 3000-5000 years ago before the patriarchal era began. Because there is feminine energy in both men and women, the suppression of the female heart underlies both our collective heart wounds and the personal wounds that afflict us all, regardless of gender.

Tantra teacher Juliana Dahl paints a picture of the central role of women in the matriarchal culture. An abundance of goddess figurines and statues dug up in excavation, archeological evidence dating back more than 30,000 years, points to worship of the Goddess. In this matriarchal era, the basis for women's power and social respect was in their ability to nourish and sustain the culture. "They brought life into the world through their bodies, through their sexuality, and sustained life through their nurturing skills. At this time, women were gatherers of food. They invented farming to make food gathering easier. They responded to the needs of the culture and to necessity."

The culture as a whole understood that it was because of women that all people continued to prosper. Juliana continues, " In this way, the feminine traits of nurturance, love, open heartedness, emotional connection and creativity were shared and upheld. Men looked at this model, saw that it worked, and were part of it. In this way, women were the initiators of men — they initiated them into a way of being that brought peace and harmony to the culture. It became obvious that the balance of male and female aspects made for a balanced culture and society." The women took the lead in the balancing.

One theory is that the demise of this place of harmony and peace came when men began herding animals. This was another food source, another way to survive. With herding came changes to the social order. To have animals required more land. Men began to wander to find land. This was the beginning of the end. Chariots and swords were developed to ward off wild beasts initially. Eventually, these swords were used against other people to protect ownership of land and animals. A primal survival instinct emerged. People now needed animals and land to survive.

The herding of animals marked the beginning of a society focused on the warrior male. In her book, **MY NAME IS CHELLIS AND I'M IN RECOVERY FROM WESTERN CIVILIZATION**, author Chellis Glendinning calls this historical moment "original trauma," when instead of being a part of nature, man now sought to control, own and dominate nature. In this warrior male culture, women were no longer revered. A war-like way of being replaced the matriarchal focus on balance, nourishment and sustainability. Women became another object to be conquered. In order for men to overcome the matriarchal culture, they needed to have power over women. The consequence was a profound suppression of female essence and a deep wounding to female sexuality and the female heart.

We pay the price for this suppression of the feminine both personally and collectively in our fast paced, undernourished, overscheduled, and as Terry Real has written, "anti-relational, vulnerability-despising" culture. As a result, our primary evolutionary task at this time in history is to reintegrate the feminine into our culture and our lives.

THE FEMALE HEART WOUND

A 30-year-old woman I interviewed painted a clear picture of how our definition of what it means to be a woman has changed over the past three generations. Her 82-year-old grandmother played the traditional role of wife and mother. Her grandfather brought home the bacon and her grandmother watched the children and prepared the family meals. "My grandmother lived for my grandfather," reflected Joanne. "She did whatever my grandfather told her to do. He ruled the house." Joanne's grandmother's closest step towards personal autonomy was securing her learner's permit. However, that was as far as she chose to go. She never learned how to drive.

Joanne's mother, who is 57, on the other hand, shaped a very different life for herself than her mother's. Like many babyboomer women, Joanne's mother pursued higher education and a career. After high school, she left the town where she grew up in Wales and attended the University of London. She obtained a Master's degree in Sociology. She met Joanne's father, married and had two children, eighteen months apart. She worked part-time substitute teaching.

The family moved to Canada, as Joanne's father had the opportunity to develop his career. "My mom felt the right thing to do was to move with her husband," Joanne noted. Joanne's mother's secured a part-time job in a department store working with kitchen gadgets. Like so many women of her generation, Joanne's mother spent time with her children when they were young, while also having one foot gently planted in the world of work. These woman pioneered a "hybrid model" of part-time working woman and full-time mom.

The family moved again to Connecticut, and as Joanne and her brother were middle school age, her mom took on full-time employment. Over the past eighteen years, her mom has progressed in her own career, and holds a significant managerial position. When I asked Joanne what it meant to her to be a woman, she replied, "To keep going to school and to keep on going to work."

When Joanne was in high school, her mother began to burn in the message, "don't get pregnant." When she started dating boys and having boyfriends, her father told her, if she ever got pregnant, he would break both of her legs. "This was my education about sex," sighed Joanne. "My mother never talked to me about what it meant to be a girl. She never told me to shave my legs or anything."

"I was curious about menstruation and the changes going on in my body. One time I saw tampax in a store and I asked my mother about it. She said she'd explain it at home. She never did." Joanne got her period when she was 12, just as her mother was having a hysterectomy. "My mother never explained much about menstruation. She just gave me her old tampax, since she wouldn't need them anymore."

Joanne feels that her heart has been wounded by always having to go to work, always having to get an education, and always having to worry about the tone of her voice. "There was a double standard for me and my brother," Joanne acknowledges. "Whenever I tried to talk, my parents always focused on the tone of my voice. They didn't listen to my message, to what I was trying to say. My brother could be rude and my parents allowed it. I could say something regular and it wouldn't be all right."

Joanne's life has lacked time and space to play or relax. "I forgot about the girl parts and the feminine parts of myself," she said. "I'm sad about having to forget about those parts. Yet, I get positive feedback from both my parents and the culture for going to school and working. My parents only focus on jobs and school. They don't ask me about myself as a person." Joanne's mother lacks the skills to reach inside and connect. While she has been professionally successful, she is emotionally insensitive. It is probably no surprise that Joanne doesn't want to have children.

Joanne's family chronology illustrates a pattern I have heard repeatedly in my interviews with women for this book: Over the course of the past three generations, women have succeeded in developing their masculine energy and have become more disconnected from the feminine within. I have come to see two different layers of the female heart wound: the heart wound associated with the traditional role of women in our culture, and a more contemporary heart wound that suppresses the essential feminine qualities that women of Joanne's grandmother's generation were allowed to have.

Joanne's grandmother and most other women in her generation built their lives around the needs of other people. They didn't think about or attend to their own inner needs. They were subservient to their husbands. They experienced a sense of powerlessness and displacement in the outer world, where men worked, made money and enjoyed degrees of freedom not available to women..

Joanne's mother's generation birthed the feminist movement. Her mother's peers fought for equal rights, equal work and equal pay. They created space for women to bring their energies and talents beyond the limited frontier of the home. They fought to remedy the symptoms of the female heart wound that came with the patriarchal era. However, these women "did battle" with the male warrior culture on its own terms.

Joanne's generation is reaping the rewards of the feminist movement on the workfront, with both permission and support to develop "self as professional being." However, these young women are also paying the price for the disconnection with feminine energy that has accompanied this social progress. My interviews revealed an increasing number of "masculinized women" who suffer from the male heart wound as much as the female heart wound. These woman have often experienced a loss of girlhood and feel disenfranchised from their soft, receptive and feminine side.

Symptoms of the Traditional Female Heart Wound

♥ disconnection from intellect, internal power and passion

♥ undeveloped sense of mature woman

♥ powerlessness

♥ self-lessness

♥ inattention to needs

♥ raw, fragile vulnerability

♥ starving for connection

♥ chronically feeling unheard

♥ depression

♥ body hate and body shame

♥ not valued for being

♥ putting others ahead of self

♥ lack of acceptance of being authentic
as a woman

THE HEART-WOUNDING SIDE EFFECTS OF "SOCIAL PROGRESS" FOR WOMEN

In 1987, Char Tosi started "**Woman Within™ Training**," a workshop that offers an initiation for women. "It's an initiation in the sense that women find parts of themselves that they have cut off and need to reclaim." Six thousand women have gone through the program in the United States, Canada, Europe and other countries. "I call us a 'post-feminist' organization," says Char. "What drove me to create 'Woman Within' was that I was wounded by the feminist movement and I felt I wasn't good enough. The part I had cut off was that I was good enough as a woman. The feminist movement told women they had to be more like men, and pull up their masculine part of themselves to succeed. I needed to reclaim the power of who I was, the innate power of being a woman."

There are many ways women have been cut off from their innate power, which they need to reclaim. Some of these ways include:

Body hatred and body shame:

A lot of women, even young women, hate their bodies. They hate who they are, how they look and need to reclaim that they are good enough. The media has a lot to do with body hate. Char cited some research that women who read Cosmopolitan magazine and other magazines of this genre are significantly depressed after they read the magazine. These magazines are all about body image, and women feel they will never measure up.

Some of the wounding around body image can come from parental teaching and modeling. A diet- and weight-obsessed mother, who is always anxious at meal-times, can exert subtle and overt pressures on her daughter. Yet it is less common for today's mothers to tell their daughters they need to be beauty queens. Char notes that body hate issues have exacerbated since she first started her trainings fifteen years ago.

"I see a positive difference in the crone generation. Women over fifty are taking better care of their bodies," reflects Char. "They are doing it from a healthy place. They are more conscious that their bodies are part of their wholeness. Many twentysomethings and younger babyboomers are still trying to make their bodies look younger and perfect — the 'Barbie Doll Effect'." Healing body shame, accepting our okayness, and embracing our wholeself physically, spiritually, mentally and emotionally is an important movement. When a woman can step into being all of who she is and recognize how all the parts relate, it is a whole different way of looking at oneself.

Looking outside, not within:

Char has observed that women in their early twenties and Generation Xers have learned to look outside for approval. Just as Joanne related earlier in this chapter that her parents, including her mother, were unable to reach inside and connect with her, many women are unable to reach inside and connect with themselves. Women in Joanne's grandmother's and even mother's generation were never encouraged to look inside and develop themselves. The messages for self-development have focused more on "what to do professionally" and how to define oneself externally, in the outer world.

To an increasing degree over the past several decades, the ever expanding media has inundated younger women with messages about how they should look, act and behave. Moving from radio to television, first black and white and then color, to cinemascope and now the Internet, these media images have contributed to anorexia and bulimia in epidemic proportions. Women have been cut off from their own inner voice, from listening to the wisdom of their bodies and trusting their own intuition.

Tosi commented, "Women have learned how to deafen themselves to their inner voice. Many women come to the training saying they have wanted to leave their husband for ten years but can't do it. They can't translate their voice into action." Women need to learn to listen and translate into action what they hear. A major barrier to listening and acting is a fear of losing connection. Many women fear if they really stand up for themselves, speak and act, they will be alone or abandoned. And this really does happen. The fear of being alone or abandoned is often a grounded fear that one must face and move through.

Masculinized women:

By sheer necessity, women have had to suffer the male heart wound to survive. To succeed in the workplace, one cannot be receptive, vulnerable, emotional and open. This is true for both women and men, and has created an energetic imbalance in the culture. Men are already overmasculinized, and now, so are women.

"My 28-year-old sister is a very strong-willed woman," reflects Marie, a thirtysomething woman. "She has a career, but is also an incredibly politically correct consciousness person. We went to a political event. The woman who headed it up is around my sister's age. My sister said she was really jealous of her. That woman was actively changing the world and my sister wants to feel that kind of power and effectiveness too. She is so competitive both with everyone else and with herself. I see a lot of masculinized women in my sister's generation. They are very active in many facets of life: politically active, professionally active, socially active. They never stop and rest. They are out in the world doing, doing, doing. They seem to be expressing only one side of themselves — their yang masculine energy."

In her sister's generation, Marie sees both women who are choosing not to think about marriage and children, and other women marrying young pursuing a retro — "Leave It to Beaver" lifestyle. She sees reverse gender role polarization in couples, including with her sister and her sister's fiance."I see masculinized woman traits in my sister and feminized male traits in her fiance. My sister's fiance is younger than she is, and less certain of his professional direction as well. He's a teacher's assistant looking to go back to graduate school to become a teacher in a public school."

"One of my friends, an artist around my age, and I talk about why is it these days you look around and see women being more proactive about saving up money to buy a house or strategizing about how to make the couple's life better materially. What are the males doing? They are sitting back saying, 'You take care of it, honey.' We see a lot more 'soft' males, who might be lighter and more fun to be with, but not as aggressively male. Were these guys brought up by ardent hippie feminist women who were trying to make changes in society and succeeded? Were they brought up in households where there wasn't a male around? I feel that things have gotten out of balance. To restore a sense of balance, men need men to mentor their masculine energy and women need women to mentor their feminine energy."

Wounded female sexuality:

Women's sexuality has been wounded in many ways since the beginning of the patriarchal era. The matriarchy's "power with" model of relating was replaced by a warrior-based, "power over" model. Women became the lesser gender, the object of the dominant gender, men. Religious institutions separated spirit from body, making spirit good and body evil, adding to the suppression of female sexuality. The sexual abuse that runs rampant in our culture is a consequence of the sex-spirit split and repressed sexuality.

Many forces conspire to prevent women from stepping into the power and fullness of their sexuality. As the media has become a more central force in our culture, its images have worked against women's desires to listen to their bodies and intuition, and define a sexual identity from the inside out. "I struggle with how to parent my 14-year-old daughter," sighed a 50-year-old mother. "On the one hand I can't bear the thought of my daughter walking around in the skimpy clothing promoted in magazines and on TV. She's a down to earth kid, and she needs time to grow into her own sense of womanhood. Yet, if all her friends are dressing a particular way, to not do so would ostracize her. She wants to fit in."

The media both oversexualizes women, and offers a disembodied, objectified model of sexuality. This has gone on for a long time. For the crone age woman growing up with the culture of World War Two, pin-ups girls became the media icon of female sexuality. A sixty-year old woman I interviewed commented, "I did not like the way women were projected sexually. I remember reacting to pin-up girls with thoughts like, 'I can't identity with that kind of sexuality.' It was too blatant. It didn't seem like the whole woman."

Today, the media pushes girls and adolescents to become sexual objects earlier and earlier without the corresponding emotional maturation necessary to grow into a sense of grounded sexuality. Adolescent and teenage girls are hungry for rites of passage. In the absence of conscious cultural rites of passage, the media takes over. Gender researcher Joan Walker speaks of the "boy woman" — symbolized by pop icons like Brittany Spears or Tiffany. These women dress like sluts and act emotionally tough like men. "My 53-year-old boyfriend's 15-year-old daughter has an unabashed aggressiveness about being sexual in the world," reflects a 35-year-old woman. "If you look at the way kids dress now, going around in little tank tops that say 'hot stuff' and low riding pants that they paint on, it is quite shocking. When I was in high school, no one would be caught dead dressing that way!"

On the positive side twentysomethings I spoke with reported a sense that there was more room for sexual exploration for young women. "More women I know are exploring bisexuality," acknowledged one twentysomething woman. "Some of my friends see this as part of their sexual development. One way of coming to know who you are as a woman is by being intimate with others like yourself. Many of the men I know find bisexuality in women a turn on. In my circles, it's less okay for the guys to explore their bisexuality. For women, there is more space to explore one's sexual identity than in my parents' generation."

Voicelessness:

A traditional symptom of the female heart wound is a wounding of the female voice. Earlier in the chapter, Joanne described the way she was silenced in her family. The silencing of women's voices is one manifestation of the cultural heart wound. Because of a collective discomfort with feelings and emotional expression, most women I know have been told at some point in their lives that they are "too much," and "too emotional." Not being heard wounds the female heart. Voice is an expression of soul, and a channel for female power. If we are going to heal the female heart, we need to support women to look inside to get in touch with their personal truth and their needs. Women need safe forums to express themselves and be heard.

Crone age women were taught to be quiet and learned to be silent. During the feminist movement, many women found their voices and broke through the socially imposed wall of silence. Speaking up about personal needs in intimate relationships has remained a more challenging frontier for many women. Char Tosi comments, "In Generation X I see more skills in speaking up in relationships. These women are more willing to say what they need and not get quite as silenced by their fears as the women before them. Perhaps this is another positive model from their feminist mothers — learning to stand up for yourself and take care of yourself." When women speak up they help contribute to ending a cycle of physical, emotional and sexual abuse. They also gain more power in creating what they really want.

Having babies versus financial survival:

The desire to have babies and to love, nurture and care for children is a very basic and essential part of female nature. The continuation of our species is based on women's ability to conceive and birth new life. This essential urge and once assumed God-given-right proves challenging to many of today's women, as they question whether they can afford to have children and raise them. Can they take time out of the workforce and give birth to children? Can they afford to stay home and mother their children? Can they afford to pay for childcare so they can remain in the workforce to financially provide for their children? Will there be a partner who stays around and helps parent the children from infancy to adulthood? How painful to ask the question, "will having babies jeopardize my financial survival?"

"I have watched my friends struggle with these questions," responded a single, childless forty year old woman. "I am wrestling with the question myself. If I have a child, I become emotionally and practically vulnerable. Someone else is depending on me and it is a major commitment to care for a young someone. With a 50% divorce rate, what are the chances of my marriage working even if I find a suitable partner? Can I do what it takes to care for a child and myself without the participation or support of a partner?"

Single mothers manage to "keep things together" for their children, but not without an unavoidable cost to self and children. They often must rely on "industrial" home management resources rather than on a partner, nuclear family or extended family, whose care includes a blood-based, lifelong emotional and relational bond. Yet they need to turn somewhere. Life today is too complex, with demands and responsibilities at many levels. No one can do it all.

Lilly, 31, sees how her mother's heart was wounded at age seven when Lilly's grandmother unexpectedly entered the world of single motherhood with two young daughters. "When my grandfather died, my grandmother was catapulted into the stressful world of single motherhood. My mother saw her own mother working hard. She was stretched really thin. My mother developed a stuttering habit. Throughout my life, my mother has been loving, but unemotional. She doesn't open up to me. My mom's sister is shut down — not available emotionally."

As the pace of our world continues to speed up, as the cost of living continues to go up, as the demands placed on any human being to survive increase, the quality of space needed to nurture children diminishes. If twenty years ago it took two people's income to provide a lifestyle comparable to a one income family in the 1950's, how many people's income will it take to provide that same protected household environment today? We need to find new ways to create supportive spaces for women, families and children and for the important work of procreation and parenting.

Having to do it all:

Beth, a 46-year-old woman I interviewed, feels that part of the female heart wound for women today is the pressure of trying to have it all and do it all. "This is a variation on the theme of sexism. Women today get stuck doing twice the work. Many men aren't doing their share on the homefront. Now women are both trying to bring home the bacon and trying to take care of the kids. Sexism is reflected in women having to do it all. I feel betrayed by the men of my generation. They have focused on making lives better for themselves, but not on making things better for women. In my mother's generation, people had lower expectations."

Margo, 30, reflects, "The fact that the sexual revolution never resolved itself is the biggest wound for both women and men. People have been left dangling trying to fill all the roles all at once. Some women have decided not to have kids. Some women focus on anti-men sentiments. Other women try to have kids and a job and do everything. People have gotten really worn out by this lifestyle. Marriages have taken a really bad toll. The economy has shifted. On National Public Radio, they talked about 'the silent revolution,' where both parents, if there are two in a household, have to work just to make ends meet. It has changed everything tremendously. Now it's not just a choice but a necessity that women are playing both male and female roles."

"Our culture makes it nearly impossible to be a well-rounded person," Beth continues. "Women become masculinized because they are trying to survive in a culture that only values certain qualities. This is just like men having to stuff down their sensitive side because those qualities are unacceptable in the workplace." Do either men or women really want to embody this social model? We need to move on to build a more human, sustainable, integrative model.

THE EPIDEMIC OF UNDERNURTURED WOMEN

While I have been a pioneer in many ways that I am proud of, one of my more humbling pioneering experiences was as an anorexic. When I was 13-years-old, before the term "anorexia" was being used, I found myself in the office of a pioneering physician at the Massachusetts General Hospital because in an effort to "control" my weight, I had lost my period for nine months. I discovered I was part of an unfolding epidemic of bright young girls and women who somehow denied themselves the nourishment their bodies needed.

A colleague of mine made a comment to me that anorexia was a disease of bright, white privileged girls trying to exert control. I found her comment judgmental, and it did not resonate with my experience. While I was bright and white, I was not privileged. My middle class parents struggled with financial issues and lived frugally. When I had to face the root of my anorexia, it had to do with a combination of messages: 1. my father's simultaneous angry sexualization and rejection of me as a girl/woman; 2. constant messages that although I was the best at many things based on performance, that nothing I could possibly do or be was ever going to be good enough; and 3. that my strong, solid — not waif-like — body was undesirable with Twiggy as the role model broadcast on television.

My father would say things like, "no man will ever want you for your body" as he repressed his own sexuality. I found myself writing in my journal that I wanted to be 5'7" tall and 115 lbs, because that was what a woman of my height needed to weigh to be acceptable. The pain of not fitting into the round hole I felt pressured to match led me to exert mind over matter. I came to discover this was a path of unintentional self-destruction. Having proudly gotten my weight down to 118 lbs, I was in shock to hear the pioneering anorexia physician tell me that with my build, I needed to gain 20 lbs immediately and never let my weight drop below 135 lbs or I might never be able to have children. Here I thought I was finally succeeding, getting closer to the socially prescribed model. Instead, I discovered, I was on a path towards first reproductive and eventually whole body suicide. What a rude emotional, physical and spiritual awakening!

In retrospect, my anorexia was a kind of slow suicide of despair, denying myself nourishment, desperately trying to find some control in a life of emotional abuse and deprivation, spiritual oppression and judgment by authority figures, including my parents. I felt the pain of emotional, physical and spiritual deprivation, as no matter how good, bright or beautiful I was inside or in deed, I could never measure up. My anorexia was an expression of my powerlessness and my disenfranchisement from the source of my power — my body, my kinesthetic nature.

I learned the hard way that self-nurturance is the foundation for a healthy, balanced and productive life. All the pressure to do, produce and conform to society's often media-generated standards can literally eat away one's inner knowing, one's spirit and one's soul.

As I interviewed twentysomething and thirtysomething women, a major theme that emerged was the lack of female nurturance they received from their mothers, who were more involved in their careers and working outside the home. The professional involvement of their mothers is a good thing on an empowerment level. Women today have more freedom to choose whether they want to have children or not, marry or not, and focus on career or relationships. We have options available to us that my mother or grandmother never even imagined. And yet, no woman can be all things to all people or even to herself. One consequence of career as a primary focus for many women is that women's energies, in the aggregate, are no longer primarily focused on mothering. This can negatively impact their daughters.

And yet, when I was growing up, daughters also suffered as stay-at-home mothers had few paths of self-expression, and lacked permission or skill to nurture themselves. How we take care of ourselves and balance our energies does impact both the nature of our relationships with our children and the model we provide through the way we live our lives. Finding a personal sense of balance is both an on-going meditation and art form, profoundly challenging and absolutely essential.

THE ALPHA EARNER

N ewsweek recently did a cover story on the "alpha earner," spotlighting households where the woman is the primary breadwinner. This article felt groundbreaking, in that it brought to public attention the reality that a growing number of women are playing the primary and sole breadwinner roles. Susan, an "alpha earner" 38-year-old mom of a 7-year-old son, told me that she feels invisible, lacking the social support both for her enjoyment of her fulfilling career and for her breadwinner role in her family. The gender role reversal works well for her stay-at-home writer husband. Her nuclear family unit works well, and even makes light of mom being the "dad" role and dad being the "mom" role. If this contemporary woman feels a lack of social support for a lifestyle that is much more accepted today, it does not take much to imagine how hard it would have been to be Susan in her mother's generation.

Margo, 35, is the daughter of a sixtysomething mother. Had she been born just a generation later, Margo's mother would not have chosen to have kids. Her career was her passion, and the family home was her tether, keeping her from fully taking off in the world. When Margo was thirteen and her younger sister was just six, her mother left the family in pursuit of a career advancing job. She made her home in another state and got together with her children and their father on weekends and holidays.

"While my mother told me it was important to think about who I wanted to be when I grew up and what I wanted to do in the world, empowering stuff which is valuable, I never got training in how to be a girl," mourns Margo. "She told me relationships weren't important. I never learned how to deal with guys as a female. How to talk to them, how to date was a complete mystery. While I was raised to be an independent, intelligent, lively young woman, there was a whole denying of girlness."

Margo's mother modeled that it is okay to go into any career, but she did not model that it is okay to nurture and receive nurturing. Margo has met many young women she describes as "tough on the outside and raw on the inside," who were never nourished and cultivated by a loving, present mother. "Yes, women deserve to have fulfilling careers. And children also deserve to have the full attention and presence of loving mothers. How can we both be out in the world and at home? How do we strike a balance?"

With so much female energy channeled into the workworld, there is definitely less female energy available to channel into homelife. Many layers of life today could use an infusion of feminine nurturance. Most all of the home management functions, once the undisputed territory of women at home, have been delegated to industry and commerce. One could call this the "industrialization" of once feminine functions. Childcare, food preparation, food and clothes shopping, home organizing, and cleaning can all be performed by commercial concerns. Working women lack both the time and the energy to do this homefront work. "It's hard to keep your armor on at work and than come home, slow down and nurture yourself and your children," reflected a thirtysomething woman I interviewed. "I feel like I need either a househusband or a wife!"

Symptoms of the Contemporary Female Heart Wound

♥ masculinization of women

♥ increased disconnection from feminine nature

♥ undernutured women and undernurtured culture

♥ distrust of body, intuition and inner knowing

♥ looking outside for identity, not within

♥ disconnection from feminine sexuality,
including sexual abuse

♥ added pressure on women who want to have children

♥ exacerbated body hate and body shame

♥ having to do it all and be it all

REVISIONING FEMALE POWER

In her book **UNITING SEX, SELF AND SPIRIT**, author Genia Pauli Haddon presents a model of understanding masculine and feminine energies. She draws from Chinese Taoist philosophy, whose two great primal powers are yin and yang. I will draw from and build upon her model to provide a new framework for revisioning both male and female power as we evolve and mature as a species.

The common understanding of yin and yang uses synonyms for yin such as receptive, containing, consolidating and dark. Synonyms for yang include creative, expansive, radiating and bright. "All life is said to reflect the interplay of these two principles," Haddon notes. Stereotypes identify masculine as yang and feminine as yin. "To be masculine traditionally has been defined as to be like the penis or phallus: potent, penetrating, outward thrusting, initiating, probing, forging ahead into virgin territory, opening the way, swordlike, able to cut through, able to cleave or differentiate, goal oriented, to the point, focused, directive, effective, aimed, hitting the mark, strong, firm and erect. Once the equivalence of penis, masculinity and yang has been drawn, any human impulse or behavior having yang-like characteristics is said to be masculine."

"Femininity customarily is said to be receptive and nurturing, as exemplified by the receiving and gestating function of vagina and womb. It follows that to be feminine is to be like a vessel: receiving, encompassing, enclosing, global, wholistic, welcoming, sustaining, protecting, nourishing, conserving, embracing, containing, centripetal, stable, holding together, inclusive — in other words, yin."

Following from the "polarization of genders" model still adopted in our mainstream culture, if a women's personality evidences "expansive yang potency," she is often looked at as "unnatural and dangerous." Likewise, if a man demonstrates yin-like behaviors such as a capacity to be comforting and supportive, he is often negatively judged or viewed pathologically.

Haddon's major contribution is expanding the traditional view of yin and yang to a four-dimensional model. The following picture illustrates the four quadrants of her model:

Yin Feminine	Yang Feminine
♥ gestating womb and vagina with its receiving and gestating function	♥ exertive womb with its pushing and birthing function
Yin Masculine	**Yang Masculine**
♥ testicles self-generating source and place of ripening	♥ penis with expanding and penetrating function

The traditional definition of "yang," which Haddon calls the "yang masculine" is built on both the image and the energy of the penis or phallus. Yet, using our physiology s a guide to our reality, there is more to a man's physical genitals than his penis. The testicles are as essential a part of male sexuality with very different qualities than the penis.

"Physiologically, the testicle is a reservoir, a holding place, where seed is nurtured to maturation. Unlike the penis, whose power acts through intermittent erection and ejaculation, the testicle is stable and abiding. It quietly and steadily undergirds the man's sexuality. It 'hangs in there.' The testicle is the germinal source, the vessel from which is poured forth the sap or water of life."

The testicles represent the "yin masculine" — expressing the yin nature of "the archetypal Great Masculine."A complete understanding of "the Great Masculine" and manhood includes both phallic (yang) and testicular (yin) qualities.

This same thought process can be applied to the vagina and womb.In addition to the receptive and gestating yin feminine, there is also a yang feminine. Again, turning to our physical reality, the birth-pushing, assertive function of the womb expresses the feminine yang. "If we were to define femininity solely in accordance with the womb's birthing power, we would speak of it as the great opener of what has been sealed, the initiator of all going forth, the out-thrusting power at the heart of being." Yang-femininity is concerned with the transformative process and the experience of self-transcendence.

According to Haddon, both men and women must realize and own all four quadrants. At this time in human evolution, we have developed a culture that is overly focused in just one quadrant — the yang masculine. Men are overmasculinized and women are having no choice but to buy into this framework. With such a great imbalance, it is no surprise that so many personal and social structures are unsustainable and are breaking down. If we continue along the trajectory of this imbalance, we will eventually destroy life on this planet, whether it be through world war with weapons of mass destruction, suffocating the collective heart with all its life-giving and affirmative functions, or making the climate for individual women so difficult that they conclude they cannot afford to bear children and raise them.

The power to heal, rebalance and transform the culture will come out of developing the yang feminine with its capacity to birth, to create, to bring forth new life. We need to support women to gather together and embrace this essential feminine capacity individually and collectively. The yang feminine includes recognizing our connection to the earth and being able to be grounded in the earth. We need to activate and harness the power of the yang feminine to balance the overly developed yang masculine energy at all levels in the culture. If we can welcome and build on the yang feminine, we can create the space to reintegrate yin qualities in both men and women.

Integrated female power balances an outer-directedness — looking out for others, their feelings and needs — with an inner directedness — being grounded in one's own needs and self-care. Female power leads with the heart and draws wisdom and voice from the soul and the body. To the degree we shame the body, we shame the soul. It is time to heal the shame that binds us, as John Bradshaw was known to say, and restore a sense of respect to the sacred feminine and its vessels, the body and soul.

HEALING THE FEMALE HEART WOUND

At the core of healing the female heart wound is restoring a sense of sacredness and dignity to feminine energy. Women need support for their feminine nature and inherent wholeness both from other women, and from society as a whole. We first need to take the feminine out of the shadowlands, where it currently resides, and create safe spaces where it is welcome, visible and valued.

As with the male heart wound, some heart healing work needs to be done by women on their own and also with other women. Healing work also needs to be done in mixed gender settings. Both genders need support to find a balance of masculine and feminine energies within themselves and with one another.

Here are some ways women can begin to heal their wounded hearts:

Educating women what healthy nurturing is:

Women who haven't been nurtured don't know how to nurture. Unfortunately, many of us have not had good role models of healthy nurturance. Women who have been incested by their fathers or mothers don't know what healthy nurturing is. Women who have been neglected or abandoned or raised by narcissistically wounded parents don't have a model of healthy nurturance either. Many of us need a definition of healthy nurturance.

Healthy nurturance can take many forms. It includes being heard, accepted unconditionally, being supported by women who are equally powerful and not having to do anything to get support. Char Tosi comments, "Many women in our on-going empowerment circles have the experience of finding out what they are defining as their nurturing is their power."

Learning to trust:

Trust is a big part of nurturing. Without trust, it is hard to let down defenses and take in the nourishment you need. We need to create safe experiences and safe environments to build trust. When women have been hurt by others, including other women, it is hard to trust. Trust has to be built first within oneself — trusting one's experience, one's feelings, one's body, one's inner knowing. Once we trust ourselves we can learn to trust other people.

Creating space where feminine energy is welcome:

Too many women have had to suppress or compartmentalize their feminine energy to survive emotionally, psychically and financially in today's world. It is rare to find spaces where feminine energy is really welcomed and valued, never mind recognized as sacred. Spaces where feminine energy is honored and embraced are necessary to soften the exterior shells of women who have become masculinized by necessity. We need these sacred spaces to allow the free flow of feminine energy and all that grows from it.

Developing the yang feminine in ourselves and our culture:

The yang feminine energy offers a powerful, creative, transformative counterbalance to our overmasculinized culture. Developing the yang feminine will not only help remedy the masculine/feminine imbalance we live with today, but will also create the space for yin-masculine and yin-feminine energies to be present. We need to both ground, soften and transform ourselves and our world. The yang feminine can help us do this important healing work.

Embracing the power of the heart:

Heart understanding is very different than head understanding. The heart seeks to find interconnections, while the head or intellect separates, analyzes and divides. As I mentioned in this chapter, the heart is a source of true feminine power. Truth knows no judgment through the eyes of the heart.

Bringing women together to do heart healing work:

While some work needs to be done by women in the privacy of their own inner lives, joining with other women to do healing work is also an important pathway. At other times in our history, women had the time, space and cultural support for gathering together.

Women's busy lives often do not allow for "organic" or spontaneous gatherings of women. Too, many women feel wounded by other women as well as men. Women need to join together to heal their relationships with their mothers, daughters, sisters, female colleagues and friends. An integrative approach to healing may be most powerful and effective, working with mind, body, spirit and body. Healing our relationship with our body, with our sexuality and with the earth are essential.

Choosing partners who are doing heart healing work:

To move towards the soul-centered paradigm of relating requires partnerships in which both people are engaged in their own heart healing work. Many of the same core principles apply whether the partners are two men, two women or a man and a woman. We all need to find authentic ways to integrate masculine and feminine energies within ourselves and within our partnerships.

ESSENTIAL QUESTIONS:

1. How have you come to define what it means to be a woman?
2. How is your sense of womanhood similar to and different from the way your mother might have experienced her sense of womanhood?
3. Do you recognize signs of the traditional female heart wound and/or the contemporary female heart wound? In what ways is your heart wounded?
4. What are ways you nurture yourself? Are there ways you yearn to be nurtured?
5. How have you been hurt by other women? How have you been mentored and/or guided by other women?
6. How comfortable are you with your feminine nature and the power of your heart?
7. To what degree can you be your whole self in your relationships? With a partner? With other women? With men? With children? At work? At home?

MEDITATION: *Honoring Your Feminine Nature*

Take a moment to get comfortable, and close your eyes as long as you are comfortable, taking whatever time and space you need to breathe. And as you inhale, see if you can feel the support of your seat, your pillow, the floor, whatever supports you....and as you exhale, allow the surfaces supporting your body to support you...taking a moment to get comfortable, and adjusting your position any way you need to be more comfortable...

And whenever you feel ready, allow your focus to be with your heart, noticing where you feel your heart, when you hear the word, "heart,".....Taking a moment to let yourself become a little bit more familiar with whatever is happening in your heart right now...Is it full? Is it empty? Is it heavy? Is it light? Is it separate? Connected? Take a moment to let yourself become a little bit more familiar with whatever is happening in your heart, now....

And whenever you feel ready, take a moment to explore your feminine nature....what qualities, characteristics and parts of yourself express your feminine nature? Which of these qualities, characteristics and parts of yourself do you feel most comfortable with? Which ones are most developed and which ones are most dormant or undeveloped?

Take a moment to explore what kind of environment would allow you to honor and express your feminine nature....If you could create a special room to honor the feminine within yourself, where would it be? What would it look like? What colors, smells, sounds and textures would you want to include in this special room? Are there sacred objects you would want to place in the room? If so, what might they be? Would other people be allowed in this room or would it be your private space? Take a moment to let yourself reflect on your ideal space to honor the feminine within yourself.....

And whenever you feel ready, take a moment to reflect on some rituals you might create to honor your feminine essence....These rituals could be simple ones you could incorporate in daily life, or more elaborate ones to do at a special time....Letting yourself reflect on ways to deeply honor your feminine essence, incorporating all of your senses, your body, your mind and your heart.....

And whenever you feel ready, at your own pace, very slowly and gently, take a deep breath, and bring your focus back into the room....And take some time to journal your reflections from this meditation....You are welcome to draw pictures as well as express with words....using whatever media best allow you to continue reflecting on honoring the feminine within yourself.

Chapter 5

THE ESSENCE OF GENDER

*"Just as gayness is not a disease to be cured
(as once was viewed by psychoanalysis) so
gender difference..is another aspect of diversity,
which is slowly becoming recognized as legitimate
and possibly prenatally determined."*

— Niela Miller,
Counseling in Genderland

In Chapter 2, I discussed the gradual unraveling of gender as we have known it over the past several decades. I suggested that this unraveling is part of an evolutionary shift in consciousness from a place of separation to one of integration. We are coming to realize that all dualities are one — light/dark, male/female, and human/non-human. We are being asked to look beyond the concrete, the physical, and the emotional to the soul/spirit or energetic level. As we recognize the energetic or soul level shift, our outward structures must also begin to change.

One of the consequences of our evolutionary shift is the confusion many people are experiencing about the meaning and place of gender. Several decades ago, most people took gender for granted. There was little reason to think about it or talk about it. Men and women were born into a culture which provided certain expectations and models for behavior based on gender. Once assigned a gender at birth, boys and girls were socialized to fit the social norm. If people did not fit this dualistic model of gender, they were silent, hidden and outside our direct line of vision.

The appearance of Rene Richards on television made me aware that a person's sense of gender could transcend the culturally defined vanilla male and female. Her story captivated me. I wished I could sit down and ask her if she still experienced her masculine energy now that her body expressed her feminine soul. Just as ice cream parlors have evolved offering countless creative flavors over the past decades, the possibilities for gender expression have also grown.

As we move through the evolutionary portal, from old paradigm to new, we need to honor two co-existing truths: 1. Male and female gender classifications are important to many people as anchors for identity and social participation, and 2. The gender boxes that once helped create social order no longer seem to fit. We are being invited to embrace a deeper, integrated, soul-based experience of gender.

Not only is there masculine energy and feminine energy, but also men and women possess both energies. Because we are living in the "awkward in-between stage" transitioning between old paradigm and new, men and women today BOTH gain meaning from our social understanding of gender AND feel chaos and confusion as that social understanding sometimes resonates with their inner and outer experience and sometimes fails. We are caught between two worlds in our gender experience, and we need to build a bridge!

As we explore the cultural heart wound in this book, we must explore both the familiar world of male and female identity and the emerging world of energy consciousness and gender integration. Some of the symptoms of the cultural heart wound impact all of us at an energetic, human level. Other manifestations are more gender specific, which I discussed in Chapter 3, Honoring the Male Heart, and Chapter 4, Hearing the Female Heart. This chapter explores our changing understanding of gender. As we build the bridge between paradigms, transgendered people are emerging as cultural educators and agents of social change.

ANNIE

In the late1980's before my first book came out, I led **LIVING WITH VISION** workshops in London. My colleague Martin Leith did the bulk of workshop organizing, but one day he introduced me to a woman who wanted to help the organizing effort. Her name was Annie.

Meeting Annie was a pivotal experience for me in beginning to look deeply at matters of gender, identity and soul. Annie was a transsexual, which was no small feat! Annie had grown up in Ireland and always felt she had a woman's soul. For the first six years of her life, she never even questioned this fact, as she spent all of her time in the company of her best friend, Eileen. The adults in her community thought it was so cute that these two children were deeply bonded and inseparable. No one blinked an eye when they would go into the girls room together. These two children seemed to be twin souls.

Annie's entire life turned upside down when Eileen died. Not only did she grieve the loss of her soul-friend, but also her relationship with the world at large dramatically changed. As Annie continued to do all the activities she had done in Eileen's company, now alone, she was greeted with judgment and scolding. How dare a little boy go into the girls' bathroom! How naughty and inappropriate was this little boy!

Annie was confused, heart-broken and lost. Nothing inside her had changed. Eileen's death catapulted Annie into a struggle of gender and soul, as she discovered her external packaging betrayed her inner truth. Annie tried for many years to learn and perform the male role. She became a nurse. She got married. She had children. She supported her family. But something always haunted her at the deepest level. The life she was living might have looked good to the outside world, but it was not her own life.

From a place of deep courage, in the early 1980's Annie decided she needed to build a new, authentic life as the woman she really was. Her decision forced her to leave Ireland, where her entire family rejected her, and try to start over in London. She went through the process of transforming her body, first with hormones and later with surgery, without support of friends, family or community. She faced the emotional, psychic and physical pain alone. She also risked the fear, anger, rejection and even violence of the world at large, who neither understood nor dared understand the deeper truth of her soul's reality.

As she healed physically in the safety of her private world, she began to build a new life for herself in this new city. She got a job working for an accountant. She made her apartment into a home. Her true identity and story remained a secret for many years. It was not until she participated in Insight personal growth seminars that she found a safe space to finally bare her soul, and break down the walls of secrecy and isolation. Her involvement in the Insight community led her to me and my work.

When I would work in London, I would reside there for two weeks at a time. I enjoyed the welcome of staying in one of my colleague's homes. Once Annie got involved in organizing my work, I would stay with her. As our friendship grew, I would learn more and more of her story.

She shared with me her struggles of building friendships with people who were both unacquainted with and frightened of her transsexuality. She craved love, intimacy and companionship in a primary way, like all of us, but finding a loving partner was far harder for Annie than for a vanilla male or female. One night several years before I met her, she was sitting in a bar having a drink and a man started to make a pass at her. Feeling it important to be honest, she gently took the man's hand and tried to tell him who she was. His response was rage. He took her outside the bar and beat her brutally. Here was homophobia at its worst — the fear of a man attracted to a woman who used to be a man!

Annie and I would have profound conversations about gender, soul and the meaning of life. She was a gifted poet, and she expressed her heart in her words. Her difficult journey forced her to ask deeper questions than I had ever confronted as a straight, monogamous female. She taught me that all gender expressions were valid and personal, and that different sexual subcultures each express an aspect of soul.

GENDER AND IDENTITY

Gender is core to a sense of human identity. Issues of gender touch the most primal layers of the human psyche. We learn to identify who we are with how we are wired, the nature of the body we inhabit, and the cultural programming that goes with being male and female.Gender is both biologically and culturally determined. And for many, it is also a spiritual assignment, an expression of soul. For the majority of men and women born with what is considered "normal" genitalia, XX or XY chromosomes and wiring that conforms with the gender they are assigned, the subject of gender can be taken for granted.

For others, such as intersexed and transgendered people, developing a sense of gender identity is a deep, complex and often painful process. The dominant culture teaches us that there are two genders, male and female, that they are "normal" and that anything else is abnormal. When these commonly defined classifications get shaken up, a primal terror is evoked. Men kill from this terrified place. In reality, gender is a continuum, with many shades of gray between the two extremes of male and female.

Raven Kaldera, author of **HERMAPHRODEITIES: THE TRANSGENDER SPIRITUALITY WORKBOOK**, notes, "In this society, gender is the primal division. You can tell that because people who cross the divide are more penalized as a group than those who cross any other social divide." Anthropologist Adrianne Dana Tabet reflects, "Defining what it means to be a man or a woman forces people to think in cliches. When we speak of 'men' or 'women' we speak of attributes, not essences. Attributes are culturally driven. Essence is intangible."

Having wrestled with the issue of sexual orientation over the last several decades, perhaps facing the issue of gender in our society is the next evolutionary step. Initially gays and lesbians were judged and persecuted in our heterosexist and homophobic culture. Over time, through political action, education, and demystification, many gays and lesbians have come to enjoy a more welcome place in many segments of our culture. How many people do you know who don't have a close friend, family member or colleague who is gay or lesbian? Once we break down the barriers of "them" and "us," our primal fears dissolve and social acceptance is more possible.

WHAT IS IMPORTANT ABOUT MALE AND FEMALE TRAITS?

Human beings like to have models and guidelines to help us understand who we are. When wrestling with essence, energy or the mythological level of existence, models help us grasp what is ephemeral by nature. Because gender is about essence or soul at one level and social role at another level, the concept of "maleness" and "femaleness" both creates a lot of anxiety about who we are and soothes this very anxiety. As we struggle to reconcile internal cues with external messages, gender provides an anchor for our identity.

Anthropologist Adrianne Dana-Tabet notes that gender provides a sociocultural representation and presentation of self. The list of qualities and traits that our society assigns to men and women helps us find a place to fit on the social map.

This sociocultural representation is like a gender job description: it tells us how we are expected to dress and groom ourselves; how we are expected to express ourselves emotionally, physically, spiritually and professionally; and what kinds of activities we are expected to engage in. In this way, expectant parents are given a road map for what to provide materially, emotionally and experientially for their new arrival. Our sense of gender as we have known it contributes to a sense of social order.

Our gender job descriptions create a commonly understood language and set of expectations. They are communicated to us visually and verbally through the mass media. Advertisements on TV and in magazines provide images and role models for who we are supposed to be as men and women, and boys and girls. The media is a powerful school for social and cultural ideas of what male and female mean.

What's Important About Male & Female Traits?

♥ sociocultural representations and
presentations of self

♥ archetypes

♥ mass media representations

♥ anchors for identity

♥ different energies

♥ the same energy — two sides of the same coin

♥ a need to label things

♥ a lot of anxiety is created by it and soothed by it

♥ social ideas and cultural ideas

One's gender assignment helps a child come to understand who s/he is, and determines how s/he is treated by family members and the world around him/her, and how s/he is socialized. As our previously understood models of gender unravel, we come to understand all gender assignments are preliminary. We discover there are different levels of gender experience, some of which take time and life experience to fully grasp and integrate. As we evolve as a species, becoming more emotionally and spiritually mature, and more aware of the soul level of experience, our understanding of gender needs to expand.

The following chart identifies four different levels of gender experience: How we are "wired," the gender we are assigned, how we feel inside at an essential or soul level, and our self-perception in contrast to how others see us.

Different Levels of Gender Experience

♥ how we are "wired"
(genitalia, hormones, chromosomes)

♥ the gender we are assigned
(with the social role that accompanies it)

♥ how we feel at an essential level
(soul level)

♥ self-perception versus how others see us
(all gender levels are preliminary)

For people whose wiring, gender assignment and sense of soul all line up, life can be free of gender angst. For transgendered people, whose wiring and/or gender assignment are incongruent with their sense of soul, developing an authentic sense of gender identity is a long, often painful, journey. Even for people whose wiring and gender assignment feel accurate, gender identity is not black and white. Some men are more feminine than many women. Likewise, some women are more masculine than some men. As I stated at the beginning of this chapter, I believe all human beings contain masculine and feminine energies within. As we integrate our masculine and feminine energies, we move beyond gender boxes into a third dimension of gender space.

GENDER IS NOT ALWAYS ONE'S BIOLOGICAL SEX

For many mainstream vanilla, straight, monogamous men and women, gender is rarely given much depth of thought. For these people, their genitalia, biological sex, gender and sexual orientation line up in a predictable way. Writer Alice Dreger points out, however, that "while the 'male' and 'female' types are relatively common, nature presents a full range of sex types."[1] We often link biological sex with one's genitals. For transgendered and intersexed individuals, this linkage is not a given. An intersexed person is born with what is often labeled, "ambiguous genitalia," challenging where the line should be drawn between male, female and something in between.

Dreger challenges us to look beyond the black and white categories familiar to us, and recognize the spectrum of human experience. "The sex spectrum is like the color spectrum," she notes. "Nature provides us with a range where one 'type' blends imperceptibly into the next. For our linguistic and social convenience, we can break that spectrum into categories."

Intersexed kids pose a tremendous challenge to both their parents and the medical community, who in response to a genderphobic world tries to assign them an 'appropriate' gender, in spite of ambiguous genitalia. The thought behind this 'assignment' is that gender is a social role that can be defined and performed, rather than an internal knowing and state of being that one discovers as one lives and grows.

Intersexed babies are a fairly common and growing population. Given our evolutionary shift towards integration, this is no surprise. Today 1 in 2000 children are born with genitals that are pretty confusing to the adults in the room. Alice Dreger notes that given these statistics, intersex is at least as common as cystic fibrosis.

Most intersexed babies are surgically "altered" to fit the norm for the gender they are assigned by their parents and the medical community. This can both psychologically and physically injure and cripple the growing being who may discover that her assigned gender is not who he really is! In 90% of cases, intersex infants undergo genital surgery to make them appear as "normal" females. It appears to be easier to craft female genitalia than male genitalia.

GENDER IS A DIVINE ASSIGNMENT, NOT A SPIRITUAL CHOICE

Raven Kaldera was born with secondary congenital adrenal hyperplasia — a genetic endocrinal condition in which the adrenal glands put out extra androgens. Kaldera was born with XX chromosomes and assigned female. However, his body thought it needed a male normal level of androgens, even though he lacked testes. Kaldera went through a double-barreled puberty. "My breasts grew, I started to menstruate, my voice deepened and my clitoris enlarged. My parents were very upset."

"When I was ten years old, I read the word hermaphrodite and I knew that was me. It was in a book of mythical creatures. I didn't tell anyone. Then it happened to me, like magic. I thought it was really neat to be this creature endowed with magical powers." Unfortunately, Kaldera's delight was short-lived. His upset parents felt like his unusual development was a horrible, shameful thing.

"The word intersexed was never said to me. It was just that I had a hormone problem. Because I knew I had something medically wrong with me and it had been pounded into my head, I had to try my best to stay female." Kaldera was put on large doses of estrogen at age 13. It stopped the masculinizing in its tracks. It also brought with it severe depression. Raven suffered from gender dysphoria, and sensed that something was terribly wrong.

"When a person suffers from gender dysphoria, there are two kinds of experience: body dysphoria and role dysphoria. Role dysphoria is not liking the social role you have been assigned. In repressed cultures, I would say most of the culture would be suffering from this. Body dysphoria is entirely different. It has nothing to do with role. It has to do with a deep discomfort with the way your body is shaped gender-wise. I am convinced it is biological, because it doesn't respond to anything else. For me, it got to the point where I could not stand the gender of my body anymore."

Kaldera had a really hard time coming to terms with this deep inner reality. "I tried for years and years to be female. I thought if I could just try hard enough I could do it. I tried two extreme forms of womanhood — being a heterosexual housewife and then being a feminist lesbian. Neither experience really changed anything. From my feminist background, I could deconstruct gender, but it didn't matter. My sense of gender affected everything I had to do with my body, so I lived from the neck up."

Kaldera's constant battle with severe depression since puberty kept his looking for alternatives. In his late 20's, working with the seventh in a long string of endocrinologists, Kaldera received a shot of something that made a huge difference. "They gave me a two-week shot of something, and within 12 hours I was no longer depressed. It was like the sun came out. Boom. I went to bed, got plenty of sleep and ran around and had plenty of energy. I felt better than I had in years."

Kaldera went back one week later and asked for more of whatever he had received. The doctors said they couldn't give it to him. It was testosterone. Because Kaldera was not a transsexual, he did not qualify to receive testosterone. Two definitions of transsexual are currently in use. "By one definition, you need to identify 100% opposite of the gender on your driver's license. The second is someone who has an overwhelming urge to change the secondary sexual characteristics of their body. The second definition was true for me."

Kaldera went through counseling, got a letter saying he wanted to be a man, gained access to testosterone and took to it like a duck to water. "My body craved it. Off it I am depressed. On it I am well. I didn't want to do this unconsciously. It was a fully conscious choice and it was a spiritual choice. When I threw up my hands and said, 'Why? Why maleness? I need it physically but I don't like it culturally,' the answer that came to me was 'I am sending you where you are most needed.'"

"Those of us who are transgendered are catalysts by our very nature. People don't decide to be transgendered. You ARE and you don't get to say no. It is a divine assignment." Transgendered people are very powerful. They have access to male and female power simultaneously. This scares many people. "I can't make someone transgendered, but I can make them think about it. My world view is contagious," acknowledges Kaldera.

GENDER AS A PROCESS, NOT A CONDITION

Joan Walker, 65, has been doing introspective work and research on the essence of gender since 1952. Joan is transgendered, but more significantly, androgyndered. "For a long time I had a theory there was another category of gender which was never defined in literature. Nevertheless, there are people to look at who embody this third category, the androgyne. This is somebody who has the masculine polarities and feminine polarities equally strong, to the point they begin to integrate." Gender is an energetic phenomenon, palpable in the electromagnetic fields around the body.

"When the electromagnetic fields around the body begin to integrate, it creates a third gender. You could imagine it as a blend of masculine and feminine, but it doesn't blend. It becomes the master feminine, a third energy. If you take the masculine polarity and put it beside the feminine polarity, the feminine polarity is more magnetic."

You can see this in relations between ordinary men and women too. "If a man who is masculine comes into the field of a genuinely feminine woman, the woman has greater power. The man may be afraid he will lose his identity, and lose control, so he pulls back. This relates to men falling asleep after intercourse. He wants the feminine woman, but not too close for fear he will lose himself. When an androgyne man experiences the feminine pull, he has enough feminine to balance it."

In her research, both with transgendered and transsexual people and with saints, yogis and spiritual leaders, Walker has come to see gender as more than a state of condition. Gender is a process, and a pathway of spiritual evolution. "Many transgendered people are going through a process. One woman I know started out being a street queen. She went through that phase and went back to wearing male clothes and became more like a guy. She went through a sex change operation with no regrets, and is now becoming more neutral. She thought she found out exactly who she was, yet she has never stayed there. She has gone from phase to phase to phase to phase." Each phase has been part of a pathway towards integration.

"Some people may spend a whole lifetime in one phase of the process." Not everyone has signed on for gender as a spiritual, evolutionary path. "There may very well be a phenomenon going on in the culture where the human body is evolving into a whole new form. If you go to college campuses, you may notice any number of college students where you cannot tell if they are male or female. Their clothes and hairstyle are soft. They are unlike the rebellious culture you see young kids get into. It is a culture of androgyny.

Likewise, some of the role models women are given today are more androgynous, including "boywomen." "Pop icons like Brittany Spears and Madonna represent the 'boywoman,'" reflects Joan. "They dress like boys and act like sluts. They call one another guys and exude a physical sexuality. They believe they can do anything a man can do."

MASCULINE AND FEMININE ENERGIES

We often confuse masculine and feminine energies with male and female genders. Perhaps our confusion is at least partially due to the similarity of the words themselves. Feminine energy and female are not the same. Masculine energy and male are not the same. Biologically, physically and emotionally, one might identify as male or female, and present oneself as male or female in the outer world. And as I have said earlier in this chapter, both men and women have both masculine and feminine energy. The energetic level exists as an inner reality and may be more subtle in its expression out in the world. The balance of masculine and feminine energies is unique in any individual.

The Tao symbol from Eastern cultures expresses the same kind of idea. Psychologist Dan Johnston, writes, "The symbol, a circle divided into two portions, each containing an element of the other, indicates that all of creation is composed of two energies held in harmony and interaction. The Yang energy is masculine in nature and is described as light, dry, directed, focused, logical and action oriented. Yin energy is feminine and described as dark, moist, diffuse, vague, intuitive and receptive."[2]

Men's psychological functioning is predominantly yang but contains a yin aspect. Similarly, women's psychological functioning is predominantly yin but contains a yang aspect. Johnston notes, "Thus human beings are psychologically androgynous with latent masculine and feminine energies awaiting development."

When the baby boom generation was growing up, men were supported in developing their masculine qualities and applying them in the world. Women developed their feminine qualities and applied them at home. In her book **PASSAGES**, which was written as the baby boomers were entering young adulthood, Gail Sheehy referred to the 'switch forties.' Having developed their masculine energies to an extreme, men became burned out from their years in the work world. At mid-life, the roles of husband and father suddenly seemed a needed counterbalance for this generation of men. Having devoted their energies to home management and child-rearing, women at mid-life wanted to leave home and engage in the world of work.

This invited a role reversal for both genders, but also facilitated a disconnection between them. During the years she was minding the homefront and family, a woman might have yearned for her "too-busy" husband's company. However, once he became aware and available, it was time for her to put her energies out into the world. Johnston noted that the potential for significant conflict arose as these two people crossed paths on different trajectories.[3]

A significant number of baby boomers and generation-Xers have had another experience. Both men and women have put their primary energy into the world of work from early adulthood on. Home and child-rearing energies are now provided by professional service providers. As a result, since both men and women have focused on developing their masculine energy, there has been an overdevelopment of the masculine in the culture as a whole. The feminine has gone underground, and a significant energy imbalance impacts us all. At mid-life, as both men and women are feeling drained from their careers, they feel a pull to balance their lives with more feminine energy.

Another model, which some couples — men and women, women and women, and men and men — and individuals of both genders have chosen, is to balance feminine and masculine energies from early adulthood on. To balance their energies and lives, baby boomers and generation X-ers have chosen contract employment, self-employment, balancing a creative pursuit with a stable job or working part-time. To find inner peace, we each need to examine the balance of masculine and feminine energies in our lives, and see what kinds of adjustments we might wish to make.

Masculine Energy	Feminine Energy
light	dark
dry	moist
directed	diffuse
focused	vague
logical	intuitive
action	oriented receptive

THE LIGHT AND DARK SIDES OF MASCULINE AND FEMININE ENERGIES

Coach and author Jeanie Marshall acknowledges that there are both dark and light sides to the masculine and the feminine.[4] The following chart summarizes dark and light sides of both energies:

The Dark Side of Masculine	The Dark Side of Feminine
harsh overly competitive violent	weak insecure tentative needy
The Light Side of Masculine	**The Light Side of Feminine**
protective eager outwardly helpful	open receptive listening nurturing

Marshall writes that both men and women who have not integrated their feminine energy can be hard or cold. "Their warmth is lacking or inconsistent. Men or women who have not integrated their masculine sides are often seen as weak or passive. They tend to hold back, allowing others to walk on them." Perhaps it is the lack of integration of both masculine and feminine energies that underlies some of the war between the genders. This includes the gender wars within ourselves as well as the gender wars between us and other people. Marshall notes "The confusion between masculine and feminine encourages unhealthy competition, dysfunctional comparisons, low self-esteem, and of many kinds."

Writer Kristopher Rafael speaks to one example of this kind of imbalance. "The reason why technology has become so destructive to life is because it is void of feminine energy. If technology were balanced with both masculine and feminine energy, it would be the magical manifestation of mankind it was meant to be."[5]

There is also a shadow side of our cultural pursuit of "gender equality." For the past several decades, women have gained more rights and equality in the workplace. Because the workplace values the masculine more highly than the feminine, women have developed their masculine professionalism and distanced from their feminine qualities in order to succeed. One result is that the our culture as a whole suffers from an energy imbalance. It has become overmasculinized and underfemininized.

Just as our religious institutions separated sexuality from spirituality in past eras, the workplace has separated sexuality from the professional environment. The result is that both men and women have learned to neutralize or suppress their masculine and feminine energies. Men suppress their sexuality in order to work alongside women colleagues. Women suppress their sexuality to be seen as equals to their male counterparts and to be taken seriously.

Is it a surprise when men and women try to meet in the bedroom, they have a hard time bringing forth their sexual energy and connecting? By learning to treat each other as "equal" in the workplace, we have, perhaps, unconsciously neutered both genders. This is an example of how symptoms of the male heart wound — disconnection from feelings and body, denial of desire and needs, and valuing doing over being — have become normalized for both genders.

GIRLS, BOYS, WOMEN AND MEN

We can see that the gender energy continuum has swung to extremes and is now being called back into more balance. Just as gender integration for professional women has pushed the feminine underground, many men and, particularly, boys in a school system dominated by women, have been pushed to develop their feminine qualities, sometimes at the expense of their masculine ones.

Kristi Meisenbach Boylan, author of **BORN TO BE WILD: FREEING THE SPIRIT OF THE HYPERACTIVE CHILD** (Perigree 2003), acknowledges, "Boys and girls learn differently. When women teach boys they don't always get it. My son needs to be throwing a football while someone is giving him spelling words. 95% of the education system is feminine. Men feel they need to be masculine, but we are telling them they need to be feminine. Little boys are feeling wrong for being little boys!"

The emergence of more intersexed and transgendered individuals is inviting us to jump out of our societally prescribed gender boxes. It is time to value and integrate the masculine and feminine energies within ourselves in more balanced, meaningful, respectful and life-sustaining ways. My hope is that we arrive at a deeper, personal and more compassionate understanding of gender, recognizing both that it is core to human identity and more far-reaching and complex than our black-and-white thinking has allowed. Understanding, balancing and integrating gender energy is part of the pathway of human evolution.

ESSENTIAL QUESTIONS:

1. To what degree has your gender been something you have questioned or taken for granted?

2. What masculine qualities or traits do you feel are most developed in you?

3. What feminine qualities or traits do you feel are most developed in you?

4. On the continuum of gender energy, where would you place yourself — towards the high masculine end, towards the high feminine end or more integrated?

5. Would your answer to question #4 been different at different stages in your development?

6. What traits and qualities, either masculine or feminine, would you like to develop more fully?

7. If you look at the gender energy balance of the people you are attracted to, how would you describe it? Are you most attracted to people who have high masculine energy, high feminine energy or more integrated energy?

8. How comfortable are you exploring questions like the ones posed above?

MEDITATION: *Getting in Touch With Your Masculine & Feminine Energies*

Find a comfortable place to sit or lie down. Get comfortable, and gently close your eyes. Take whatever time and space you need to breathe, letting your chest and belly fill with air as you inhale and letting your chest and belly relax as you exhale....Taking a moment to see if you are comfortable or if you need to adjust your position in any way to be more comfortable. Whenever you feel ready, allow your focus to be with your heart, noticing where you feel your heart when I say the word heart...And if it helps to put your hand on your heart to help focus there, you are welcome to do so...And take a moment to notice how your heart is feeling, physically and emotionally...Is it full? Is it empty? Is it heavy? Is it light? Is it separate? Connected? Take a moment to let yourself become a little more familiar with whatever is happening in your heart right now.

And whenever you feel ready, take a moment to get in touch with your masculine energy...the part of you that is focused, directed and puts your energy out into the world....Take a moment to notice how you experience this energy in your body....Where do you feel it? Is the current strong or weak? Do you feel open to this energy or blocked? As you bring your attention to the focused, directed, energy giving part of you, do you feel comfortable? uncomfortable? strong? tentative? invigorated? resistant? Take a moment to let yourself become a little bit more familiar with whatever is happening in your body, mind and heart right now...And take a moment to create a symbol which represents the essence of your masculine energy. You may want to take a few deep breaths and bring your focus back to the room for a minute to write about or draw the symbol for the essence of your masculine energy... and whenever you have noted or drawn what you feel moved to, very slowly and gently close your eyes, take a few deep breathes, and return to your comfortable meditation position.

And whenever you feel ready, take a moment to get in touch with your feminine energy...the part of you that is receptive, intuitive and soft...The part of you that can surrender and let go...and see what comes to you in the flow of life....Take a moment to notice how you experience this energy in your body...Where do you feel it? Is the current strong or weak? Do you feel open to this energy or blocked? As you bring your attention to the receptive, intuitive, soft part of you, do you feel comfortable? uncomfortable? strong? tentative? invigorated? resistant? Take a moment to let yourself become a little bit more familiar with whatever is happening in your body, mind and heart right now....And take a moment to create a symbol which represent the essence of you feminine energy. And whenever you feel ready, take a few deep breaths and bring your focus back to the room. Take a few moments to write about or draw the symbol for the essence of your feminine energy.

You may want to make notes on how easy it was to get in touch with the masculine and feminine parts of yourself...how you experienced the masculine and feminine aspects of yourself in your body....and which parts were most comfortable, uncomfortable, accessible, blocked....Which energy is easier for you to connect with? Do the energies feel separate or interrelated? Make notes about your experience from this meditation. When you want to focus on your masculine or feminine energy, you can use the symbols you have created, as well as referring back to your bodily experience of each energy. You can also experiment with moving back and forth from masculine to feminine to masculine to feminine...and with imagining the two energies coming together and integrating within you...seeing how it feels in your body, and what symbol you might create to represent this integration of energies.

Notes:

1.. Alice Dreger article can be found on *www.isna.org.*

2, 3. From *"Anima and Animus"* by Dan Johnston on *www.lessons4living.com.*

4. From *"Masculine and Feminine Energies"* by Jeanie Marshall on *www.mhmail.com.*

5. From "Nagual Series V — The Flow of Gender Energy" on *www.toltecnagual.com.*

Chapter 6

THE LONELY COUPLE

"No one gets away without some share of (sorrow).
We all grieve life's inevitable losses.
We fear the inherent uncertainty and vulnerability of existence.
And increasingly, as a population, we are familiar with
the despair of troubled relationships, unexpected traumas,
inner emptiness and global degradation and terror.
As much as joy, wonder and love,
the dark emotions are part of our human endowment,
however much we may sometimes wish they weren't."

— Miriam Greenspan
"Healing Dark Emotions"

Our idea of what we want in love relationships is evolving. Once, a stable partner with a steady job who could share the tasks of daily life and provide companionship through both good times and bad times was enough, and even something to be grateful for. In cultures where men and women were paired off in arranged marriages, love, sexual-spiritual connection and soul partnership were not part of the discussion the parents of the bride and groom engaged in while negotiating the marriage contract.

Today, love relationships are being asked to provide more than food, shelter, clothing and companionship. While necessary, these things are not alone sufficient. As the human species evolves emotionally and spiritually, we are seeking a deeper level of connection and expression in our love relationships. The term "soul-mate," once confined to new age circles, appears in even mainstream vocabulary. Media images portray the fantasy of meeting one's soul-mate, someone with whom one can share a sense of deep loving connection, and enjoy a sense of intimacy and everlasting relational bliss. More and more people are recognizing that love relationships can be part of the spiritual journey of our lives, and that love relationships themselves can offer a powerful spiritual journey.

Yet, even though many people I know are holding visions of meeting soul-mates, and succeeding at meeting people who feel like soul-mates, in time their dreamy bubble bursts. "I was overjoyed to meet a man who felt like my soul-mate," recounted a forty-something professional woman. "I expected to sail off to a life of joy and fulfillment. Everything was supposed to be easy. Things would just work. All past hurts and difficulties would be healed. But it didn't work out that way!" To her dismay, this woman discovered that the very same stumbling blocks that had plagued her previous intimate relationships had reared their unwanted heads in her supposedly perfect, sacrosanct relationship with her soul-mate! "I am disheartened and confused," she reflected. "What went wrong?"

I have heard this sentiment echoed by both men and women of all ages, straight, gay or lesbian, and bisexual, sharing their experiences of short and long-term relationships. How can the perfect couple unravel into the lonely couple? This chapter will explore this question from many different angles.

THE MEDIA AND THE COLLECTIVE FANTASY

Today, a marketing culture permeates the sound waves and visual space of daily existence. The media has emerged as architect of collective images, role models and fantasies. Like the tale of Cinderella and Prince Charming, we embrace a cultural mythology about love, romance and intimate relationships. These media-generated images leave us vulnerable and unprepared for the actual path most intimate relationships take. In spite of our sophistication, at some level many of us still hope for easy, natural, storybook relationships, but end up in initially wonderful relationships that are hard to sustain, breakdown or end.

While media images evolve with the times, they still provide a fantasy to overinvest in. Male and female icons are one-dimensional characters devoid of the depth, complexity and uniqueness of real human beings. The men and women we are taught to dream of are twenty-first century hybrids who still look like movie stars or models and stay eternally young. The men are strong yet sensitive and the women are coiffed, thin sex kittens who also hold high-powered jobs in the corporate world. Everyone is rich, white and heterosexual.

Our fantasy couples take exotic vacations and drive SUV's or luxury cars. When it is time for a family they have their 2.3 children and live in beautiful homes in the suburbs. They never sweat, fight, get tired or depressed. They don't go through lay-offs, divorce, menopause or financial hardships. In spite of being extraordinarily busy, they appear to have everything in their lives under control at all times. Our culture is enamored with a false, superficial and limited concept of relationships created by our commerce driven way of life. As a result, too many people are ill-prepared for both the real challenges of relationship and the real fruits that meeting the challenges brings.

I had a taste of the power of media-created images when I used to work in England about fifteen years ago. I remember visiting a childhood penpal in Manchester. I was approached by sincere people at a party who asked me how it felt to be rich, drive a Cadillac, and host parties at my swimming pool. I was floored. They had been watching the show "Dallas," and believed all Americans were like the characters on the TV show. What a distortion! The closest I had come to Dallas was a layover at the airport on one cross-country business trip. I drove a 10-year-old Toyota Corolla, lived in a modest Cape style house in Shrewsbury, Massachusetts, and didn't even know anyone with a swimming pool. I was trying to build a new therapy practice, having given up my middle-class corporate job to pursue my lifework as a therapist and healer. My friend's friends' fantasy could not have been farther from the reality of my life.

In similar fashion, the scarcity of images and role models depicting both the struggles and possibilities real people encounter in love relationships leaves us unprepared for reality. We imagine one thing and experience something completely different. The difference between fantasy and reality is often painful, difficult and disappointing. We lack good role models, guidelines and roadmaps to help us navigate the terrain of intimate relationship. We need a more grounded picture of what actually happens as intimacy unfolds. I hope to offer one here.

THE EVOLUTIONARY SPIRAL OF RELATIONSHIP

Love relationships proceed along the pathway of an evolutionary spiral. The chart below depicts the three major stages in the spiritual evolution of a relationship: 1. The "Getting to know you stage," 2. The Shadowlands, and 3. Spiritual partnership.

The "Getting to Know You Stage": This stage at the beginning of a relationship, when we experience the bliss of "new relationship energy" is the one the media has indelibly imprinted in our minds. Meeting another person with whom there is a sense of connection, attraction, and sometimes lust, and infatuation feels exciting and wonderful. With this stranger we barely know, it is easy to put our best foot forward, focus on only the positive qualities in ourselves and the other, and experience the relationship as fun, easy and light. In the "getting to know you stage," people often feel, "I'm in love," "This is it!" and "Things are right!" The "getting to know you stage" can last from one month to several years depending on the pace of the relationship. As intimacy increases, the relationship will cross over the threshold from this first stage to the second stage.

Because our culture is ripe with images of the "getting to know you stage," we begin to assume that relationships are always supposed to look, feel and be this way. When we find our relationships evolving and deepening we are not prepared for what follows as we grow beyond the "getting to know you stage."

The Shadowlands: Once the level of intimacy has deepened in the safety and trust that develops in a growing relationship, the relationship inevitably enters the second evolutionary stage, which I call "the shadowlands." Few of us have ever been told that ALL deep, emotionally intimate relationships hit the shadowlands — a place that most of us wish to avoid or make go away. In the shadowlands, the new relationship energy and bliss of the "getting to know you stage" seems to be lost and sometimes forgotten. Past wounds surface to be healed. Undeveloped parts of ourselves emerge for cultivation. Differences we never knew existed become crucial. We find ourselves "emotionally triggered" by our supposed beloved, and our good communication skills can be thrown to the wind.

In the shadowlands many people feel lost, frightened, disempowered and despairing. Too few of us have been taught that the basis of a sustainable relationship with another is a grounded, secure relationship with oneself. To navigate the waters with another person, one first needs to be clear about one's own boundaries and needs. Yet, "need" is treated like a "four-letter-word" in our culture. Rarely do we find opportunities where it is truly safe to get in touch with and learn to articulate our needs. As a result, too many of us are out of touch with our needs. We develop rigid boundaries or none at all. We may do things for others that don't work for us or make sacrifices that we later resent. I watch people struggling to find an authentic, connected way of living from moment to moment. Many lack the sense of presence and self-knowledge this requires. I watch earnest people experience barriers to the intimacy they want and need or get enmeshed with a primary partner and lose touch with their own personal needs. Intimate relating becomes bumpy and difficult.

In the shadowlands, common responses are "It isn't working," and "This is too hard." Both partners and the relationship as a whole feel stuck. As a result many couples break up, believing the relationship is the problem and leaving is the solution. Others stay together by putting up walls to keep them from the pain and necessary work of a deepening relationship. They remain together, but intimacy is compromised. A small percentage of couples recognize that the shadowlands are a necessary and important evolutionary stage, and then find the resources, inner and outer, to do their work, so that the relationship can continue to deepen and grow.

Without doing shadow work, the relationship cannot progress to the third evolutionary stage. By trying to avoid shadow feelings and shadow work, many relationships remain stuck at this stage of relationship evolution for very long periods of time, sometimes forever. Because fear of emotions and relational conflict is so prevalent in the culture as a whole, many relationships are stuck in the shadowlands.

Spiritual Partnership: The third stage of the evolutionary spiral is reached when partners do the often painful emotional and spiritual work brought forth in the shadowlands. The reward is greater intimacy and a sense of spiritual partnership. By healing pain, conflict, miscommunication and woundedness, partners can experience a sense of mutuality and oneness in addition to a sense of self. At this stage, both partners have learned to love themselves. They also can feel that the relationship has a life of its own — that there really is a "we."

By tending to the "we" as well as to self and other, the partners can grow together and experience a sense of a higher purpose for the relationship. This higher purpose might be having and raising children, creating a loving home or doing a project of service out in the world. Whatever the purpose, the partners recognize that by working together, they can be more powerful and effective than either could be alone. In this way, the spiritual dimension of intimate relationship grows. Sexuality and spirituality often integrate at the spiritual partnership stage.

Because relationships progress in an evolutionary spiral, as we do the work at one level, we will continue to cycle through the others in an on-going way. Periodically, shadow issues emerge even in a spiritual partnership. However, as the relationship matures spiritually and emotionally, the partners recognize the shadow work for what it is and take steps to work through and integrate new shadow parts as they emerge. The partners appreciate the intimate dance of relationship and develop skills and language to feed, nurture, value and sustain their relationship.

The Evolution of Relationship

Responses include:
- ♥ Mutuality
- ♥ Growing together
- ♥ Sexuality/Spirituality
- ♥ Higher Purpose

Spiritual Partnership

greater intimacy

THRESHOLD

our shadow parts emerge

Shadowlands

WORK!!!

Responses include:
- ♥ It isn't working/too hard
- ♥ Break-up
- ♥ Putting up walls to stay
- ♥ Doing the work

harder   deeper

THRESHOLD

easy   fun and light

Responses include:
- ♥ I'm in love
- ♥ This is it
- ♥ Things are right

Getting to Know You

projections of fantasy

Intimacy Increases

THE TRAUMA OF OPENING OUR HEARTS

Through loving another person, we receive a mirror of our own soul. In the Human Awareness Institute's Love, Intimacy and Sexuality workshops, intimacy is defined as "in-to-me-I-see." When we feel loved — when we are seen and heard for who we are — our defenses start to melt. We encounter and reveal parts of ourselves that may be less familiar to both ourselves and others, and less developed. The closer we get to another person, the deeper we are asked to go in our relationship with self.

As deepened intimacy brings us into the shadowlands of relationships, our issues of attachment, trust and connection are often brought to the surface from the bowels of our psyche. When we emotionally invest in another person, we become vulnerable. And while vulnerability can lead to intimacy, historically, for most of us, vulnerability has led to hurt, betrayal, abandonment and loss of love. This happens to us with our parents as children. It happens all through our development into adulthood. And it happens in adult relationships.

There is something in our very chemistry that invites relationships to be a ground for emotional healing and a restoration of self-worth and love or a re-enactment of traumatic moments past. Sherry Cohen, a psychotherapist in Newton, MA, described to me how when we open our hearts we experience a post-traumatic stress response (PTSD). Pheromones are an active player in attraction and run wild as we connect with another person and open our hearts to love. "Pheromones drive the sense of wanting to be with another person, of longing, of wanting to connect, of wanting to be physical and emotional. With pheromones comes the excitement, the love and the sex, AND the symptoms of PTSD. If people get close and get pulled with pheromones," says Cohen, "their issues around attachment are pulled."

Our capacities for attachment, bonding and constancy are often damaged in our development, so as we open our hearts, we experience a chaotic attachment which is accompanied by PTSD. The fear of going too far too fast, the experience of being overtaken by a deep primal terror that seems greater than one would expect as a rational adult, fixating on "doing it right" or on possible mistakes that seem to have larger than life stakes, repetitive thoughts and feelings replaying good or bad moments again and again, all reflect the shadow of a PTSD response as we open our hearts.

"It's hard for people to connect around all of this," notes Cohen. "Pheromones are most up in a new relationship because of the level of excitement and risk.Getting close to another person can be a beautiful and exciting time and it can be a terrifying time."

Some have the context with which to view this passage into intimacy and find resources, inner and outer, to weather the initial storm. Many lack the roadmap and respond to the intensity of feeling in both themselves and their partner by disconnecting after going deep. Pulling away, numbing out, dissociating, experiencing a sudden "change of heart," even abandoning entirely the person who was once the object of such passion and love, are all reactions to the terror of intimacy and opening the heart.

Why are there often such dramatic estrangements in families? Why do accomplished professional adults often melt into 3-year-old terror in the presence of their now elderly father? Why do lovers get close and then abandon each other? Why do committed partners eventually and perhaps inevitably end up in intense and intimate fights? Close relationships invite us to go deeper into our woundedness, into our primal terror, and either run for the mountains never to be heard from again or find the resources, inner and outer, to create a new kind of intimacy and safety that allows us to heal.

EXERCISE: Intimacy and Bonding: *Your Inner Responses*

Take a moment to get comfortable, sitting up or lying down, and allow yourself to take a few deep breaths. As you inhale, allow your body to be supported by your seat, your pillows, the floor — whatever supports you. And as you exhale, allow yourself to very slowly and gently relax into the support of your seat, your pillow, the floor — whatever supports you. And take a moment to see if you are comfortable, allowing yourself to adjust your position any way you need to be more comfortable....And allow your focus to be with your heart... noticing where you feel your heart in your body...If it helps to place a hand on your heart to help focus there, you are welcome to do so...And take a moment to notice how your heart is feeling physically and emotionally...is it full? is it empty? is it heavy? is it light? is it separate? connected? Take a moment to let yourself become a little more familiar with whatever is happening in your heart right now.

And take a moment to reflect on what it is like for you to establish intimacy with a love partner....See if you can recall a person you felt attracted to, someone you thought might be a potential partner....You may find that you recall the beginnings of a current partnership or a past partnership...or the beginnings of another significant relationship ....Taking a moment to notice what attracted you to this person....and how you felt initially upon meeting this special person...

Take a moment to notice what's happening right now in your breath, in your body, in your heart, in your thoughts....as you focus on your experience of meeting this special person....And whenever you feel ready, take a moment to notice how you felt as the relationship began to unfold and deepen....Did you feel frightened? Did you find yourself wanting to spend as much time as possible with this new love? Did you want the relationship to move slowly? Did you find yourself "falling in love?" Did you find yourself thinking of all the reasons NOT to be with this person? Take moment to let yourself become a little more familiar with your inner experience of deepening this love relationship ...noticing what's happening in your breathing, your body sensations, your heart and your thoughts....

And take a moment to see if there was a time in this relationship where you started to feel "triggered"--where the experience of getting close to this person evoked a primal terror....where you were afraid of getting close to this person, only to have the relationship not work out... where you were afraid of showing this person your deepest vulnerabilities ...where you felt numb, pulled away, experienced a change of heart or abandoned your beloved....Notice what happens inside of you as you explore feeling frightened... Do you recognize what I called "the trauma of opening your heart?"

Take a moment to notice what's happening in your body right now — in your breath, physical sensations, in your heart....And take a moment to notice what your heart needs most when you are building intimacy with a love partner.... What helps you feel safe? What does your heart need to know, feel, heart, experience, give or receive to feel safe as you open your heart?

Whenever you feel ready, very slowly and gently take a deep breath....feel your body supported by your seat, your pillow, the floor, whatever supports you...and whenever you feel ready, very slowly and gently take a deep breath and bring your focus back into the room.

QUESTIONS for journaling and/or discussion:

1. What was the experience that came to mind in the meditation? Describe it.

2. How did you feel when you first met this special person? What did you notice in your breath, your body and your heart when you focused on this person and the experience of meeting them?

3. As the relationship deepened, how did you feel? What was comfortable? What was scary? What are your emotional, thought and behavioral patterns in a love relationship?

4. Have you experienced "the trauma of opening your heart?" If so, was your experience like? (Feelings, thoughts, body sensations, behaviors)

5. Do you have any primal fears or reactions that surface as intimacy deepens? If so, what are they?

6. What do you need to feel safe as you build intimacy in a love relationship? What do you need to experience within yourself and with another to feel safe as you open your heart?

THE MALE HEART WOUND MEETS THE FEMALE HEART WOUND

The wounds to our male and female hearts contribute to the trauma of opening our hearts. Men and women suffer differently but equally as we are unable to relate to each other in all our depth, power and vulnerability. If the male spirit is suppressed and the female voice is silenced, we become trapped in relationships that deny us the joy of true intimacy.

My colleague, Mark McDonough, reflects, "Men and women have lived out an unspoken deal. There are three elements to the deal. First, men have asked women to be their hearts, and in exchange, the women haven't had to put on a hard shell and go out into the world." This was certainly true in the "traditional family" model promoted in the 1950's.

"Second, head and heart functions have been split between the genders rather than developed in each gender." Women were taught to let men be the rational thinkers. In exchange, women handled the emotional level of life.

Third, each gender has had a different and complementary response to the narcissistic heart wound that I described in Chapter 2. The male response has been, "These people can't take care of me. So, I will become big and strong and take care of myself. I can make it on my own and I don't need anyone." The female response has been, "I can't make it on my own. I'll find someone who can protect me, because I don't have the power to do it on my own." As a result, men were asked to be overly tough and self-reliant. Women were expected to be overly fragile and dependent. In reality, both men and women can be strong and fragile. Both genders can stand alone and can gain value from relating with one another.

Whether by nature or through socialization, men and women learn to give emotional energy differently. To be overly simplistic, women give emotional energy through nurturing. Men give emotional energy through providing. Both genders get a sense of empowerment through expressing their hearts. To nurture, women have to fully connect with another human being. They are able to plug in to the other person, experience what they are feeling and empathize with them. Through acting, men connect with the resources of the world. They do what needs to be done and move things forward.

Unfortunately each gender may miss the heartful expression of the other. Men may take women's nurturing efforts for granted. Women may not recognize the expression of emotional energy by men. When women nurture and when men work, it comes from the heart. Through these actions, both genders express their intention to emotionally be there for one another. It is their way of trying to emotionally connect.

As gender roles have come undone, the landscape of male and female emotional expression has grown more complex. The next generation (18 - 35 year olds) has grown up with not only the unraveling imagery of the traditional male and female gender model, but also masculinized women and feminized men. Divorced parents, at-home dads and corporate moms are all part of their home landscape. Babyboomers grew up with both two potentially contradictory and polarized models: "traditional" gender roles of inequality and feminist values of full equality for men and women. Pressure has been put on both genders to be everything and nothing. Finding a personal solution for expressing manhood or womanhood can be an uncertain and overwhelming task.

THE VOICELESS BODY: GETTING LOST IN THE WORDS

M any of us are afraid of our deepest feelings. This is often especially true for men, yet can be true for any of us as a consequence of the cultural heart wound. When a man or woman has strong feelings and expresses them, the person on the receiving end may feel uncomfortable and threatened. I am a deeply feeling person, and have worked for many years to be able to experience my feelings fully in my body. As a result, I have been told by both men and women that I have a big presence and can overwhelm some people with my energy without speaking or doing a thing.

Our fear of strong emotions is compounded by the lack of a mutually understood emotional language. Feelings carry an electromagnetic charge and can permeate another person's emotional energy field, sometimes intentionally and sometimes unintentionally. Because of the presence of this electromagnetic current, it is possible to read another person's pain, anger or sorrow without their uttering a word. This happens at a primal level that we are often not taught to consciously monitor or manage. I have found when others are uncomfortable with emotional energy, what they say to the object of their discomfort can be a defensive, blaming, judgmental response. For example, a close friend of mine who was very scared of his own emotional stirrings, used to tell me I was "too much."

Communicating felt experience often requires non-verbal sensory language, including gestures, energy and touch. In the preface to his book Touching, anthropologist Ashley Montagu reflects on the way words have come to replace sensory experience in our culture. "The one-dimensionality of the word becomes a substitute for the richness of the multidimensionality of the senses, and our world grows crass, flat and arid in consequence. Words tend to take the place of experience. Words become a declarative statement rather than a demonstrative involvement, something one can utter in words, rather than act out in a personal sensory relationship."

Women, in particular, have learned to use words to express pain, anger and deeper needs, sometimes at the expense of connection. In an article I wrote entitled, "I Really Don't Want to Talk About It: Just Hold Me," I speak of "the compensated woman." In intimate relating, so often a woman turns to her words when she just needs her partner to reach in and hold her. In her heart, she feels the yearning to make contact. Yet in this body-scared, touch-averse culture, she may be out of touch with the fact that being held is what she needs to fulfill her yearning. Or she is afraid to ask to be held, if she is aware of what she needs. So, to compensate, she goes on and on and on with her words.

In our culture, as we have separated mind from body, heart and soul, we have rendered our deepest selves voiceless. Heart wounding has created a culture of voiceless bodies walking around attached to talking heads. The soul's language is in the body and needs to be expressed non-verbally in order to produce embodied words. Most people I have worked with need to feel emotionally safe to dig down deep inside, feel what they are experiencing, and find a way to put that experience into words. The words that follow have a completely different quality than words produced by a brain at work. And at times that language is non-verbal. The body may speak most fully through a look, a touch, a hug, a gesture or movement, an embrace or an invitation to dance. I think back to the 60's television show "The Flintstones," a cartoon that depicted the life of "a modern stoneage family." Supporting characters Betty and Barney had a son, aptly named Bam-Bam. When Bam-Bam had something to say, he communicated at a primal level. He took his stone bat and whacked it on the ground yelling, "Bam, bam, bam, bam, bam!" When I sit with both individuals and couples in my therapy office, I often watch earnest people spinning a web of words but cut off from the feelings and sensations in their bodies and hearts. My task is often to help them find a more integrated, and often primal, language like Bam-Bam's!

MUTUAL DEPENDENCE AND EMOTIONAL SECURITY

"Need" is a four letter word in our culture. With needing comes vulnerability and dependence, which often lead to being hurt and judged. Yet needing is both human and central to our ability to be connected to self and others.

Psychologist Susan Johnson has found that our need for emotional security in relationship is so central that she has developed an approach to couples therapy based on this fact. Emotionally Focused Couples Therapy (EFT) asks partners to recognize that they are both emotionally dependent upon each other for love, comfort, support and protection, much like a child depends on a parent. In a culture that fosters a sense of rugged individualism and self-reliance — part of the male heart wound when taken to an extreme — this is a hard pill to swallow.

Johnson's approach drew from psychiatrist John Bowlby's attachment theory, concluding that everyone has an innate yearning for trust and security or attachment. Children need to feel attached to a parent. Adults need to feel attached to another adult, usually a romantic partner.[1] When those we are attached to cannot respond to our needs, we become frightened and anxious or numb and distant. We protect our hearts and shield our vulnerability. We no longer make clear, authentic contact from heart to heart. Instead, isolating and distancing patterns of defensive relating unfold.

At my school, the Institute for Emotional-Kinesthetic Psychotherapy (EKP), I developed a useful model that depicts both how defensive layers form around our hearts, and what is necessary to create the safety and rapport to melt our defenses so we may give and receive the love and other qualities that we really need.

HOW DEFENSES FORM AROUND UNMET NEEDS

I magine you are an infant, about three months old. The world is new and full of fascination. Your life is one of just being. You use your senses to take in information about the world — what you see, hear, smell, taste and touch. Your young body has not yet developed the motor skills to sit up, crawl or move about. You can make gurgling sounds, but not yet words. Take a moment to take a few deep breaths and just notice what happens in your body and heart as you let yourself imagine what it feels like to be a 3-month-old child.

For such a young baby, the energetic level of communication is very tangible. If a mother is in tune with her baby, a subtle shift in the baby's energy alerts her to the baby's need for food, comfort or sleep. When my son was an infant, I could intuitively tell when he was hungry, when he needed me to just hold him and when he wanted me to nurse him to sleep. His heart and body would emanate an energetic cue to me, and I would pick up on it and respond. Now imagine that a 3-month-old baby reaches a point where s/he is hungry. Because such young infants need to eat frequently the sensation they feel in their stomach calls urgently for nourishment. My son nursed 30 - 40 minutes every two hours around the clock. I remember feeling daunted by the huge responsibility that came with nursing a very young child. I realized my vital, thriving infant son was also fragile and dependent on me! My ability to provide a regular supply of breast milk and to respond to his nursing signals played an essential role in keeping him healthy and alive.

Without the benefit of the spoken word, a hungry baby sends out the energetic signal "I need." If the baby's mother or caregiver is close by and recognizes the signal, the baby is fed. S/he gets what s/he needs, and his/her metabolic energy can be used for growth and development. Need expressed. Need fulfilled. Content baby. End of story.

But imagine if the baby is hungry and sends out the energetic signal "I need," and no one responds. Perhaps the baby is in another room from his/her caregiver. Or perhaps the caregiver isn't attuned to the subtle shifts in the baby, the energetic expression of his/her need. So, time begins to pass, and the baby feels the pain and discomfort of being hungry without receiving the nourishment s/he needs.

As the discomfort builds, the baby begins to cry. As more time passes, the baby's urgency increases. His/her cry becomes louder and more desperate. If a caregiver now responds to the baby's cry s/he will need to find a way to comfort the crying baby before attending to his/her original need. More energy and skill are required from the caregiver to meet the baby's need. More of the baby's energy is required for communication and survival, to be sure that his/her needs are attended to.

But what if the caregiver is out of earshot of the crying baby or is unable to respond to the cry of need? Then more time passes and the urgency of the baby's need for nourishment increases, along with his/her fear and anxiety that nobody is there to meet his/her need. The baby uses more of his/her energy to call the caregiver. It becomes a survival cry. If the caregiver now responds to the thrashing and screaming baby, it will take more time and skill to help the tensed up baby relax and stop crying. Until the baby is soothed and calmed, s/he will not be able to take in what s/he needs.The longer the time that passes between the energetic expression of need and the caregiver's response to that need, the more work the baby has to do to get someone's attention to meet his/her needs. And in the event someone finally responds to the baby's efforts, the more attention s/he needs from their adult caregiver to meet their original, basic need.

So, imagine that no one responds to the thrashing, screaming baby....A baby can only scream for so long before s/he collapses in exhaustion and despair. The baby will eventually become quiet. This is not necessarily a good thing. As the exhausted baby collapses, s/he concludes from his/her experience,

How Defenses Form
Around Unmet Needs

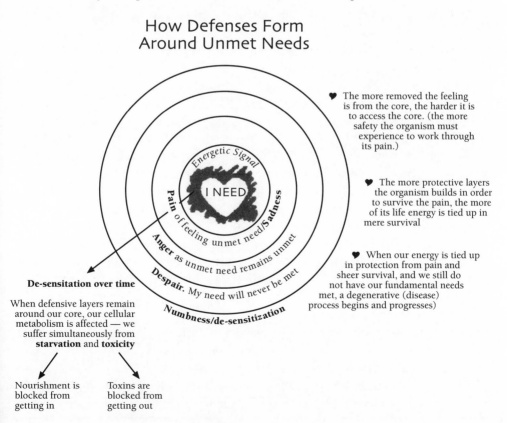

♥ The more removed the feeling is from the core, the harder it is to access the core. (the more safety the organism must experience to work through its pain.)

♥ The more protective layers the organism builds in order to survive the pain, the more of its life energy is tied up in mere survival

♥ When our energy is tied up in protection from pain and sheer survival, and we still do not have our fundamental needs met, a degenerative (disease) process begins and progresses)

Energetic Signal

I NEED

Pain of feeling unmet need/Sadness

Anger as unmet need remains unmet

Despair. My need will never be met

Numbness/de-sensitization

De-sensitation over time

When defensive layers remain around our core, our cellular metabolism is affected — we suffer simultaneously from **starvation** and **toxicity**

Nourishment is blocked from getting in

Toxins are blocked from getting out

"I cannot get what I need." The baby may cry him/herself to sleep. This is NOT a peaceful sleep, but a sleep of resignation and powerlessness. Sleep becomes a dissociation or detachment from the unending pain of the situation.

The baby may now be quiet, yet the energy of this baby does not feel the same as the energy of the quiet baby who expressed his/her hunger and was responded to right away. The life energy of the collapsed baby is just a little less vital. The caregiver will be "off the hook," but at a psychic and emotional cost to the child. The baby is now several layers removed emotionally and physically from his/her original need. To try to make contact with the vulnerable part of the child that first expressed need will be difficult for not only a caregiver but also the child him/herself.

And if no one reaches in to the collapsed, despairing baby, s/he will eventually become numb. Even despair takes energy to maintain. When a baby reaches his/her limit, feeling anything at all is too painful and energetically too costly. The baby has learned to dissociate from the rhythms of his/her own bodies and needs, and from others.

THE WOUNDED HEART AND BARRIERS TO INTIMACY

While I made the central character of the story a baby, this story could be told about a person of any age, child or adult. The story illustrates the way our hearts develop protective layers as our needs go unmet. While these protective layers allow us to survive unbearable pain, they also provide a barrier that keeps us from giving and receiving love. The protective layers can become rigid and hard, like tectonic plates which keep danger away from the vulnerable heart. A child or adult has learned that needing and being vulnerable is unsafe and painful. Many layers now stand between a person's need and the point of contact that is safe to make with another person. This kind of emotional and energetic armor provides a barrier to contact and connection in love relationships. In our wounded state, we are protected against further wounding, but we can become lonely and isolated as we are also defended against love. To connect, we need the safety to be vulnerable and relate directly heart to heart.

I witnessed this struggle for intimacy in a couple I was working with who had hit barriers in their relationship they could not surmount on their own. While at a core level they really loved one another, they both seemed blocked and unable to access this deeper sense of love. Zachary emanated a genuine warmth when he walked into the room, but also a sense of emotional detachment. When threatened or confronted, he resorted to silence, analysis and the safe battlefield of the head. Marsha appeared more tentative at first, but soon unleashed what Zachary called "the angry bitch goddess" as soon as the session started.

"He never listens to me," screamed Marcia. "I feel like I am talking to a stone wall." Zachary remained characteristically silent and pulled back in the face of

Marcia's anger. I could sense a deep sense of hurt underlying both Marcia's anger and Zachary's silence. However, their conflict postures left little room for the emotional safety needed to get closer to the heart of the matter. To use the concentric circle diagrams, what they both really wanted looked like this:

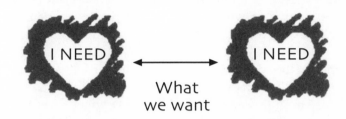

But in their state of defended woundedness, the way they were relating looked like this:

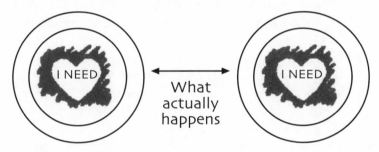

Marcia's angry layer was relating to Zachary's numb layer. By helping Marcia get in touch with the pain beneath her anger, I could help Marcia express her hurt, her vulnerability and her need. By helping Zachary get in touch with his feelings, I could help him recognize and express his own hurt, and his vulnerability and need. As I facilitated first Marcia and then Zachary, the energy in the room dramatically softened. Tears came to both Marcia's and Zachary's eyes, and they reached out to one another to physically embrace.

If we go back to the heart's electromagnetic field which I discussed in Chapter 1, imagine what it feels like physically and emotionally to try to reach out and make loving contact with a person with a protected, wounded heart. The layers in the concentric circles diagram illustrate the emotional and energetic walls we build around our hearts when we are wounded. The power of the wounded heart is mobilized to maintain this emotional energetic wall. If Marcia reached out to Zachary in his numb bordering on dissociated state, she would not feel received. She might conclude that Zachary was so far removed there was no way for her to connect with him, to touch his heart. If you have ever had the experience of trying to connect with someone who was unreachable, you know how much it really hurts!

THE WALL AND THE VOID

If Marcia is in touch with her vulnerability, and from this place expresses what she needs, and if Zachary is in a distant, defended state, the couple enters into an emotional, energetic dance I call "the wall and the void." Marcia's need for emotional contact triggers and intensifies Zachary's emotionally protective wall. I want to note that I could be writing about this dynamic between two men, two women, or a man experiencing his vulnerability and a woman experiencing a distant, defended state. When the male heart, wound meets the female heart wound, the dance of the wall and the void often unfolds.

One symptom of the female heart wound is being cut off at the throat. So, Marcia struggles through her words to find her voice, and the emotional intensity of her struggle triggers the woundedness in Zachary's male heart. Zachary is scared by the intensity of Marcia's emotions and is overwhelmed by the deluge of her words. He evokes the wall over his heart to protect him and distance himself from Marcia, and from the inundation of her words. As Zachary distances, Marcia falls farther into the emotional void of aloneness and disconnection that is already ravishing her heart.

Zachary and Marcia, now enter a downward spiral of triggered relating. The pain frequency of Marcia's voice and energy increases. Zachary perceives Marcia's intensified "need" as a stronger demand and greater threat. This promotes more distancing and fortifies his emotional wall. Both Marcia and Zachary feel unsatisfied and disconnected — one feeling so much and the other working hard not to feel.

The wall and the void collide. And in this dance, both men and women emotionally starve. Both parties feel hurt, hopeless and inadequate. If the cycle is unending, the relationship can be damaged. A piece of the soul dies.

The story reminds me of the plight of a food-addicted person. You can't get enough of what you don't really need. So, the words can drone on and on, creating more frustration and exhaustion for both partners. And the deeper need for contact goes unmet. If only Marcia could utter, "I really DON'T want to talk about it, just hold me," and Zachary could respond in kind, the pain could move through his body and out of her heart. She could find peace, comfort and quiet in his arms. And he could feel effective, connected and whole, to give free of demands.

Many couples lack the awareness, the skills or the facilitation often needed to safely melt the defensive layers that surround their wounded hearts. As a result they feel the pain of the love they wish to give and receive but can't. They experience a simultaneous starvation and toxicity: unable to let in the love they need, and unable to let held pain out. It is no wonder their relationships gradually breakdown and erode.

CREATING AN EMOTIONAL/ELECTRICAL LANGUAGE

Given that much of our knowledge about the electromagnetic field of the heart and its properties is relatively new, I find it interesting that we have evolved language to describe emotional experience that has an electrical meaning as well. The following words are the foundation of an emotional/electrical language:

Triggered: We say a person is "triggered" when s/he becomes emotionally reactive to another person's words, actions or energy. When we are triggered, one emotional current may become so strong that it overtakes us. If you have ever been emotionally triggered, you may have noticed a surge of energy running through your body. The experience may feel similar to what happens when an electrical switch is triggered and the current rushes forth. When triggered, the magnitude of a reaction may be disproportional to whatever we are reacting to. Acting out road rage is an example of a triggered response.

Grounded: In electrical language, wires must be "grounded" to be able to safely carry a current along a desired pathway. If you touch an ungrounded wire, you can receive a shock. Our bodies are conduits for life energy currents. When I am grounded, I feel centered, fully present in my body and connected to the earth. I feel the earth's energy, and feel strong and present in the moment. When I am grounded, I am less likely to be triggered. Being grounded provides safety and awareness. We need to be grounded to inhabit our bodies and consciously experience the stream of emotional and physical sensations that runs through us.

Containment: The word "containment" evokes an image of a vessel that can hold the contents I pour into it. Our bodies are vessels in this sense. When I am emotionally, physically and spiritually grounded, I experience an internal sense of spaciousness. This spaciousness allows me to hold and embrace my emotional experience. The more emotional space I develop, the more readily I can contain both difficult and joyous feelings and maintain my composure in the face of another person's triggered behavior. When we can contain feelings, we can work consciously with their energy. This is the opposite of being reactive.

Emotional circuitry: One way of thinking about our emotional circuitry is "how we are wired." In my body-centered psychotherapy practice over the past twenty years, I have observed that people have an "emotional circuitry" that reflects both an innate capacity and ways we become wired through our life experience. Some people are inherently more mellow than others. On the other hand, trauma can "wire" in hypervigilance for mellow people as well as for more innately tightly wound people. Our emotional circuitry can reflect habits. A male client of mine many years ago had only one channel for emotional expression: anger. Growing up in his family, people yelled at each other when they were scared, when they were sad and even when they were proud. My client internalized this model and had not had the chance to "wire in" other emotional pathways.

Capacity: Each person has a "capacity" for experiencing and containing emotional energy. When we feel safe, connected and grounded in our bodies, our capacity is at its greatest. When wounds become wired into our emotional circuitry, they can diminish our capacity. If our wounds are activated, our emotional circuitry can experience a sense of overload. Heart wounds both require and deplete emotional and psychic energy.

Overwhelm can be understood as the experience of an emotional charge that is larger than our emotional holding capacity. When we feel overwhelmed, the intensity of feeling is too great to contain. If we cross the threshold of "too much," it is as though an emotional switch flips, like an emotional circuit breaker, and we shut down emotionally. We may numb out or dissociate.

I have found that the more grounded a person becomes, the more safety they experience with their feelings and body sensations. Safety and groundedness increase emotional holding capacity. Strong feelings like anger, fear, sadness and joy have more room to be experienced viscerally and emotionally. A person has the room to feel the feelings and let them pass through.

All of these concepts can be applied in exercises to help heal the wounded heart.

EXERCISE: *Breaking the Cycle of Triggered Relating*

Once triggered relating begins between two people, a downward spiral often follows. The fact that the electromagnetic current generated by one person's heart registers in another person's brain waves when they are in close proximity helps us understand why this happens. As one person is triggered, their heartwave has 60 times the electrical current of the other person's brainwave. The electromagnetic force of their heart is 5000 times a powerful as that of the other person's brain. Unless the second person is incredibly grounded, the electromagnetic energy generated by the first person's triggered heart will become an overpowering force.

This is what happens in fights that escalate. Once the fight is started, both people get stuck in the electromagnetic force field of fighting. Neither person can extract themselves or change the dynamics. The fight seems to take on a life of its own.

Here is a seven step model you can try to use to break the cycle of triggered relating:

1. *RECOGNIZE*
   that you and your partner are feeling triggered. Notice the tensions in your body, the thoughts that go through your mind, and the emotional

sensations you experience when you are triggered. As you become familiar with these emotional, mental and physical clues, they can help you recognize when you are triggered.

2. *STOP*

   the action and the dialogue. In a triggered space, little emotionally grounded or productive communication can happen.

3. *NAME*

   that you are in a triggered space. Becoming conscious of what is happening and articulating it grounds the situation and begins to diffuse the triggered energy.

4. *RESIST*

   the temptation to get sucked into the spiral of triggered relating. The energy of triggered relating exerts a strong pull. It may take time and work on grounding to be able to resist the seductive pull to keep engaging in triggered relating.

5. *TAKE SPACE*

   with yourself, away from your partner. Getting out of the energy of the triggered relating breaks the cycle, and allows you to reconnect with yourself and reground. Take some deep breaths. Go for a walk. Write in your journal. Sit quietly for a while. Call a friend to vent or for feedback.

6. *RECONNECT and REVISIT*

   the triggered incident when you and your partner are both more grounded. From a distance you both may be able to look at the original incident and the triggers it provoked in a more spacious way.

7. *SEEK 3rd PARTY FACILITATION*

   if you can't navigate this territory on your own. Often it takes a 3rd party to contain a triggered relating pattern. Consider seeking help as an investment in the success of your relationship. It is a form of self-care and relational care.

ESSENTIAL QUESTIONS: *Questions for reflection and discussion:*

1. How comfortable are you with your needs? How readily can you identify them and articulate them?

2. How comfortable are you hearing and responding to another person's needs?

3. If you are currently in a partnership, how able are you to articulate and respond to one another's needs? What are your greatest strengths and greatest challenges in working with one another's needs?

4. What ground rules could help you work with each other's emotional, physical, spiritual and sexual needs?

5. How do you feel when a relationship hits the shadowlands? What tools have you developed to navigate shadow terrain in an intimate relationship? What are your learning edges?

6. Have you experienced "getting lost in the words?" What ways of non-verbal relating feel most connecting for you?

MEDITATION: *Connection and Disconnection*

Take a moment to get comfortable, closing your eyes as long as you are comfortable, taking whatever time and space you need to breathe. As you inhale, allow your chest and belly to fill with air. As you exhale, allow your chest and belly to relax, feeling the support of your chair, your pillow, your bed, the wall, the floor, whatever supports you....And take a moment to see if you need to adjust your position in any way to be more comfortable...continuing to take whatever time and space you need to breathe.

And whenever you feel ready, allow your focus to move to your heart, noticing where in your body you feel your heart...and if it helps to place your hand on your heart to help focus there, you are welcome to do so...And take a moment to notice how your heart is feeling physically and emotionally right now...Is it full? Is it empty? Is it heavy? Is it light? Is it separate? Connected?...Take a moment to let yourself become a little more familiar with whatever is happening in your heart right now...

And whenever you feel ready, take a moment to recall a time when you felt connected....If you are in a love relationship right now, you may wish to recall a moment you felt connected with your current partner.... And if you are not in a love relationship right now, you can recall a moment at any time in your life that felt connected.....Take a moment to remember that time of connection.... where are you?...who are you with?....what are your surroundings?... what are you doing?....just letting yourself recall the moment and what happened....take a moment to notice how your body is feeling right now as you remember a time of feeling connected .....noticing physical sensations and emotional currents, as well as the thoughts that are going through your mind....Take a moment to notice what's happening in your breathing right now....as you reflect on what it feels like to be connected...

And whenever you feel ready, take a couple deep breaths, and allow your focus to shift to a time when you felt disconnected....and again, if you are in a love partnership right now, you can recall a disconnected moment in this relationship....or you can recall a disconnected moment in any relationship you have been in....letting yourself notice what comes to mind....Taking a moment to recall that time of disconnection...where are you? who are you with? what are your surroundings? what are you doing?...just letting yourself recall the moment and what happened.... notice physical sensations and emotional currents, as well as the thoughts that are going through your mind....Take a moment to notice what's happening in your breathing right now, as you reflect on what it feels like to be disconnected.

And whenever you feel ready, take a few deep breaths, and allow yourself to explore what creates connection and disconnection? What helps sustain connection? What helps remedy disconnection?

Whenever you feel ready, at your own pace, very slowly and gently take a deep breath, and bring your focus back into the room. You are welcome to write down your experience from this meditation in your journal as well as whatever thoughts and feelings emerge as you start to write.

Notes:

1.. From *"Save Your Relationship"* by Susan Johnson, Ph.D. in *Psychology Today*, April 2003.

Chapter 7

Birthing the
Soul-Centered Relationship

"Love one another
as deeply and fully as you can each day...
Remember that you are journeying together
in this lifetime for a sacred purpose...
That is, to grow, to learn, to expand,
to discover your own deep spiritual essence
and to honor your beloved's..."

— Caroline Joy Adams

The word "relationship" has taken on a very limited meaning in popular culture. When the word "relationship" is uttered, the image most commonly understood is a romantic liaison between two people, most often one male and one female, with a long-term goal of marriage. To allow for a little more diversity with the passing of time, we now use the term "primary relationship" to refer to this union. In contrast, other emotional ties are deemed less important and less central. When a man or woman utters, "I am having problems in my RELATIONSHIP," we seem to understand this verbal shorthand.

As a young person I used to find this verbal convention confusing. After all, wasn't my connection with my brother, with my best friend, with my co-worker and even my dog ALSO a relationship? Didn't "relationship" refer to all emotionally meaningful human bonds? Wasn't a love partnership just one kind of relationship? Didn't all intimate, emotionally involved connections take us to the same place if we chose to follow the path of the heart?

My little girl's heart asked good questions. ALL intimate, emotionally involved bonds ARE relationships. And when we get emotionally close to others — primary partner, best friend, co-worker, parent or child — our emotional triggers emerge and our wounded places ask for our healing attention. Love partnerships have simply been the relationships societally sanctioned for emotional and physical intimacy. Other relationships were not expected to be as central or run as deep.

As the human species matures emotionally and spiritually, our concept and practice of intimate relationship is also being asked to evolve. As I look both at myself and the people around me, we want relationships which provide emotional and spiritual depth and substance. Old time personality-based relationships are no longer enough. We are yearning for spiritually anchored, soul-centered relationships.

Evolving and maturing is a birthing process. We struggle with the shadow aspects of ourselves and our partners. We work hard, sometimes not knowing if our efforts will bear fruit. We live with uncertainty and not knowing, learning to find our strength in being present to each moment. In time, the fruits of our efforts emerge from the birth canal as we create deeper, more authentic, soul-centered ways of relating.

EVOLVING FROM THE PERSONALITY-BASED RELATIONSHIP TO THE SOUL-CENTERED RELATIONSHIP

When I was growing up, the relationships I witnessed were rooted in what I will call "the personality-based model of relationship." This remains the current paradigm in the mainstream of our culture, although more and more people seem to be feeling the evolutionary currents and growing beyond the limitations of this model. In the "personality-based" model of relationship, the relationship is rooted in external aspects of relating:

Role performance: Roles may be delineated along gender lines, like the traditional model of man as provider and woman as housekeeper, or along functional lines — enough income needs to be earned to support the household, dinner needs to find its way to the table, and the dog needs to get fed and walked. The two partners come together to negotiate their functional roles and allocate the tasks necessary to have a home and life.

Packaging: This ranges from height, weight and hair color to years of education and professional status, religious affiliation or the kind of car one drives. Personal ads often include a list of this kind of adjectives or criteria for a potential mate.

Common interests or hobbies: The theory goes that if you have common interests, like playing tennis, riding motorcycles, or fine dining you will enjoy one another's company and be a good match.

Outcome-directed: Just as the dating process centers on "is s/he the one?" once a personality-based relationship starts, the timer ticks towards goals of marriage, a house in the suburbs, two SUV's and children. A romantic relationship is supposed to produce a life that fits a traditional set of cultural specs.

There is less attention to inner attributes and emotional and spiritual compatibilities. The "personality-based" relationship is an evolutionary step forward from the arranged marriage. Here, an individual has free choice of who s/he chooses to partner with, within a set of socially acceptable parameters.

Limitations of the personality-based model of relationship include:

1. The skills needed to build and sustain intimacy are often not considered when forming or attempting to live out a personality-based relationship. As discussed in Chapter 6, as intimacy deepens,the partners find themselves in the Shadowlands, unprepared and unaware of where they are, how they got there, and what to do about it.

2. Partners often lack a language or tools to navigate relational challenges that emerge in any growing relationship. There may be significant limits in each or both people's communication skills.

3. Partners are often scared of conflict or conflict averse. Conflict evokes fear of loss of relationship, abandonment, or triggering the other's anger. Conflict is, therefore, suppressed.

4. Because dark feelings, like anger, sadness, fear and disappointment are threatening, one or both partners may avoid them. As a result, the relationship may take on a superficial and inauthentic quality.

5. When either or both partners hit places of emotional vulnerability or unhealed woundedness, they often act out, blame, withdraw or finger point, without a conscious awareness that they are triggered and reacting. These are the behaviors that were modeled in many people's families growing up.

6. Emotional and physical violence can often emerge from the shadows in the forms of yelling, name calling, making the other wrong, judging, hitting, pushing or verbally attacking. Either or both individuals may lack skills for containing or working with difficult emotions.

7. One's deeper needs may be overlooked, suppressed or avoided. As discussed in Chapter 6, "need" is often perceived as a four letter word. Needs are a source of shame. This creates barriers to intimacy and connection.

8. People commonly live with a silent, unspoken tension or high drama, as a result of discomfort with the natural emotional fluctuations that emerge in life and relating. Strong feelings can

be suppressed or repressed. When inner tension gets too high, this can lead to explosive expression.

We are evolving to a new paradigm which I call, **"the soul-centered model of relationship"**, which is rooted in the emotional, spiritual and process aspects of relationship:

Relationship is understood as a spiritual partnership as well as a practical partnership: Both partners recognize an intimate relationship can be a path of personal and spiritual growth, as well as a practical arrangement.

The partners understand the importance of emotional awareness and more sophisticated communication skills than was expected in personality-based relationships: Both partners recognize good relationships require time and communication, including talking about one another's needs, triggers, and feelings. The relationship offers a safe space for expression of a full range of emotions — light, dark, delicate and intense.

Needs are recognized as points of human vulnerability, connection and exchange: They allow both independence and interdependence. We give and receive.

A primary partnership is viewed in the context of a system of significant relationships: Each partner recognizes that some needs can be met with a partner. Some needs also need to be met with one's own inner resources. Other needs are met with others — be they friends, family, children, colleagues, animal companions or God. As a result, each partner has a stronger base of support and is more emotionally rooted.

Two people come to a partnership anchored in a clear, grounded sense of self: Each partner knows him/herself well enough to be able to say "no" and "yes." With grounded self-knowledge, boundaries become a point of contact. Both partners can really show up when they choose to relate. Deeper intimacy — emotionally, physically, spiritually and sexually — becomes possible.

CONTRASTING PERSONALITY-BASED AND SOUL-CENTERED RELATIONSHIPS		
	Personality-based relationship *Current paradigm*	**Soul-centered relationship** *New paradigm we are evolving towards*
Paradigm	Relationship rooted in doing, externals, role performance	Relationship rooted in being, internals, intimate connection

	Personality-based relationship	Soul-centered relationship
Relationship with conflict	Conflict averse. Fear of conflict leads to suppression of differences, feelings and needs. Few skills for managing conflict in growth-promoting ways.	Conflict is understood as something that naturally emerges when two people disagree or feel strongly in different ways. Skills for managing conflict in growth-promoting ways.
Fighting	Fighting unravels to blaming, power struggles, finger pointing withdrawal, and sometimes violence...or is repressed.	Fighting for something and for the relationship rather than against one another. Skills for fighting fair. No blame, no pain.
Intimacy	Relationships often hit blocks to intimacy. Fear of vulnerability, fear of abandonment and fear of loss of freedom get in the way.	Intimacy continues to evolve and unfold through personal and inter-relational work. The couple turns to third party facilitation when needed to help work through blocks.
Conflict & Intimacy	Fear of conflict limits intimacy	Recognition that conflict is an invitation to go deeper allows for increased intimacy.
Emotional Expression	Fear of strong feelings — dark (anger, fear and disappointment) and light (passion, joy, pleasure and love). Fear both of own feelings and partner's feelings.	Comfort and facility with full range of emotional expression. Fluidity with feelings. Respect for self and partner.
Needs	Need is experienced as a four-letter word. Needs are a source of vulnerability and discomfort. Fear of needs leads to extremes of excessive self-reliance and co-dependence.	Need is understood to be part of the human condition — points of vulnerability, connection and exchange. We give and receive. Comfort with needs leads to interdependence.
Boundaries	Often rigid or undefined boundaries. Boundaries may be adopted from outside the relationship — society, religious thought, gender definitions — and may not fit the needs of the two partners or the relationship.	Grounded boundaries based on each person's sense of self and their own needs, and the needs of the relationship.
Triggers	People become triggered and act out from triggers, but may not be aware about the nature of triggers. Emotional suppression and explosive expression are common.	Partners recognize we all get triggered sometimes and try to act responsibly when triggered. Learning how to get grounded when triggered and to name "I am triggered" reduces acting out.

	Personality-based relationship	**Soul-centered relationship**
Sexuality	Sexuality may be viewed primarily as a means of procreation. Sexuality may be a source of power struggles or a way to control another. Partners may not know their own sexual needs or lack language to communicate about sexual needs	Sexuality integrates spirituality. Sexuality is recognized as a pathway to soul deep connection. Having children is seen in more of a spiritual light.
Gender	Understood in terms of socially prescribed roles and the physical packaging we are born with.	Understood as energy or essence. May or may not be reflected in our physical wiring or plumbing.
Relationship With Our Body	Body as object. We like it or don't. We color it, package it, and try to make it fit external standards.	Body as temple of the soul. Body as conduit for connection and exchange. We learn to care for our bodies.
Spirituality	Often confused with religion. Comes with a list of beliefs, do's and don'ts.	Understood as life force energy. Expressed in many forms.

BUILDING A SOUL-CENTERED RELATIONSHIP

I remember a time in my mid-20's when I really embraced the pathway towards soul-centered relationship. Much as I wanted to get married, make a long-term commitment and build a life with another person, I was aware something seemed to be missing inside of me.

I had lived with a wonderful man for several years, yet felt numb and unable to fully receive his affections towards me. I could go through the motions of partnership, play the role with great competence and sincere care, yet something still felt incomplete within me.

We entered couple therapy, and the therapist asked early on why I was with this man. I said, "because he is a nice person." That was fine and good. Yet, I was aware of an emotional deadness within me when she asked and I responded. I felt a passionlessness within myself. And I knew it wasn't about him so much as it was about me. I was numb to his sexual advances, even though I wanted to connect with him. "Was there simply a lack of chemistry?" I asked myself, "Or was there something else I could not see?"

So, in 1985, I turned my life inside out and made a commitment to embark on a journey to date, court and eventually marry myself. I had no idea what the path would look like or how long it would take. I just knew I had to clear the decks, and travel through deep, sometimes dark, and unknown spaces within myself physically, emotionally, spiritually and sexually.

I broke off my relationship with my friend. I quit my corporate job and set out to do my real life work. I chose to live alone for the first time in my life. I dated no one but myself. I jumped off a cliff into the unknown, committing to God that I would follow the path of my heart and see where it led.

I entered into a period of voluntary celibacy. I decided I needed to learn to be my own most intimate lover and explore what turned me on, opened my heart and made me melt. I engaged wholeheartedly in bodywork and therapy, well aware of my sexual trauma history which was blocking my aliveness. I spent hours and days and seemingly weeks alone with myself, sometimes in peace and quiet, and sometimes in pain and discomfort. I laid the foundation for my first book **LIVING WITH VISION: RECLAIMING THE POWER OF THE HEART** during this time, and found opportunities to take my work abroad.

I had no idea how long this passage would last when I entered into it. It turned out to last two years. During this time I learned how to touch myself, soothe myself, pleasure myself, comfort myself, listen closely to my heart and find a sense of my own pace. I found more comfort in solitude than I ever had imagined possible. When I felt ready to self-marry, I decided to create a sacred ritual to signify my deep, lifelong commitment to marry myself.

I created a ritual ring with a jeweler friend of mine. I discussed ritual design with a friend from Connecticut. When the time was right, I surrounded myself with beautiful flowers, took my ring and made a self-wedding vow. I began to wear my self-marriage ring as a symbol of the lifelong commitment I had just made to myself.

As I re-entered the world of dating and attraction, I felt like a new woman. My sexuality was more available to me and felt connected to my heart. Although my self-work continued, this was a turning point in my readiness to marry another and be a soul-centered partner.

There are many components involved in building a soul-centered relationship. Here are some important ones.

1. *Self-marriage as the first commitment.*

   As I learned in my journey, before we can be fully available to love another, we need to be fully available to ourselves. Authentic self-knowledge, self-healing and self-love are prerequisites for forming a deep, intimate and sustainable bond with another person. To the degree we are unavailable to ourselves, we are not able to be there with another. To the degree we are numb to or unaware of our own feelings and needs, we are insensitive to and unable to respond to a loved one's feelings and needs. To be ready and available to build an intimate partnership with another, it is valuable to first commit to a lifelong marriage with oneself.

2. *Recognizing that the relationship is a living organism: 1+1=3.*
   Too often people don't recognize that when they form a partnership there are three beings to care for: you, me and we. The partnership, like each partner, is a living being, and needs time, care and attention to grow and thrive. When we neglect the "we" dimension of relationship, the effects are palpable by the individual partners.

3. *Learning about space needs: separate space and relational space.*
   In my years of private practice, I have heard countless people wrestle with how to be in relationship and get the space they need. I have watched members of a couple argue over their space needs, without realizing they are speaking different languages. I have found there are two kinds of space that need to be balanced for both partners and the partnership to feel vital and alive: separate space and relational space. Separate space is alone time, cave time, reflective time on one's own. Often a partner needs time apart from their partner to meet their separate space needs. Relational space is the kind of space one gets being with their partner "in relationship." Relational space feeds one's need for connection, for intimacy, for being with. When two people come together, it is common for one person to have higher relational space needs and the other to have higher separate space needs. When unrecognized and undiscussed, these differences lead to tension in the relationship and can be the source of conflict and struggle.

4. *Cultivating connection.*
   Feeling connected is central to love, intimacy and an experience of nourishing partnership. Staying grounded in our connection with self is a prerequisite for being available to sustain connection with a partner. Different people feel connected through different means. For example, a woman I know feels most connected when doing activities with her partner. "When we've been out biking together, I want to throw my arms around him and get physically close." Her partner is more kinesthetic and feels connected through lots of stroking, massaging, touching and holding.

   Other people feel connected when they can laugh together, when they feel safe enough to open their hearts and talk to one another, when they can rest silently with one another, when they can make music together or cook dinner together. We can use all of our senses to connect. Experimenting with different ways of connecting can be a fun and learningful exercise.

5. *Taking time for relationship process work.*
   Many people I know hate to talk about the hard stuff, the challenges and even the fine tunings that emerge in a working relationship. These same people may also find it hard to acknowledge what they appreciate in their partner and in themselves. Building in regular times to talk deeply, about hard stuff, fine tunings and appreciations is part of the care and feeding of a soul-centered relationship. It allows for nipping shadow issues in the bud as they arise, rather than leaving them to fester. It also allows for exciting new ideas to grow. When a couple cannot work through pieces on their own, bringing in a third party, often a professional, to hold the space and facilitate the process is an invaluable choice.

6. *Making time to touch each other emotionally, physically and sexually.*
   To stay connected and keep intimacy alive, we need to make regular time to touch and be touched. This includes time to speak and listen from the heart, to hold and nurture each other with non-sexual touch, and to have a free, abundant, loving sexual connection. Often emotional touch and physical touch go hand in hand. When we feel deeply touched on the inside, we often want to reach out and touch one another physically. When we touch one another physically with love and care, we feel emotionally connected. In Chapter 1, emotional, physical and sexual contact were listed as basic human needs.

7. *Developing a shared vision which incorporates both partners' dreams.*
   Since a soul-centered relationship often has a spiritual purpose beyond just daily companionship, it is important the partners take time to cultivate their own sense of vision and build a shared vision together. Our individual and joint visions evolve and unfold over time. The more deeply we know our heart's desires, the more consciously we can fulfill them.

8. *Incorporating play, fun and pleasure into the relationship.*
   Our culture places a great emphasis on working and too little emphasis on fun, joy, pleasure and play. Pleasure is an essential ingredient to keep our spirits healthy and vital. Pleasure feels good. Laughter is a kind of medicine for the soul. Recognizing the value of play and pleasure is an important part of sustaining a deep, intimate relationship. We need to make time for fun, pleasure and play.

CHALLENGES FOR THE SOUL-CENTERED RELATIONSHIP

The need for the soul-centered relationship and the richer, fulfilling quality of life it brings are both clear. However, the path towards soul-centered relationship is still marked by some significant challenges. These include:

Discerning stuck places from unworkable differences.

For many of the individuals and couples I have worked with, one of their greatest challenges is figuring out when a relationship is truly unworkable versus when the relationship has simply hit a painful piece of process work. "How do we know when it's time to call it quits?" asked two members of a thirty-something couple who were wrestling both with their own inner demons and with practical concerns. "How can we tell the difference between a difficult passage that ultimately, with the right help, can be worked through and when our relationship is truly unworkable?"

Many people cannot face working through the pain of relationships, which can be incredibly grueling at times and require deep inner work. "People will divorce because they cannot bear the discomfort of working through change, because they are too filled with 'me' to do anything but leave when the going gets tough," reflected a middle-aged woman. "People commonly leave relationships after six months or after five years. They never reach the place of safety and trust that can take years to develop."

On the other hand, how often do people stay in stagnant relationships, where the two partners have grown in different and sometimes incompatible directions? To break-up a relationship is so earth-shaking to the foundation of one's life. "How do I know I haven't been wasting the last fifteen years of my life?" asked a 37-year-old man who had lived with his girlfriend since he was twenty-two. "How can I tell if this is a healthy relationship? We have been together seemingly forever, but are we really equipped to get married and have kids?"

Discerning when a relationship is stuck or in need of focused attention and when it is no longer workable requires deep soul-searching on the part of both partners. Honest, heartfelt communication is essential, including taking the risk to speak the unspeakable or the hard but essential truths. Sometimes, this very process of deepening communication creates the space to work the pieces and builds a path of enhanced intimacy. Sometimes, the process illuminates what isn't workable, so the decision to separate can be made thoughtfully, with respect, love and care. Third party facilitation is often needed to do this depth of work.

Lack of support structures for partnerships.

As I was contemplating getting married, I was deeply touched when an older gentleman told me that one of the purposes for gathering others together for a wedding ceremony was to ask them to commit to supporting the couple to live out their wedding vows. Just as it takes a village to raise a child, it takes a village to hold a couple. The conditions of our current times do not help sustain long-term relationships. Community is virtually non-existent. We live in a mobile society with no extended family down the street. We embrace few traditions which extend the continuity from the previous generation.

A 52-year-old woman I interviewed commented, "No one sticks around long enough to get to the place of safety where they can trust one another. Living in a mobile society, we've created a fascination with change. People who are deprived of hope/faith, grounding and connection to oneself, one's family, community, the land and God rarely understand what is necessary to rectify their problems."

With our busy lives and the conflicting demands that pull us all in many directions at once, remaining centered and grounded in ourselves and our relationships takes great commitment and discipline. It is hard to nurture relationships in a culture that values worldly production over being and relating. We need to become more creative in finding ways to build support structures around our important relationships.

Transmuting the cultural shadow.

Individual and couple therapy can help provide a first level of emotional and spiritual healing for people pursuing soul-centered partnerships. However, there is a whole other dimension that requires a larger forum in which to dialogue, heal and grow. We need to evolve our collective consciousness so that forums can be created where we can dialogue with one another about gender-healing and soul-centered partnership matters. Creating safe spaces in which we can both hear and be heard can help sort our unique individual struggles from collective challenges facing us all. We need to collaborate to evolve social, political and economic structures that reflect a balance of male and female energies as we heal our wounded hearts.

Molly Dwyer, who along with Will Keepins, brings together men and women to do gender reconciliation work notes, "The dynamic is larger than can be confronted on a psychological or sociological basis. It is a spiritual dilemma. We need to work with larger forces. We won't solve it through human ingenuity, through political processes, through psychological efforts. We see it as something bigger than just a human dilemma or a human dilemma that is so large that it needs a larger force to address it. Opening ourselves to the listening and guidance that can emerge in the moment is an essential part of the healing process."

The process unfolds based on the people who come together, not a set of ideas or tools. Dwyer continues, "A collective alchemy emerges. We are transmuting the cultural shadow into the gold of relational communion."

FORMS OF RELATIONSHIPS AND CONFIGURATIONS FOR LIVING

While some soul-centered relationships will simply be deepened versions of our traditional heterosexual, monogamous marriage relationships, this time of cultural evolution presents an expanding array of choices for forms of relationships and living configurations. A member of one of the groups I lead cited a figure that more than 50% of households today are other than straight married couples. Considering the numbers of people who are single by choice, divorced, single parents, same sex couples, and unmarried partners, this statistic is not hard to fathom.

As I was sitting at my son's gymnastics class, talking with the grandmother of a girl who attends my son's school and the mother of a boy in my son's gymnastics class, we started making our own calculations. In the granddaughter's second grade class, there are two children of divorced parents, one child adopted from China by a single mom, two children whose parents never married, and one child who has two moms. In my son's school, many of the teachers and administrators are themselves single parents and same sex parents. The mom of the other boy in my son's gymnastics class was nodding her head as she realized four children in her son's second grade class had two moms. One of the two-mom families had two children, one birthed by each mom, both sharing the same father.

I know several unmarried women, both straight and gay, who have searched for male partners with whom to father and raise a child without the complication of a personal romantic relationship. One mom of a six-year-old daughter chose a male friend of hers to father and co-parent her child. Both parents are equally committed to their daughter's best interests. They worked hard to negotiate a co-parenting contract prior to the birth of their child.

In addition to the many forms of "family" that people are creating today, the meaning of "home" is also changing with the times. The mainstream norm of a single family unit occupying a house or apartment of their own is being challenged with alternatives. With the costs of housing becoming unaffordable in many parts of the country, people choose to share their living spaces with other adults, be they friends, family or housemates. Sometimes people live together for the company as well as the economics. Co-housing is a living form that is growing in popularity, as people come together to find new ways of building community.

CONSCIOUS RELATING: THE NEW PARADIGM FOR LOVE

While we have made progress in accepting same-sex relationships between men and men and women and women, the culture as a whole still offers a pretty narrow view of what constitutes an acceptable loving relationship. Our high divorce rate illustrates that even straight heterosexual men and women struggle in the most accepted form of relationship called marriage.

Deborah Taj Anapol, a pioneer in the field of exploring conscious relating, speaks of a new paradigm for love. We are moving through a shift in consciousness where a marriage or blending between the masculine and feminine is taking place. "With this shift comes an understanding of love as consciousness, rather than feelings for an object or love as something finite. The new paradigm for love is one of partnership, rather than a dominance/submissive form of relating."

In the old paradigm, when relationships fail, partners often distance from themselves and one another with lies of omission and commission. When intimate relationships are formed from a utilitarian base, responding to social expectations, economic necessity, or gender role expectations, it is hard for men and women alike to find an authentic way of relating. When relationships are formed from a more spiritually integrated place, one comes to a partner freely, from a place of unconditional love and choice.

When people are afraid to admit their needs to themselves, never mind their partner's, it is hard to have a paradigm for love. Learning to know one's emotional, sexual and intimate needs becomes a spiritual journey. For many people, alternative lifestyle options are needed for authentic and vital relating and expression. As we move through the paradigm shift, forms of relationship may need to adjust to accommodate our individual and collective growth and change. Committed relationships may range from marriage to God with a celibate lifestyle to polyamorous relationships where people are both emotionally committed and sexual with more than one partner. Some people commit emotionally to a primary relationship with a person of one gender, yet engage sexually with another person or other persons of the other gender. Some individuals and couples choose to study and practice sacred sexuality to increase both their sense of connection and pleasure.

Bob Francouer, a teacher of graduate and undergraduate classes in Human Sexuality at Fairleigh Dickinson University and the editor of **THE INTERNATIONAL ENCYCLOPEDIA OF SEXUALITY**, comments on the shifting paradigm: "I think the outcome is going to be a much greater, more open, tolerant diversity. Once premarital sex was taboo. Today, in many circles, including mainstream circles and even churches, premarital sexual relationships are taken for granted. We will see different lifestyles that are socially responsible and fulfilling for the individuals. As we live into our 70's, 80's, 90's and beyond, some people will change their pattern of relationships."

15 TIPS FOR A GREAT RELATIONSHIP *by Chip August*

1. The question we must keep asking ourselves is how much do you want to love and be loved?

2. What you find hard to say, you must say.

3. I own my thoughts and behavior. You own yours.

4. I own my genitals and body. You own yours.

5. Practice surrender. Find out what your partner wants and offer it.

6. Great relationships require time investment.

7. Talk is very important.

8. Loving, intimate touch is more important than talk.

9. Instead of arguing or debating, reflect your partner's feelings back.

10. Choose love over any other thought, feeling or behavior.

11. When you have forgotten to choose love, choose love again.

12. Pleasure is healing. No pain, no pain.

13. Whoever has a problem, has the solution.

14. Would you rather be right or happy?

15. Sexuality lives in the inner child. Play. Laugh. Be creative.

ESSENTIAL QUESTIONS

1. What are the benefits and limitations you have experienced in personality-based relationships?

2. In what ways have you tried to create or succeeded at creating soul-centered relationships?

3. What are the greatest challenges you envision or have encountered as you seek to deepen your intimate relationships? Which of these challenges are personal and which are socio-cultural?

4. What emotional and relational process skills do you bring to an intimate relationship? What skills do you need to learn?

5. What is most scary about soul-centered relating?

6. What is most exciting about soul-centered relating?

7. How do we teach our children about soul-centered relating?

MEDITATION: *Connecting the Dots*

Take a moment to get comfortable, closing your eyes as long as that's comfortable...and take whatever time and space you need to breathe...

letting your chest and belly fill with air as you inhale, and allowing your chest and belly to relax as you exhale....Feeling the support your seat, your pillow, the wall, the floor--whatever supports you, provides for your body as you inhale....and as you exhale, letting your seat, your pillow, the wall, the floor — whatever supports you — support you....Taking a moment to see if you are comfortable...allowing yourself to adjust your position any way you need to be more comfortable...and allowing your focus to be with your heart.

Take a moment to notice how your heart is feeling physically and emotionally ....is it full? is it empty? is it heavy? is it light? is it separate? connected? ....Take a moment to let yourself become a little more familiar with whatever is happening in your heart now....

One of the things I have found most sad about many people as they explore the mysterious terrain of love relationships is that they don't really know their hearts in a sustainable, grounded way. This applies both in long-term committed relationships and in new, potential dating relationships. How often have we experienced being on either the giving or receiving end of declaring love, attraction and passion in one moment, only to disappear from the scene in a heartbeat....as though one moment had no relationship to the next. When this happens, are we or is our partner being deceptive or insincere? Or can the feeling of the moment be ephemeral, as we discover that we or they simply do not know our/their own hearts? What is it like when we cannot "connect the dots" from one moment to the next? Werner Erhard used to say, "When you get what you want, can you take it?" Have you ever had the experience of pursuing and getting closer to what you seemingly wanted, only to encounter terror and run away? Take a moment to let yourself reflect on your experience right now....

How can we build safety and trust in relating if one moment's truth has no relationship to the truth of the next? What does it take to train our hearts and minds for relationships to be more like marathons, a long term journey, rather than a short-term "hit" or "intimacy fix?" How do we need to shape our social fabric as well as our personal relationships so that intimacy is not so terrifying and seemingly life-threatening in a primal way? Take a moment to reflect on what you need to experience, create or learn to really know your own heart....

And at your own pace, very slowly and gently take a deep breath and bring your focus back into the room. And you are welcome to make notes on your experience in this meditation... recording whatever thoughts, feelings, questions and ideas emerge as you begin to reflect and write.

Chapter 8

INTEGRATING SEXUALITY AND SPIRITUALITY

What happens between you and me before sex
Lives on, during sex
Long before we have touched each other on the skin
We have touched each other inside
The atmosphere between us outside of sex
Deeply affects the way I experience you within sex

— Aron Gersh,
Deeply Touched Inside

Sexuality is as magical and miraculous as life itself, a special gift we have each been given to enjoy and share, an invitation to participate in the creative dance that is life. Sexual energy is life energy, the feeling of the life force pulsating within us. It allows us to become one with self, nature, God and another human being. At its fullest, sex is soul energy exchange, the deepest and most intimate level of human contact, where mind, body, heart and spirit come together for the meeting of two souls, Sexuality allows the sacred dimension of human experience to be fully embodied. Soul energy exchange can be both genital and non-genital.

And yet, how rare is the experience of a fully embodied, spiritual sexuality as I have just described? Our culture tends to look at sexuality prudishly — existing for the sole purpose of procreation — or hedonistically — existing for the sole purpose of recreation. We are not taught to consider the body as a sacred vessel which prevents many people from appreciating sex as a sacred activity. Our religious institutions tend to promote the prudish viewpoint and condemn the hedonistic viewpoint. Rarely are we offered the road map for sexuality as a spiritual path or spirituality as a sexual path. We live with a sex-spirit split that has been operant for thousands of years.

When you hear the words sexuality and spirituality, do you automatically link them? Or do you wonder what they have to do with one another in any way, shape or form? Are sexuality and spirituality words you have defined for yourself based on your life experience? Or is one or both of these two "s-words" imbued with cultural connotations, shoulds, shouldn'ts, pain, disconnection and shame?

Many years ago when I was teaching a stress management course in a large corporation, I experienced the level of discomfort a lot of people have with the topic of sexuality. While brainstorming strategies for managing stress, a group of five adults between the ages of 30 and 60 came up with sex as a stress reduction tool. The woman who voiced the word "sex," turned red in the face, as the other members of her group started giggling like school children. This group of five exuded both a silent tension and an expectant curiosity. The energy of just uttering the word was exciting and palpable.

Other class members looked towards this group eager to learn what was going on that was so fun and juicy. They shared the giddiness when they realized the "s-word" had been mentioned. Some classmates did not stray from the "serious" assignment at hand, ignoring this unsolicited diversion and focusing on the "professional" context. While I would have been happy to deepen a discussion on the topic, I could see clearly this was NOT the thing to do.

The room grew really silent. In the silence were feelings of relief, discomfort, titillation and fascination. Beneath the business suits lived the spirits of a group of 5-year-old children emerging as sexual beings, and being cut off from their emerging sexuality. Their sexual curiosity was overshadowed by the fears of their parents, the workplace, religious institutions and our culture overall. Having never had a safe place to take this conversation to the next level, these adult professionals were emotionally stuck at the developmental age where they had learned to separate sexuality from self. I observed this pattern in other Stress Management classes as well. In fact, it became a classic happening when the "s-word" managed to emerge briefly in almost every class I taught.

THE SEX-SPIRIT SPLIT

A t times of transformation we live with the simultaneous existence of deconstruction and convergence. Today there is a resurging interest in spiritual practices in many circles, and also a breakdown in the patriarchal, hierarchical church structures. The spectre of clergy sexual abuse intermingles with a worldview promulgated by the church about the nature of relationships and sexuality that no longer has meaning for people today — men and women, young and even middle-aged. As I discussed in Chapter 5, the gender roles we were raised with have broken down and blurred. The image of nuclear family as mom, dad and 2.4 children has been superceded by a far greater spectrum of family possibilities. Bisexuality, androgyny, gender fluidity and polyamory are more and more common, especially among the twentysomething generation.

As we live with breakdown and deconstruction at so many levels, one thread that emerges is a hunger and longing, both spiritual and erotic. "We are in a culture of dis-remembering in a lot of ways including the natural flow of erotic energies through and around us," comments Suzanne Blackburn, a massage therapist and energy worker whose participation in sexuality and spirituality work has catapulted her personal and spiritual growth. Alex Jade of the Body Electric School uses the term "erotic amnesia." Many bodies of work are now available to help us "re-member." I list some of them in the Resources Section at the end of the book.

Living with splits between mind and body, head and heart, heart and pelvis and sexuality and spirituality, we have lost touch with many of the most beautiful pleasures and experiences possible in being human. So many people today are searching for meaning and purpose, most often expressed through job dissatisfaction, addictions and broken and troubled relationships. We have become disconnected from our bodies, hearts, souls, spirits, and the divine, and also from one another. The rise of industrialization, urbanization, the nation-state, global dislocations, war and poverty all contribute to the sex-spirit split for us both individually and collectively.

LIVING THROUGH A PARADIGM SHIFT

Bob Francouer, a teacher of graduate and undergraduate classes in Human Sexuality at Fairleigh Dickinson University and editor of the **INTERNATIONAL ENCYCLOPEDIA OF SEXUALITY**, notes, "Sexuality and spirituality have always been joined and interwoven from the very beginning of the human race. It is only in the last 2000 - 3000 years of Western civilization that the two have been separated. And they have not just been separated, but have been seen as antagonistic to each other. The split between sex and spirit came out of the Greek philosophy of dualism, and a dichotomous view of humans as matter/evil/female and spirit/good/rational/male."

Just as Western civilization went through a period of major cultural upheaval 2000 - 3000 years ago, we are undergoing a period of major cultural turnover and paradigm shift now. "The institutional churches are losing their credibility in dealing with sexuality and spirituality. They are losing their authority," continues Francouer. Francouer is well versed in the changing paradigm worldwide. **THE INTERNATIONAL ENCYCLOPEDIA OF SEXUALITY** is written by 300 experts in 60 countries on 6 continents. The encyclopedia includes in-depth reports of all aspects of sexuality. Each country has a section on religious and ethnic influences. Having collected information from many cultures all over the world, "it becomes very clear the spiritual traditions are undergoing major revolutions in their patterns of thinking. People in many cultures worldwide are now not thinking in terms of marital and procreational values, but in terms of individual self-enrichment and fulfillment. The spiritual is a very important part of the new perspective."

"When the human psyche reaches the point of convergence and breakthrough into a new level of consciousness," reflects Francouer, "diversity is the first thing that happens. The energy spreads out and explores all kinds of possibilities.

There is no one ideal paradigm nor five ideal paradigms. All the models we have had in the past have real difficulties being applied in today's world. So, people are creating their own models and patterns." The new paradigms created need to include and consider the collective as well as the individual.

HEART WOUNDEDNESS AND SEXUAL WOUNDEDNESS

Alexander Lowen, developer of Bioenergetics, stated, "The primary nature of every human being is to be open to life and love." Sadly, the heart woundedness I have been describing in this book disconnects us from our primary nature and contributes to the sex-spirit split.

In Chapter 1, I talked about the electromagnetic power of the heart and how the electromagnetic field generated by our hearts touches others within 10 - 12 feet of our physical presence. Imagine what the energy exchange might look and feel like when two people with safe, present, open hearts are engaged in soul energy exchange. In contrast, if our hearts are wounded and we are cut off from our souls, our ability to be sexual is drastically limited and sometimes inaccessible. Individually and collectively, we have lost touch with the natural place of sexuality in life and love.

In our disconnection, we swing between polarities of sexual repression and indulgence. Indulging, you repeat habits in a mechanical way. Repressing, you never discover what sexuality can be. We see the paradoxical juxtaposition of indulgence and repression every day. On the one hand, sexual imagery abounds. This past Christmas, I couldn't tell whether it was the Gap, Old Navy or some other commercial as I watched twentysomething models in tight jeans gyrating their way across the television screen.

Everywhere we turn, the billboards on the highway, the magazines on the newsstand, the websites on the Internet, offer provocative and erotic imagery. Yet, in spite of its abundance, this imagery is neither real nor embodied. It reflects thousands of years of the mind-body-spirit-sex split and dualistic thinking. We have learned to separate sexuality not only from spirituality, but also from our natural body.

In his book **JOURNEY OF THE HEART: INTIMATE RELATIONSHIPS AND THE PATH OF LOVE,** John Welwood points out that "only human beings make love through sex, because only human beings lie and linger front to front, with the softest parts of our bodies fully exposed and in contact. At least two main feeling centers are located in the midsection of our soft front. The lower center, around the navel, is the home of our gut feelings, where we experience erotic resonance with another person. The upper center is the area around the heart, where we sense more delicate feelings of openness and surrender...Only human beings exchange chi — the energy of aliveness — by making love face to face, belly to belly, heart to heart." Yet sadly, so many people experience splits between these different energy centers and are cut off from the energy flow that can happen amongst and between them.

Sex therapist and researcher Gina Ogden, who has conducted the first nationwide survey on sexuality and spirituality reflects, "We have been taught how to be sexy, but not how to be sexual." We have been taught to fantasize and create sexual thoughts in our minds, but have not been educated about learning what pleasures us and how we both express ourselves and connect with others in our skin and energetically. Fundamentalist religions have spent hundreds of years telling people what is and what is not appropriate. "Many women come into my office having known sex only as an 'out-of-body' experience," continues Ogden. So, while sex is in our faces, it is too often disconnected from our hearts and souls, our bodies and the very life energy that sex is about."

This disconnection is emotionally and psychically costly. How many of us yearn for passion, meaning and fulfillment in our lives, not only sexually, but at all levels? How many of us override our body wisdom, our inner knowing, in pursuit of external, socially prescribed ideals and goals? How many men and women suffer from what we label as "sexual dysfunction," unable to experience their bodies as instruments of pleasure, connection, union and surrender?

Sadly, as we have been socialized to be good boys and good girls, we have embraced an out-of-balance model of living and relating, which includes a distorted understanding of what sexuality is, who can be sexual, and how sexuality relates to spirituality and love. Good boys "fuck" and good girls "don't." Neither gender is given the tools, the experiences and the support to develop a personally fulfilling sense of sexuality. We are taught to "function" and "perform" sex rather than BE sexual. We are taught to fragment, to compartmentalize, to dissociate and not to integrate our sexual selves.

Some of the results of heart woundedness and sexual woundedness are:

Disappointment: Our media has sold us an image of finding our magical soul-mate with whom everything easily just works. This is the modern day version of the Cinderella myth, which leads to a version of the Cinderella complex. No matter how wonderful a partner appears to be initially, shadow issues eventually rear their unwelcome heads and the bubble is burst.

A wall of resentments: Following from our Cinderella or soul-mate fantasy, when we experience disappointments, we build a wall of resentments about how our partner is not good enough or unable to meet our emotional, physical, spiritual, practical and sexual needs. Since we lack the empathy and communication skills to work through our disappointments and resentments, as the wall grows bigger and thicker, it sets the stage for spiritual divorce.

Spiritual divorce: A couple remains together, but in a shell of a relationship. Emotional, physical, spiritual and sexual intimacy are gone. The couple may either function as two ships that pass in the night, or divide up external roles and perform them in a business-like manner.

Sexless marriage: This phenomenon is becoming more and more visible. It isn't clear whether the fast-paced, overwhelmed-with-demands way of life so many people are leading has created this distance, or the fear of intimacy and emotional breakdown in our relationships turns our energies in other directions. "Dual-income, no sex" has become a popular media buzzword.

Mutual abandonment: Lacking a mutually understood language to work through differences, woundedness and needs, partners disconnect and abandon one another. Psychiatrist Miguel Liebovitz comments, "People operate on assumptions without checking out each other's feelings."

Lack of empathy and communication skills: Men and women lack empathy for self and partner, and lack the communication skills to both express their own feelings and needs effectively. Nor do they hear and respond to their partner's feelings and needs.

Asking our partner to be the cosmic tit: In a partner, we look to find the ideal mother (or father) to latch onto, to feed our deep unmet needs. "Men go to their female partner to have an emotional bond and emotional grounding," notes Mankind Project Executive Director, Carl Greisser. "It becomes a central need in a relationship." Because most men don't have other close emotional relationships, a burden is placed on his primary partner to meet all of his emotional needs. Women may "latch on" to their male partners for protection or material providing needs. Taken to an extreme, we relate to each other as wounded boys and girls looking to be taken care of by mommy or daddy.

Exercise: *Sexual and Spiritual Wounding*

This is an exercise you can do yourself or share with a partner or group. Begin by reflecting on each of the following questions, and making notes in your journal. Once you have completed your reflective time, you can share your answers if you like.

About Your Spirituality:

1. To what extent do you feel clear and comfortable with your spirituality?

2. What is most clear about your sense of spirituality?
   What is most unclear?

3. Are there ways you feel spiritually wounded? If yes, how do you feel spiritually wounded and how did the wounds originate?

4. What might you need to heal any sense of spiritual woundedness?

5. Are there any ways you feel undeveloped spiritually? What might help you develop spiritually?

6. What do you need to feel whole and at peace with your sense of spirituality?

About Your Sexuality:

1. To what extent do you feel clear and comfortable with your sexuality?

2. What is most clear about your sense of sexuality? What is most unclear?

3. Are there ways you feel sexually wounded? If yes, how do you feel sexually wounded and how did the wounds originate?

4. What might you need to heal any sense of sexual woundedness?

5. Are there any ways you feel undeveloped sexually? What might help you develop sexually?

6. What do you need to feel whole and at peace with your sexuality?

About Integrating Your Sexuality and Spirituality:

1. To what extent do your sexuality and spirituality feel integrated? Separate?

2. What does it mean to you to integrate sexuality and spirituality?

3. To what extent do you suffer from a sex-spirit split?

4. What might you need to heal any sense of a sex-spirit split?

5. How might you express your spirituality through your sexuality? How might you express your sexuality through your spirituality?

6. What kind of environment would you want to create to support the integration of your sexuality and spirituality? For yourself? With a loved partner? In community?

SEXUALITY AND THE MALE AND FEMALE HEART WOUNDS

Just as the cultural heart wound has male and female expressions, sexual wounding also has different expressions for men and women. A classic scenario is the wounded male heart separates sex from love, and links sex with mental fantasies, visual imagery and "sex is sex" thinking. The wounded female heart fears sexual power, sexual expression and often never develops a sexual self. When wounded male and female hearts meet in the bedroom, we have the chemistry for misunderstanding, power struggles, hurt and anger. Neither gender understands the heart wound or the sex wound of the other. In fact, often neither gender understands the heart wound or the sex wound that they carry themselves!

Therapist Lidia Rodrigues comments that men are supposed to have all the knowledge, yet they never get an education except in the locker room. Women don't say anything because they feel embarrassed and ashamed. "A woman thinks she's the only one who feels the way she feels, so she complies. Women are afraid if they don't comply with the man's sexual requests, the man will leave them for another woman. Women are not empowered around sexuality."

Because men have been taught to sacrifice their hearts and their lives for the forward movement of civilization, their sexuality and intimacy needs have gotten disconnected. Intimacy and vulnerability are defended against rather than promoted. Both genders suffer as they bang up against the thick walls of protection that surround their wounded hearts. We lack the tools and a common language to navigate this painful territory where we may find a safe, mutually respectful way to connect and heal.

"I don't think I've met a man so far who doesn't have deep doubts about his sexuality, what it means to be sexual, what it means to be potent or effective as a man," acknowledges Mankind Project Executive Director Carl Greisser. "Every man I have met carries a pretty heavy burden of shame around sexuality. Men rarely speak about sexuality outside of a safe container like the one we create in the Mankind Project trainings."

In this context, it is no surprise that sexual anorexia and sexual addiction proliferate, two sides of the same coin:

The sexual anorexic represses his/her passion. Out of fear, trauma, anger or hurt s/he disengages from sexual need, sexual passion and sexual expression. Work, children and life's busyness fill the gap where healthy sexuality would live. My colleague Tracy MacNab commented that some of the men he sees in his practice self-castrate with work and marriage. Many of the women I have seen in my practice have never had a context to explore emotionally safe sexuality. Childhood sexual abuse, religious shaming and body image wounding have made sexuality a painful and dangerous subject.

The sexual addict cannot distinguish passion from the sensual high of what is often emotionally and spiritually dissociated sex. In his/her relentless pursuit of sexual connection, s/he turns both self and other into sexual objects instead of sexual people. Sex becomes mechanistic, a momentary haven from life's loneliness and pain. Intimacy is too scary and vulnerable. Sex becomes destructive rather than life enhancing and bonding.

We lack a model of integrated sexuality that is rooted in connection with the life force, the earth, our own body and soul, our lover and the divine. Characteristics of male and female sex wounds are listed here:

The Male Sex Wound	The Female Sex Wound
♥ sex is separated from heart, love and intimacy	♥ sex is separated from passion, power and self-expression
♥ men are expected to know everything without any formal education	♥ women are expected to let men know everything without any formal education
♥ men aren't taught to recognize their emotional needs	♥ women aren't taught to recognize their sexual needs
♥ sexual energy gets channeled into work and worldly doing	♥ sexual energy is repressed and undeveloped
♥ sexual anorexia and sex addiction	♥ sexual anorexia is more common than sex addiction
♥ difficulty connecting sex, love and intimacy	♥ difficulty connecting sex, love and intimacy
♥ objectification of sexual partners	♥ being treated as sexual objects, not sexual people
♥ sex-is-sex, not about connection	♥ sex becomes about reproduction, not pleasure and connection
♥ not being acknowledged for what they do	♥ not being acknowledged for who they are

Rich Tosi and his wife Char have each led workshops for members of their own gender for many years. Together, they lead workshops for couples. They include an experiential exercise in which through meditation, participants travel back to when they were young children and have a chance to recall times when they were wounded and hurt by the other gender. "We grow them up through high school and college," comments Rich. "We have both men and women put stickers on themselves in those places that represent where they were wounded. We sometimes color code them — spiritual, emotional, sexual and physical wounds each having a particular color — and have the participants attach them in silence."

"We then ask them to silently stand up, mill around and find someone of the opposite gender and stand before them in silence. They then walk around and look at the wounds their gender has caused to the other gender. Some people will have 15, 20, 30 stickers on their body, on all different parts of their body. What happens is without anything being said, a lot of tears are shed. Men and women will start crying. It just happens in a space where you look in a way that allows you to see what has happened. The energy goes to a deep heart level, beyond blame. It turns into an incredibly compassionate moment. We then have people sit in small groups and invite anyone who is willing to talk about their wounds."

Some of the ways women have been wounded that come up frequently include:

Father wounding at puberty: Many women experience a disconnection or distancing from their fathers when they reach puberty. When she is clearly a "little girl" she has a close and friendly relationship with her father. Once the father recognizes his little girl is becoming a woman, he doesn't know what to do with it, so he rejects her. This wounds women emotionally and sexually. When a young woman who is experiencing her sexuality had a loving relationship with her dad up until she started developing sexually, as she feels rejected, she does not know what to do with her sexuality.

Confusing sexuality and looks: As women experience the externally generated pressure to be "pretty enough" and be a certain way, they can develop confusion between sexuality and looks. Wanting to be attractive — be it pretty enough or thin enough or whatever enough — women feel they need to measure up to this culturally generated image to be "okay." This can be mistaken for intimacy and sexuality.

Sexual abuse: Sadly, a very large number of women have been sexually abused as children. This impacts their adult relationships with men in a number of ways. Some women seem to be looking for dad, having had a special relationship with their father, which they are now looking for from other men. Other women go to the other extreme, shutting men out entirely. In his work with couples, he has observed women who will be either excessively or inappropriately sexy or will go the other way and make themselves very unattractive to men. Sexual abuse creates wounds that rob women of the opportunity to be in their heart and sexually present in a safe, grounded way.

Some of the ways men have been wounded that come up frequently include:

Mothers who sexualize their relationships with their sons: Rich has found a surprising number of men who as a child have experienced their mothers being overly sexual with them. This occurs not in the experience of having sex, but walking around nude, being suggestive or somehow suggesting to a young boy, be he 6 years old or 10 years old, that they are sexually attracted to them in a way that is confusing to the boy. This is a surprisingly deep and little talked about wound, about mothers who replace their husbands with their young sons. "This is a very difficult wound to identify," acknowledges Rich. "It takes men a long time to acknowledge that possibility exists."

Being put down and diminished: Men are far more sensitive than they first appear. A woman doesn't have to say much to wound a man sexually by suggesting he's not much of a man. A legacy of criticism and put-downs can start with a boy's mother and father when he is young. Adult men put each other down, measuring how much money they make, how pretty the woman they are with is, always trying to be better than. Respect is very important to a man. While disrespect may not sound like much, to the male psyche it is very significant.

Men's fear of other men: Carl Greisser reflects, "Our culture fosters fear between everyone, especially men. This relates to the competition that is part of the culture." Competition between men shows up at work, in their relationships with their fathers, brothers and male peers. One way men betray each other is in their competition for women. "When men don't trust each other, in effect, they wound each other," notes Rich Tosi. "If I don't trust another man, and I do something to him and I hurt him because I don't trust him, he has to do something back. We get in a battle and it started because we didn't trust each other."

SEXUALITY, SPIRITUALITY AND INTIMACY

In the **ART OF SEXUAL ECSTASY**, Margo Anand describes intimacy as "closeness — the fine-tuning of a relationship that allows increasingly subtle levels of feeling to be explored and shared." In order to be intimate with another we need to first learn to be intimate with ourselves. To open up and let our energy come forth in relationship to another, we need to be comfortable opening up and learning how our own energy flows and works. To show who we are to another and receive the other person as they show us who they are, we need to first have a clearly defined, grounded sense of self. As we are secure in ourselves, we can take in and appreciate another person's essence.

Both spirituality and sexuality can be pathways towards intimacy, on their own and together. A participant in one of my workshops defined spirituality as "the ground of all sexuality and intimacy." When a person is spiritually connected, there is an energy flow that runs between them and the universe, that brings a sense of comfort, connection and sense of self. Some people call this energy the lifeforce. Others call it God or a higher power. Spiritual connection also transpires with other people, groups of people and the natural world. Spiritual connection can help us address issues of meaning: figuring out who you are, what you are, and what you are doing here in this world.

Sexuality is also a dance of energy and connection. A participant in one of my workshops commented, "There are a lot of sexualities. Hedonistic sexuality is doing something that feels good. Sexuality can also be an energetic intuition about the universe. And there is a lot in between. Sexuality can invite the most powerful negotiation of space and energy. Sexual energy can be forward moving, directive and aggressive. Or it can be receptive, still and opening — two people merging as one, feeling a sense of union as the boundaries of ego melt and convergence takes place at a soul level. Marriage is a particular form of sexuality." Sexuality can be an art form for spiritual expression. The body is the medium for exploring and expressing our spiritual selves.

Through meeting in the body, you can very directly open up emotionally and spiritually and let another person see a piece of your soul. Margo Anand reflects, "Many people believe that sex is the quickest way to open the door to intimacy...In reality, it is not sex that opens the door to intimacy, but intimacy that opens the door to good lovemaking." In fact, Anand feels that "sex happens as the crowning act of intimacy."

Some combination of enculturation and wiring has tangled up the relationship of sexuality and intimacy for both men and women. Many men are socialized that sex is the safe doorway to intimacy. Until many men experience the closeness of sex, emotional involvement cannot unfold. Sexual contact may be considered intimacy in and of itself, even without emotional contact. Some men lack a broader context in which to view a woman's choice to be sexual or not with him. If a woman is not ready to receive or respond to his sexual advances, a man may feel deeply rejected rather than recognizing the time just isn't right at that moment.

For many women, emotional contact has been socialized as the safe doorway to intimacy. While some women can engage in casual sex, many women cannot be sexual with someone they don't feel an emotional connection with. Too many women have learned to submit to sexual contact in order to be loved, putting their partner's needs ahead of their own. A woman might just need to be held, but might also feel, "I will be rejected by my partner if I am not sexual right now.

Writer David Steinberg comments, "Sex opens people up and suddenly there are these feelings they didn't realize they had. People get scared by seeing the reality of themselves that sex reveals. Mutual ground is when both men and women are willing to honor and acknowledge their intimacy needs and their physical needs."

Because of the difference in socialization for men and women, both genders can suffer from misunderstandings of sexuality and sexual intention. They may find themselves speaking a different language from one another. Misunderstandings and feelings of rejection can lead to distancing and conflict. Men and women can both objectify their partners as "sexual objects," rather than seeing them as people who are sexual.

Therapist, author and workshop leader Margaret Paul comments, "For some people a core problem is that having control over sex is more important than having sex, just as control over getting love may be more important than receiving love." Sadly, in some relationships, control is really the issue rather than sex itself.

The culture portrays women sexually as the ones who say no; it is men's job to coerce them into being sexual. Many men are simply not prepared for women who have claimed their sexuality and sensuality and who really love sex. A 38-year-old client of mine worked hard to develop her sexuality and become comfortable sensually in her own skin. "Here, I thought I had become the fantasy woman so many men dream of. Yet, what happened again and again, is men found out about my sexual energy and run for the hills," she mourned.

"I was dating a man who complained that he had never been with a woman who could satisfy his libido," she reflected. "I love sexuality and physical closeness, and can make love every single day. I thought that when he met me, he would be happy. But what I discovered was that once he had the very thing he complained he never could get, he did not really want it. My passion, my power and even my tenderness frightened him. He felt pressure to have to perform, to have to keep up, even when I was not consciously exerting pressure. He ended up leaving me and choosing another sexually unavailable woman and married her. Go figure!"

The parallel for men is when a man works hard to develop his emotional side and their vulnerability, and discovers that women cannot tolerate the expression of his feelings and his vulnerability. "My partner kept telling me she wanted me to talk about my feelings," related a 42-year-old man, "And I worked hard to get in touch with my feelings and learn to express them. But I feel like it all backfired. Once I had a language to talk about my needs and my feelings, my partner didn't seem to like what was coming out of my mouth! On the one hand, she wanted me to be sensitive, but on the other hand, once I showed my vulnerability, she walked right over me."

Once we get past the cultural training and focus on the human core, Steinberg believes the differences between men and women are much smaller, if they exist at all. The men have been taught to be the keepers of emotional distance for a lot of reasons. Primary among them is to get them to do difficult jobs and to go to war. Women have been given the job of sexual gatekeepers and naysayers — keeping sex repressed. "Coming off those radically different trainings and looking for common ground is hard," reflects Steinberg. "As women become more independent and are willing to acknowledge their sexuality, and men become more aware of their grief and pain — the emotions real men are not supposed to feel according to cultural training — then there is more common ground."

SEX AND POWER

In the thick of the gender wars, sex is linked not with spirituality and intimacy but with power. "In matriarchal communities," notes therapist Lidia Rodrigues, "Women had power. Men were terrified of the sexual power women had, so they annihilated it. Patriarchal substituted for matriarchal. Women have forgotten their power at a cellular level. They forgot they had orgasmic power and sexual powers."

Lidia traces the roots of today's male-created model of sexuality back to the **KAMA SUTRA**, written in 400 BC by men, for men. "The **KAMA SUTRA** teaches men how to get women to provide for their needs. It enables men to learn about their sexuality and to teach women about male and female sexuality from a man's point of view. In this era, men taught women about sexuality, which included how to excite men. This translates into today's culture as how to use femininity with make-up, clothes, and high heels so men will be excited. This model exploited women."

This model gave men the dominant position, and even women's power as seductress still conformed to male-generated rules of female role performance. To take her power back, a woman could manipulate by not delivering what the man wanted, by withdrawing. "With women's lib there was an awakening," adds Lidia. "However, women fought men with the same weapons they criticized men for fighting with. Women became militant and engaged in another power struggle."

Inherent in sexual desire and sexual fulfillment is both vulnerability and surrender. Sadly enough, these conditions can lead to oppression when respect for self and other is not at the root of relationship. Because many people have been dominated and controlled as children, their sense of personal power is wounded. As a result, they may lack sensitivity and skill in their ability to negotiate their intimate needs with another person.

I have known people, both as friends and clients, who have engaged in BDSM (bondage and domination, sadism and masochism) circles to try to heal their relationship with power, so that they can relate to others out of a place of clarity, choice and mutual respect. "There can be a spiritual dimension to BDSM play," commented a woman in her late twenties. "There is a concept in the BDSM world called the 'safe word,' which has helped me have permission to learn where my boundaries are and communicate them to another person. The 'safe word' is a word that is chosen by me, like the word 'red,' that means stop at the moment I utter it. When something feels unsafe, uncomfortable or just plain unwanted by me, I voice my safe word, and all contact is stopped, no questions asked. By learning about my real needs and limits, I have regained a sense of personal, sexual and relational power."

Many men and women reawaken, or in many cases develop, their sense of personal power working in groups with members of their own gender. In another generation it may have been more organic for men to gather with men and women to gather with women. As our sense of community has broken down in the culture as a whole, it has become harder to gather a circle of men or women. We need community contact with members of our own gender to grow into and embody the natural power of maleness and femaleness.

Trainings like the Mankind Project's **New Warrior Training** for men, **A Woman Within** for women, and the Sterling Institute's men's and women's weekends provide sacred circles where men and women can define and reclaim a sense of wholeness. "The power of a woman emerges when she is whole within herself. The power of men emerges when they are with other men," says A Woman Within founder, Char Tosi. If we don't learn how to honor each other, there is no win. If we can gain a clear sense of power with our own masculine and feminine energy, we can then find a space of mutual respect with one another.

TOWARDS AN INTEGRATED SEXUALITY

How do we get from discomfort, dissociation, addiction and anorexia, and other out-of-balance sexual states to a more integrated sexuality? How do we heal the sex-spirit split in our own relationships and lives? Here are some steps you can take both on your own and with beloved partners.

1. *Emotionally safe sex.* Emotional safety allows us the possibility of noticing the emotional, sensual and electric currents that run through our bodies from moment to moment and over time. These currents provide information about what attracts us, what connects us, what feels good, what our pacing is. When we are not emotionally safe, we numb ourselves, shut down and leave our bodies. Emotional safety allows the internal and interrelational space to reawaken our sensations, thoughts and feelings. We can explore, experiment, give and receive and see what truly pleasures us and our partners.

2. *Reconnecting with our bodies and coming to our senses.* To have a fully integrated experience, you have to get into your body first. The most spiritual sex is also the most embodied sex. Gina Ogden notes, "One of the characteristics of truly spiritual sex is that the sensations are heightened. These are not only physical sensations, but also emotional sensations and spiritual sensations."

3. *Touch with permission and respect.* In sexual contact, one partner might feel that they can touch their partner anywhere, any way at any time. Many people I have worked with have never felt it was okay to say where, how and when they like to be touched, and where, how and when they didn't like to be touched. An integrated sexuality is one of respect for self and partner. Having the freedom and permission to say what works and what doesn't, when the time is right and when the time is not is important even in a context of love and good will. Emotional safety and space are created as partners learn to ask permission to touch and be touched, and have the freedom to say "yes" or "no."

4. ***Expanding our understanding of sex beyond just intercourse and the quest for orgasm.*** Intercourse and orgasm can be enriching and fulfilling, but these experiences alone are not all there is. Sex is the interchange of energy, and at the deepest level soul energy exchange. Sexual energy can touch you, without genital contact and without the laying on of hands. Just as the electromagnetic field of the heart can be felt by others within 10 feet of our bodies, sexual energy can reach beyond the boundary of our bodies and skin. Same gender couples and transgendered individuals may not be able to have sex through penile-vaginal penetration, but they can still engage in meaningful and fulfilling sexual contact. Our definition of sexual contact can also include sex with ourselves and a sense of sexual-spiritual connection with the divine.

5. ***Improving sex education.*** Performance artist and sex educator Annie Sprinkle reflects that regarding sex education, "Most people are left to their own devices. They experience only one, two or three sexual relationships in their whole lives. How are they going to learn?" Good sex education is not just about sperm fertilizing eggs or techniques you can try with a partner or how to avoid STD's. Good sex education is by its very nature experiential. We need to learn how to live more in our bodies and experience sexual energy. People crave experiential workshops, rituals and classes.

   Sprinkle acknowledges, "I have seen over and over people learn a lot when you do hands-on, physical stuff, exercises or demos. It is very powerful to learn about sex in groups. People share their thoughts, feelings and experiences." This gives others reference points, points of comparison, and allows wisdom to be shared in the most personal way. While books can be helpful, it is a paradox that we expect to learn about an embodied process from reading a book.

6. ***Respecting differences.*** Everyone is in a different place in their sexual evolution. We get into trouble when we have this ideal that everyone should be a particular way. Sexuality is so individual. Some people are hard-wired straight or hard-wired gay. Others are bisexual. Some people are naturally monogamous and others are naturally polyamorous. Some people have a vanilla male or female identity, and some people have a more complex sense of gender identity. Others are on a journey to define their sense of gender and sexuality. People need the freedom to come to know

their sexual self in an authentic way, and to be received with respect when they share it with others.

7. *Thinking about developing our sexuality as a process.* Sexual development is a journey, when we allow it to be. It is not linear and it never stops. "People go through difference phases," says Sprinkle. What happens when a woman hits menopause? When a couple gets divorced? When you feel you really want to explore? Or be celibate? "Some people want to explore their kinky side. Others have done that and are ready to do something else. Some people know exactly what they want and are happy doing that their whole lives."

8. *Recognizing that sex, like food, comes in many different packages.* Our culture provides many different food alternatives which we choose based on our lifestyle, our consciousness and our personal preferences. People with fast-paced lifestyles find fast food convenient. For others, junk food tastes good, provides momentary comfort and offers calories. As their consciousness evolves, some people are choose "whole" foods, which are often higher quality, more sensually appealing and more nourishing in health-promoting ways.

    Sex comes in many packages too. It can be a quick release of tension. Sex can be anonymous or deeply personal. Sex can also be a kind of soul food, which nourishes our bodies, minds and spirits. Integrated sex can be "whole" sex or "gourmet" sex, deeply satisfying and incredibly intimate. Yet, like with food, people have different tastes, so sexual preferences are very individual, like culinary preferences.

9. *Getting to know our sexual and spiritual needs.* Earlier in the book, I noted that in our culture, "need" is a four-letter word. We are rarely allowed, never mind encouraged, to explore and talk about our needs. As a result, we don't share our sexual and spiritual feelings with each other, and often don't define them for ourselves. Learning about self as an exploratory process is often shamed in our culture. We are expected to just "know" who we are in a mechanistic way. In actuality, we learn who we are and what we need through experience, through living life as a journey. We need safe spaces where there is permission and support to get to know our sexual and spiritual needs, and other parts of ourselves. Only when we have had experiences that help us define our needs can we know, pinpoint and articulate what we need both to ourselves and to others.

10. ***Embracing our shadow side.*** Just as we lack a "journey" model for defining one's sense of self, we lack both a tolerance and appreciation for the importance of conflict and the shadow side of life. Therapist and workshop leader Rich Tosi comments,

> "There is a short distance from conflict to intimacy. But that is where all the work happens." Through our fear of difficult feelings, conflicts and disagreements, we cut ourselves off from the roots of a deepening intimacy. Rich Tosi continues, that in intimate relationships, "like the image of a tree, transformation occurs underground." An integrated sexuality embraces the dark side, the deeper and often unexplored aspects of self and other, as part of the work that inevitably needs to be done along the path of intimate relationship.

11. ***Healing our wounded child's hearts and developing our sense of adult man/woman.*** When the primary base of relating is wounded boy looking to partner as mommy to be his emotional anchor or wounded little girl looking to partner as daddy to make her feel safe in the world, the emotional and spiritual potential of the relationship is limited. As both men and women develop the emotional space of adult man and adult woman, a relationship has more potential for emotional and spiritual partnership. As men learn to connect with other men and get their emotional needs met there, a huge burden is taken out of a primary relationship. "For men to get their emotional needs met with other men makes it easier for their primary partners to be receptive and freely connective," comments Carl Greisser.

ESSENTIAL QUESTIONS:

1. What are your emotional, sexual and spiritual needs?

2. How have you learned about what you need emotionally, sexually and spiritually?

3. What do you still want to be able to learn, explore and discover about your emotional, spiritual and sexual needs?

4. What kinds of environments and experiences might you wish to have to grow emotionally, sexually and/or spiritually?

5. What would you want a partner to know about your emotional, sexual and spiritual needs?

6. What might be difficult to share with a partner about your emotional, sexual and spiritual needs?

MEDITATION: *Creating Sacred Space*

Take a moment to get into a comfortable position, whether you are sitting or lying down. Take a few moments to see if you are comfortable or need to adjust your position in any way. Allow yourself to take a few deep breaths, and whenever you feel ready, close your eyes, as long as that's comfortable.

Take whatever time and space you need to breathe, letting your chest and belly fill with air as you inhale...and allowing your chest and belly to relax as you exhale...feeling the support of your seat or the floor...supporting your head, your neck, your shoulders, your arms, your back, your pelvis and tailbone, your legs, your feet....and as you inhale, feel the physical contact of your chair or the floor, supporting your body...and as you exhale, very slowly and gently, let yourself melt and relax into whatever supports you....allowing yourself to be comfortable...and allowing your focus to be with your heart, noticing where you feel your heart. And if it helps to put your hand on your heart to help focus there, you are welcome to do so. And take a moment to notice how your heart is feeling right now...is it full? is it empty? is it heavy? is it light? is it separate? connected? Take a moment to let yourself become a little more familiar with whatever is happening in your heart right now.

And whenever you feel ready, take a moment to explore what it means to create a sacred space, a space that is safe and welcoming to soul-level experience, a space that invites you to cherish yourself and others....Take a moment to include all your senses in your exploring, imagining what a sacred space might look like, feel like, smell like, taste like, and the kinds of sounds or silence you might experience in this sacred space....Where might you find such an environment? Does one already exist for you? If you have created sacred space before, what have you done to make the space sacred? If creating sacred space is a new experience, what might you do to make a space sacred for you? What kinds of rituals might help create sacred space? Are there flowers or scents or images or symbols you might want to include? What special items might you want to bring to or include in your sacred space? What qualities of self might you wish to bring to this space? And would you want to invite another or others to join you here? If you would like this sacred space to be your special place, free from others, just take a moment to acknowledge that...and if you would like to share this sacred space with others close to you, just take a moment to acknowledge that for yourself....

Now imagine that you have created this sacred space, and you are having an opportunity to spend some time there....take a few moments to let yourself bask in your sacred space, in the qualities and objects you have chosen to bring to this space....and just notice what happens in your body, in your mind, in your heart, in your soul, in your spirit....And I invite you to spend just as much time there now as feels right for you, letting yourself experience the sights, sounds, smells, tastes and sensations that arise in this special place.

And whenever you feel ready, take a moment to acknowledge yourself for creating this sacred space, and for letting yourself enjoy its qualities.... knowing you can visit again when you feel so moved....And whenever you feel ready, very slowly and gently, take a deep breath and bring your focus back into the room.

And if you wish, you are welcome to make notes about your special sacred space, and what came up for you during the meditation.

Chapter 9

ALTERNATIVES TO VIOLENCE: EMPOWERING THE HEART'S VOICE

I will not play at tug of war.
I'd rather play at hug of war.
Where everyone hugs instead of tugs.
Where everyone giggles and rolls on the rug.
Where everyone kisses and everyone grins,
and everyone cuddles, and everyone wins.

— Shel Silverstein

In Chapter 1 I described the violent attack that I experienced when I was 16-years-old. Having lived through an attempted rape/murder, I gained a first-hand view of the inner workings of the heart and mind of the perpetrator. For this man, it was clear that both the sexual impulse and the desire to kill were an expression of rage masking pain buried deep inside his tormented psyche. He did not want to hurt me, really. But the depth of his unexpressed pain was so powerful, that he had no other outlet to release it except in such a violent act with a stranger.

When I trained body-centered psychotherapists at the Institute for Emotional-Kinesthetic Psychotherapy, we explored the sadomasochistic struggle and learned that sadism is the power of the powerless. This man, by trying to rape me and take my life, was expressing a desperate, powerless, voiceless cry.

Violence occurs when one or more people do harm to another person or persons. Violence is an invasion, an attack on another person or on self, and can take place at emotional, physical, spiritual, intellectual and sexual levels. The sudden emergence of repressed energy in a primal, uncontained or explosive manner is the underpinning of violence.

When we are deeply hurt or violated, we are not able to process or integrate the full magnitude of what has happened to us emotionally, mentally or somatically. What we cannot process, integrate or express gets "warehoused" in our neural circuitry, in our body-mind, in our heart-brain. This energy becomes repressed.

Repressed energy, while often inaccessible, does not disappear. Instead, it lingers, trapped in the bodymind, under the surface, exerting a psychic pressure. It is unconscious and often inaccessible in the ordinary relating of daily life, but when triggered by another's energy, action, words or the stress of life, can emerge suddenly, abruptly and intrusively in a way the crosses the boundaries of another in its path.

THE ROOTS OF VIOLENCE

Lynn Thomas, whose sister was murdered 13 years ago, understands how deep and powerful the roots of violence are. Violence is usually done by people who have themselves been violated in a profound and searing manner. If a person has been violated, and as a result, is emotionally, physically, spiritually and/or sexually repressed, that person needs an equally powerful experience to bring their feelings and sensations up and out. Thomas reflects, "If I am ten degrees repressed, I need something ten degrees powerful to get the repression out of me. I need something very intense done to me to feel I am alive because I am numb from all the violence and repression."

Violence may be a natural phenomenon, primal and wired into our biology.

"I am not sure that violence and peace are opposites," notes sexologist and author Gina Ogden. "It's like saying a good relationship never has any fights or an ocean never has any storms. If you look at the subatomic level of how things change and evolve, there is always a period of disorganization before things reorganize again. Peace or love is like a container, a universal big bowl of water. If you agitate the bowl, it will get turbulent, then smooth out again. It is a question of balance."

"In nature there is violence. Tigers leap upon other animals and tear then to shreds. Is that the same as banging into the twin towers? I don't think so. Violence is not by its nature a bad thing. When you've been hurt or brainwashed in some way, when you've disowned parts of yourself, then violence can be used to control and hurt other people."

Violence may have its roots in a "power over culture," where violence is a means of personal control.

In our personal relationships and those of tribe-to-tribe and nation-to-nation, time and time again we see violence rather than peace and cooperation. Riane Eisler, author of THE CHALICE AND THE BLADE AND SACRED PLEASURES, explores this subject in great depth. She discusses dominator cultures versus partnership cultures, power over structures versus power with. Her research explains how the power over religions of dominator cultures and competition for land led to men seeing women and children as their property, violence and the split of sexuality from spirituality.

"Terror and fear of loss of control is at the root of the dominator culture," Ogden reflects. "Somebody wants to control somebody else. From this place you move towards violent relationships. When there is violence, you get violence back. Cultural violence is rooted in the violence of our personal relationships."

Physical violence may be a misguided attempt at connection and intimacy that is often modeled and perpetuated in the male subculture.

Men used to relating through violence in a power over culture can even turn it around, using it as a way to connect. Joseph Kramer, sexologist and founder of the Body Electric School, comments, "I came from a family where physical violence played a role and where pleasure was not held in high esteem. I had this spartan idea to endure whatever is happening. Being introduced to massage in my early 20's was a transformative experience. It was the first time in my life that my body woke up and I felt something."

"I used to teach high school and saw how friendly intimacy among boys involved rough poundings," continues Kramer. "That was what was appropriate. It you are not going to caress someone, it is very likely that your contact might be hitting them. The movie The Fight Club exemplifies this. In the movie, the men pound each other, make each other bleed and put each other in the hospital, not out of anger, but out of intimacy. The only way open to these men to be intimate was to be violent. Much physical harm was done in this attempt to connect."

Violence may be an expression of low self-worth.

"I think violence emanates from a sense of low self-esteem and frustration in expression that starts out in childhood," reflects Thomas. "Someone is unable to control their impulses and then starts to believe it is okay to respond in this way. In my homicide support group, we believe that for a person to murder another person, they had to get a clear message as a child that they did not matter. It had to be repeated over and over. They came to believe they were not important."

"Children are just little human beings. We are not a society that values the integrity of children or finding other ways to express difficult feelings. Because we are not allowed to feel so much, feelings are kept inside and repressed. When feelings finally come out, they do so in explosive ways."

Shame may also be at the root of violence.

The relationship of shame and violence has been explored with the violence that has erupted with kids killing kids in the schools. "We shame kids. We shame teenagers and young adults. Men and women are shamed. The main reaction to shame in this culture is to reach out and attack others. Those receiving the attack are often not responsible for the shame," acknowledges Kramer. "Other people who are shamed attack themselves. People get drunk, do drugs and withdraw from social realms because of their shame."

"We are ashamed of our bodies in our culture," continues Kramer, "for not having socially acceptable desires. This shame is critical in teen years, and is at the root of the high school violence we have seen in the last several years. I have a clear understanding of those kids who kill. In most cases, they were almost constantly mocked and shamed and put down. So, they burst out and attack others."

DEGREES OF VIOLENCE

Violence, at some level, results from a special kind of heart wound. The degree of violence relates to the degree of the heart-woundedness. While I have written about the extreme kinds of violence that result from profound woundedness, it is worth reflecting on other kinds of violence as well.

Peter Smith, an architect and planner who works for the Central Artery Tunnel Project in Boston, MA, has been involved with a movement called Beyond War since the early 1980's. "Beyond War was initiated due to the threat of nuclear war to attempt to transform individuals' thinking towards elimination of all violence," recalls Smith. "In order to help people see the terrible threat of nuclear war, it was important to open up opportunities for them to see how each of us in our culture holds violence as part of our way of life, and how changing that use of violence could be a positive change in our lives and could lead to world peace."

How do each of us hold violence as a part of our way of life? "Each of us does that differently," notes Smith. "An exercise we did in Beyond War was to think in terms of what was the smallest amount of violence that we do in our lives. In order to do that exercise, we looked at the definition of violence. The dictionary describes violence as doing harm to other people or property. Therefore, if you back up and ask what is the smallest amount of harm we do to people or property, we would go through that exercise thinking what it would be."

"What I came to when I did that exercise personally, was when I go into the office each day, if I don't say good morning to people that I work with each day, if I just walk by them and ignore them, that would be harmful to them. They would wonder why I was ignoring them. So, that is how I would answer the question how do we use violence. I see it in our relationships with other people."

If any one of us chooses to take our personal inventory and list ways we hurt or harm other people in our lives, even in what seem to be small and seemingly insignificant ways, we begin to become aware that violence isn't just rapes, murders and bombings. And finding ways to live and relate that are non-violent are very personal and within our grasp.

MOVING BEYOND VIOLENCE: EMPOWERING THE HEART'S VOICE

In her book **AWAKENING IN TIME: THE JOURNEY FROM CODEPENDENCE TO CO-CREATION**, author Jacquelyn Small writes, "The

Heart...is the first level of consciousness beyond our ego's limited intellect. When we enter the Heart, we are in an inner sacred temple where true forgiveness and understanding become possible. This is the consciousness level, where we clear out our old hurts, where we grieve and where we heal."

Engaging the power of the heart can both heal the wounds of past violence and help prevent the conditions that lead to wounding and violence in the future. As we heal the splits between mind and body, head and heart and sexuality and spirituality, we need to call upon and empower the heart's voice. Jacquelyn Small notes, "While the ego's limited intellect can study isolated facts without linking them, the Heart just naturally links them, seeing the relationships among them all. What often remains a mystery to the intellect is not a mystery to the heart. Where the mind's intellectual arguments divide us, the Heart unites us; almost any controversy can be solved through heart-felt communication."

In this spirit, I would like to offer some concepts and exercises from the body of work that comprises Emotional-Kinesthetic Psychotherapy, the heart-centered, psychospiritual body-centered psychotherapy method that I developed and have both taught and practiced for nearly twenty years. These tools can help you come to know your own heart more fully, and create spaces where you and your loved ones can relate consciously and deeply, heart to heart.

HEART SPACE

The heart is multi-faceted. We are most familiar with its physiological function, as the natural pump that lives in our chest whose rhythm signals that we are indeed alive. Jacquelyn Small expresses this beautifully as she writes, "The heart is a space — not a thing." It is too big to be understood through the analytical ways of the intellect. It is something we know through what we sense and feel both physically and emotionally. When we feel hurt, our hearts are heavy. When we are angry, our hearts are tense. When we are happy, our hearts may overflow with joy.

In the space of the heart, we connect with a deeper sense of self. Jacquelyn Small notes, "It is in that place in consciousness where our identities are not just ideas we think about who we are, our identities here are intuitively felt. And in this way they (we) are known."

Heart space is important for peaceful relating. While the mind's intellectual arguments divide us, and even lead to war, the heart unites and integrates. When we speak and listen from the heart, we relate from the heart, we relate from an open, curious, receptive, compassionate level. Jacquelyn Small acknowledges that almost any conflict can be solved through heartfelt communication.

Heart space allows for and cultivates intimacy. When two people come together in the space of the heart, there is the safety and space for self and each other to be seen at a soul level.

EXERCISE: *Getting to Know Your Heart Space*

This is a meditation you can do to get to know your own heart space. It is an exercise you can try many times at different times. You can begin to notice if there are themes and patterns to what you sense and feel when you allow yourself to be with your heart space. You can also become sensitive to differences in your heart space at different times.

Take a moment to get into a comfortable position. Take a few slow, relaxed deep breaths, letting your chest and belly fill with air as you inhale and allowing your chest and belly to relax as you exhale. As you inhale, allow yourself to feel the support of your chair, the wall, the floor — whatever supports you. And as you exhale, allow yourself to very slowly and gently melt and relax into whatever supports you.

Whenever you feel ready, allow your focus to be with your heart, noticing where you feel your heart when you say the word "heart." If it helps to put your hand on your heart, you are welcome to do so. Take a moment to notice how your heart is feeling physically and emotionally. Is it full? Is it empty? Is it tense? Is it relaxed? Is it heavy? Is it light? Take a moment to let yourself become a little more familiar with whatever is happening in your heart now. And take a few moments just to let yourself sense and notice the physical and emotional sensations in your heart, in your breath, in your body right now. Take a few moments to let yourself experience the space of your own heart now.

And take a moment to notice what it is like to "see" through your heart and to "think" through your heart. If you think about someone close to you who you really care about, imagining they are near you, what happens in your heart? What sensations do you feel? What happens in your breathing? Do you feel energy shift or move in your body or heart? Take a few moments just to let yourself experience the space of your own heart right now.

And whenever you feel ready, at your own pace, very slowly and gently take a deep breath and bring your focus back into the room.

You are welcome to make notes or draw a picture that expresses what you experienced and what stands out from this meditation.

☙ How do you experience your heart space?

- ✞ What physical and emotional sensations stand out?
- ✞ What happened in your mind over the course of the meditation?
- ✞ Does your heart space feel any different when you are thinking about someone you care about than when you are just tuning in to your own sensations and feelings?

EMOTIONAL SAFETY

Emotional safety is a cornerstone for deep, intimate and honest communication. Emotional safety is an emotional, physical and spiritual experience. When you feel emotionally safe, you may feel warm, relaxed, open and connected to yourself and others. As I've asked people in the workshops I lead to describe how they feel when they are emotionally safe, here are some of their answers:

- ✞ "My stomach relaxes."
- ✞ "It's easy to let go."
- ✞ "I feel a sense of freedom and fullness inside."
- ✞ "I know I won't be judged."
- ✞ "I know everything is going to be okay."

When emotional safety is lacking, you may feel cold, tense, closed and disconnected from yourself and those around you. Many of the physical sensations and emotional responses people experience could be classified as symptoms for which people seek medical care or psychotherapy. Here are examples of physical sensations, emotional responses and thoughts people in the workshops I lead have shared when they feel emotionally unsafe:

Physical Sensations:	Emotional Responses:	Thoughts:
"A knot in my stomach"	"Afraid"	"My head starts to work overtime"
"A lump in my throat"	"Alone"	"I wonder when the other shoe will drop"
"Can't let down or relax"	"Angry"	"Wanting to hide"
"Fight or flight"	"Feeling trapped"	"Wanting to disappear"
"Heart pounding"	"Hypervigilance"	"I don't want to think about it"
"Restlessness"	"Anxiety"	"Spacing out"

Removing the factors that cause emotional unsafety is as important as learning how to create a space for relating that is emotionally safe.

Exercise: *Exploring Emotional Safety*

The following questions will help you explore emotional safety. You can do them on your own or with a partner.

Questions for individual or partner work:

1. What makes you feel safe?
2. Can you remember a time when you felt safe? If so, where were you? Who was with you? What happened?
3. When you feel safe, what physical sensations do you experience? What emotional feelings do you have? What thoughts run through your mind?
4. What makes you feel unsafe?
5. Can you remember a time when you felt unsafe? If so, where were you? Who was with you? What happened?
6. When you felt unsafe, what physical sensations did you experience? What emotional feelings did you have? What thoughts run through your mind?

Questions to do with a partner:

1. What do you want your partner to know about what makes you feel safe and unsafe?
2. In what ways does your partner help you feel safe? Are there ways your partner relates to you that feel unsafe?
3. What might you request from your partner to increase your sense of safety with him/her?
4. In what ways could you contribute to the sense of safety in the partnership?

SEXUAL AND SPIRITUAL SAFETY

While emotional safety is at the root of respectful, authentic and intimate communication, sexual and spiritual safety are also important to connect fully as partners in a love relationship. If we rarely ask ourselves what feels emotionally safe, it is even more rare that we even think about, never mind ask ourselves what is sexually and spiritually safe.

The words "safe sex" in our culture are usually assigned only to matters of birth control and prevention of sexually transmitted disease. For two people working together to build an intimate partnership, sexual safety has a much deeper and more personal meaning than just those two dimensions.

"Spiritual safety" often evokes connotations of religious freedom, freedom from persecution for one's practices and beliefs. These connotations, once again refer to one's relationship in society, and less to one's experience in intimate partnership.

When I have asked people in the workshops I lead what sexual safety and spiritual safety mean to them, what often emerges is the inter-relationship of the two. Safe sexuality is often a spiritual experience. And safe spirituality occurs when people feel loved, accepted, connected and as one in the body.

I have developed an image of two overlapping hearts, with safety in the middle to represent sexual-spiritual safety.

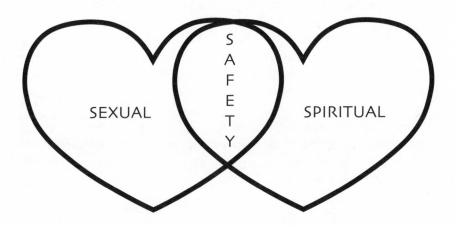

Here are some examples of responses people have given about sexual and spiritual safety:

- ☙ "Knowing where one person ends and another begins"
- ☙ "When two people can come together as separate beings and not lose self"
- ☙ "I'm newly created when I am in that sexual-spiritual space."
- ☙ "Crossing over but not eclipsing"
- ☙ "Joined for a while, then movement"
- ☙ "The stronger the container, the more room for both separateness and closeness"

When I have asked what is needed to create an environment that is sexually and spiritually safe, responses have included:

"Trust"   "Acceptance"   "Presence"   "Warmth"   "Authenticity"   "Pacing"
"Communication"   "Balance"   "Being"   "Respect"   "Grounding in oneself"
"Respect for one another's boundaries"   "Knowing what comes next"
"Knowing your own boundaries"   "The difference between expectations and intentions"   "Clear, grounded intentions"   "A mutually understood commitment"

You may want to explore, both for yourself and with a partner, what sexual safety and spiritual safety mean to you, and what creates an environment that is sexually safe and spiritually safe. Finding a language to express what is most important to you and what you most intimately need can help deepen your bond with your partner and build a solid foundation for communication and relating.

DEVELOPING HEARTFELT COMMUNICATION

In our head-dominated culture, the voice of the heart is often dwarfed or overridden both in social conversation and even within ourselves. When the Institute for Emotional-Kinesthetic Psychotherapy was in full swing, one of the short-hand phrases that emerged in our culture was "hearts can hear heads, but heads can't hear hearts."

For this reason, developing the capacity to consciously engage in heartfelt communication is like going to the gym and working to strengthen undeveloped or unfamiliar muscles. For some of us, heartfelt communication comes easily. For others, it is at best a concept, and elusive as an experience. This exercise, Speaking and Listening from the Heart, provides a model to become more aware at emotional, physical and mental levels, what is involved in the two sides of heartfelt communication: speaking and listening.

One of the behaviors that most frequently cuts off communication is when a speaker is opening up and sharing something personal or vulnerable and their listener seems distant, not present or preoccupied. Becoming more aware of your own physical heart, and the emotional and energetic sensations you feel when your heart is really engaged in listening to another, will help create a climate where others can feel safe, heard, and grateful when speaking to you.

Likewise, many people have a hard time opening up, keep things to themselves or just don't communicate easily. Becoming more aware of your physical heart, and the emotional and energetic sensations you feel when your heart sincerely wants to share itself with another caring and engaged person, will help you recognize what you have to say and the conditions you need to be able to say it.

Exercise: *Speaking and Listening From the Heart*

This is a wonderful exercise to do with a friend or partner to improve communication and deepen intimacy.

Step 1: In this exercise, there will be a chance for each partner to speak from the heart and listen from the heart. Decide who will be speaker first and listener first.

Step 2: Meditation for the first round of speaking and listening from the heart

Once you've decided who will speak and listen first, get into a comfortable position and close your eyes. Take as much time and space as you need to breathe, letting your chest and belly fill with air as you inhale, and allowing your chest and belly to relax as you exhale...Allowing yourself to be comfortable...and adjusting your position any way you need to be more comfortable....Allowing your focus to be with your heart...Noticing where you feel your heart as you say the word, "heart." If it helps to put your hand on your heart to help focus there, you are welcome to do so...and take a moment to notice how your heart is feeling physically and emotionally....It is open? receptive? closed? tight? calm? agitated? Take a moment to let yourself become a little more familiar with whatever is happening in your heart now.

And if you are going to be the speaker, this first round, take a moment to imagine what it will feel like to speak from your heart to someone listening from their heart....Is there anything in particular you feel moved to say? Is there anything that would be important for the listener to know?....Just take a moment and prepare yourself to speak, in whatever way feels natural and organic, from your heart to a listener who is listening from their heart. And if you are going to be the listener, this first round, take a moment to imagine what it will feel like to listen from your heart to someone speaking from their heart....What kind of space might you want to offer from your heart to the person speaking from their heart? What kind of presence might invite heartfelt sharing?

And take a few moments to breathe and be with whatever you are sensing, thinking, feeling...and whenever you feel ready, take a deep breath and bring your focus back into the room and prepare to speak and listen.

Step 3: First round of speaking and listening from the heart. Set a timer for two minutes, so you can focus on the speaking and listening. When the two minutes are up, find a way to respectfully acknowledge one another, and very slowly and gently, take a deep breath and close your eyes.

Step 4: Meditation for the second round of speaking and listening from the heart

Take a moment to feel the support of your seat, your pillow, the floor, whatever supports you as you inhale and exhale...and take a moment just to be still and notice the feelings, sensations and thoughts that are running through your body right now.... If you were the first speaker, what was it like to speak from your heart to someone listening from their heart?...and if you were the first listener, what was it like to listen from your heart, to someone speaking from their heart? Take a few moments to breathe and just notice your emotional, physical and mental experience right now.

And whenever you feel ready, get ready to switch roles...and the person who spoke first is about to become the listener...and the person who listened first is about to become the speaker....And if you are going to be the speaker this next round, take a moment to imagine what it will feel like to speak from your heart to someone listening from their heart....Is there anything in particular you feel moved to say? Is there anything that would be important for the listener to know?...Just take a moment and prepare yourself to speak, in whatever way feels natural and organic from your heart to a listener who is listening from their heart.

And if you are going to be the listener this next round, take a moment to imagine what it will feel like to listen from your heart to someone speaking from their heart....What kind of space might you want to offer from your heart to the person speaking from their heart? What kind of presence might invite heartfelt sharing?

And take a few moments to breath and be with whatever you are sensing, thinking, feeling...and whenever you feel ready, take a deep breath and bring your focus back into the room and prepare to speak and listen.

Step 5: Second round of speaking and listening from the heart. Set a timer for two minutes, so you can focus on the speaking and listening. When the two minutes are up, find a way to respectfully acknowledge one another, and very slowly and gently, take a deep breath and close your eyes.

Step 6: Meditation to reflect on the experience of speaking and listening from the heart.

Take a moment, once again, to feel the support of your seat, your pillow, the floor, whatever supports you as you inhale and exhale...and take a moment just to be still and notice the feelings, sensations and thoughts that are running through your body right now....If you were the speaker this time, what was it like to speak from your heart to someone listening from their heart?...and if you were the listener this time, what was it like to listen from your heart, to someone speaking from their heart? Take a few moments to breathe and just notice your emotional, physical and mental experience right now.

And just take a few moments to reflect on what is was like to play each role, speaker and listener...and what you noticed about each role...how it felt...what happened in your body and breath....the thoughts that went through your mind....if one role felt more comfortable than the other...if one role felt more uncomfortable than the other...taking a moment to let yourself reflect on whatever your experience was doing this exercise.

And whenever you feel ready, at your own pace, very slowly and gently, take a deep breath and bring your focus back into the room.

Step 7: Debriefing the exercise.

If you wish, you and your partner can now talk about your experience doing this exercise. What was it like to speak and listen from the heart? What did you notice about yourself? About your partner? Was one role more comfortable or uncomfortable? What did you learn from this exercise.

If you prefer to make notes about your experience before talking, or just to make notes about your experience without talking just now, that is fine too.

When you are done sharing or writing, take a moment to acknowledge both yourself and your partner for participating with you in this exercise. Know you can choose to use this exercise whenever you want to create a sacred space for heartfelt communication.

WHERE WE GET STUCK: TRIGGERED BEHAVIOR

As I discussed in Chapter 6, as we go deeper in intimate relationship, sooner or later we hit "triggers," places where we become emotionally reactive to another person's words, actions or energies. Because we all have wounded, undeveloped and disconnected places within, it is inevitable intimate relating will bring these shadow places to the surface for healing and integration.

Many people are afraid of being triggered, and more afraid of what lies underneath a trigger, waiting to surface. "Sometimes couples regret ever having started therapy," comments sex therapist Karen Engebretsen-Larash, "Because what they find when they turn over the stone and see all the creepy crawly unresolved issues underneath, they feel overwhelmed. They use the relationship in and of itself to keep the lid on. When that barrier isn't there anymore, when the lid is removed, there is nothing left for them. Some couples use chaos as the glue to keep them together."

Karen described a couple for whom chaos was the point of contact. There was no other way of having contact. "One couple I knew went from one crisis to the next. Each crisis was enough for both partners to say they would stick around to work through whatever was needed. When one partner made a decision that this wasn't good enough anymore, the other partner did not know how to respond.

He would create situations and end up defensive at even the littlest things. What the other partner realized is that even his tone of voice was an automatic set-up for a fight. When she stopped going there, there was nothing left. She didn't want to fight anymore. When she attempted to use healthy negotiation skills, things got turned around and it backfired."

This couple did not have the joint space to recognize triggered behavior for what it was, and develop skills to get underneath the triggers and do deeper relational work. Developing skills to work with your and your partner's triggered behavior is essential to evolving a healthy, sustainable, emotionally engaged intimate relationship.

When we get triggered, most often it is nobody's fault. Whatever unfolds — be it our partner's words, actions, lack of actions, choices, etc. simply pushes a button within and the triggered reaction is evoked. Occasionally, a partner (usually out of a triggered place themselves), may behave in a way that is intended to push our buttons. But most often, triggering is less premeditated.

What is significant is not that we get triggered, but what we do both to take care of ourselves and in relationship to our partner when we are triggered. At times, we lose our grounding, our communication skills go to the wind, and we act out. If only one person is triggered, there may be enough relational space to contain the trigger and work it out in a positive, productive manner. At other times, we need to engage a third party to create the relational space to work out the issues evoked in the triggering process.

In Chapter 6, I presented a seven step model to help break the cycle of triggered behavior. In addition to using that model when you find that both you and/or your partner are triggered, you can also take steps to prevent triggered behavior from happening in the first place.

1. **Become aware of your own triggers and your partner's triggers.** Talk about them. Explore how you both can communicate most effectively not to consciously trigger one another.

2. **If you sense that you are on the verge of being triggered, stop, slow down and take space.** When we are tightly wound, we are more easily reactive. If when you sense you are approaching a triggered place, you can slow down, relax, take a few deep breaths, feel your feet on the ground and create more internal space. The more spacious and grounded we are, the less triggerable we are.

3. **Take responsibility for your own experience.** When you speak, use "I" statements, rather than "you" statements. "You" statements, even unintentionally, can feel like finger pointing and blaming. Avoid the "blame game." Blaming may make you feel good when you feel disempowered, but in the long-term it is a no win.

4. **Be aware of your needs for emotional and psychic space.** The more aware we are of our emotional and psychic space needs, the better care we can take care of ourselves. If we take care of ourselves emotionally and psychically, we will have more space for relating and receiving our partners. When we are unaware of our emotional and psychic space needs, we become tightly wound, and more likely to be triggered by even small things.

5. **Be receptive to both your own needs and your partner's needs.** The better you each understand your own needs, the more effectively you can communicate them to your partner. The more grounded you are in your sense of self, and your right to take care of yourself in all the ways human beings need care taken, the more receptive you can be to a partner's needs.

ESSENTIAL QUESTIONS

1. How has violence touched your life? What impact has it had on you?

2. What are even small ways you have been on the receiving end of violence?

3. What are even small ways you have been on the delivering end of violence?

4. What is one small way you can act to contribute to ending violence in your relationship with yourself and others?

5. How well developed do you feel your heart space is? How readily accessible is it to you and those you love?

6. What steps might you take to further develop your heart's capacity and heart's voice?

7. How can you bring more qualities of heart to the ones you love?

RESOLVING THE GENDER WARS: *Guidelines for Peaceful, Deep and Intimate Relating*

1. **Create emotionally safe spaces.**
   This allows us to risk vulnerability and intimacy and to show up as we really are.

2. **Heal the gender wars within ourselves.**

Integrate both male and female aspects within.

Find our humanness as well as our male and female sense of self.

3. **Heal our relationship with our own gender.**
   Journey, share and heal in the company of our own gender.
   Explore how we have been hurt by our own gender and how we need
   to heal.

4. **Recognize the uniqueness of each man and woman.**
   We are each unique human beings, no matter what our gender identity.
   Move beyond stereotypes, seeing the place of labels for understanding
   patterns, yet not being limited by them.

5. **Care to learn what it is like to live inside another's skin.**
   Until we know what it is like to live inside another's skin, we really
   DON'T understand.

6. **Speak and listen from the heart.**
   This enhances our ability to be fully present with self and other.
   Connection organically unfolds.

7. **Practice non-judgment.**
   Curiosity opens minds and hearts.

8. **Communicate non-verbally as well as verbally.**
   Eye contact, walking beside someone, or holding hands offers
   connection in addition to (and sometimes deeper than) words.

9. **Explore what you need and the other person needs.**
   The better you understand each other's needs the more likely you
   will be able to meet them.

10. **Listen to how others have been hurt by your gender and the other gender.**
    Giving voice to our hurts and being heard is part of the healing process.

11. **Take responsibility for your experience.**
    Use "I" statements.
    Avoid the "blame game."

12. **Speak appreciations whenever possible.**
    Appreciation is a kind of soul food we can all use!

PREVENTING THE GENDER WARS IN THE NEXT GENERATION

*"Many of our culture's problems come from objectifying
other human beings and treating them as objects, not people.
The gender wars are just a symptom of this greater dysfunction.
If we can stop viewing ourselves as separate creatures,
and instead as part of the world, subject to natural forces
like all the other creatures, the conflict will melt away."*

— Amy Hughes

When a legacy of pain, violence, conflict and hurt run through our culture, our families and our lives, few of us want to pass it on to our children and our children's children. Sometimes it seems inevitable that the solutions to complex, multi-dimensional social challenges take many years and multiple generations to unravel. Unraveling and healing can take place as part of an evolutionary process. It both feels better and is more effective when we embark on prevention and healing consciously.

This chapter will explore what is needed to prevent the genders wars in our next two generations: today's young adults, the twentysomethings, and today's children who are growing up as we are evolving towards a soul-centered way of relating.

SEXUALITY, RELATIONSHIPS AND THE NEXT GENERATION

Today's young adults grew up in a climate dramatically different than their babyboomer parents. Unlike the "Father Knows Best" and "Leave It to Beaver" images of their parents' childhoods, today's twentysomethings grew up in the feminist era. Women demanded equality, and in many cases got it.

Kevin, 23, grew up in a family where his mom was the central breadwinner as a tax attorney, and his dad supported his mom in her career happiness and success. "My dad had a business of his own during the 1980's and did okay with it," recounts Kevin. "When our family moved to Cleveland in the late 1980's, his business began to take a back seat to family concerns. When we later moved to Richmond, he no longer had the contacts he needed to continue his business. So, he became the housemaker. He is also good at stocks, so he focused his energy on that and household matters. Before we moved to Richmond, my mom had been unhappy in her job. My dad saw the toll it was taking on her and supported her career move. I felt good my dad was supportive of my mom."

Kevin envisions himself having a primary partner and family down the line. The fact that his parents have had a long-term relationship has made it a goal of his to do the same. He has learned from their example that men and women can balance home and work functions. He has also learned through their difficulties communicating with each other that being able to express whatever it is you are feeling to a partner is central.

"My parents are very different at a basic level. My mom tends to worry a lot. My dad is just the opposite, an extremely laid back guy. As a result, my mom doesn't always feel comfortable expressing her concerns. She ends up feeling like a nag or worry wart, even if my father doesn't say anything directly to make her feel that way. My parents are on different wavelengths, and I have watched them really struggle with communication. They have now identified this as a problem and have started working on it a little bit. I want to be able to communicate well with the person I am in primary relationship with."

Today's twentysomethings have also grown up as the myth of traditional marriage has entered the shadowlands. "The traditional male/female monogamous model has been wearing thin for quite some time," acknowledges Jen, 27. "I came from a Conservative family in the South, where our models were the traditional mom and pop operations bickering for forty years over the color of the carpeting. My parents married before they turned 21 as their parents had before them. Sex was not a topic of conversation at home, but it was expected that I would be a virgin until I married, just like my mom was. My parents seemed to be playful in their early years, but that evolved into a coldness after many stressful years together. They rarely seemed to be on the same wavelength and showed little interest in each other as the years passed."

"As a generation we have witnessed more fragmented families than ever before. We know well that family can be two moms, three dads and a slew of kids from all over. With that fragmentation comes the freedom to explore and create new models. It has become infinitely easier to traverse the gender/sexuality spectrum. Creative relationship design is a bit trickier because there are still so few models for healthy non-monogamous relationships. Many times it seems that no model truly works. We are all constantly tinkering but never reaching that great 'Eureka!'"

"As a kid I thought I had good role models in my parents," recalls 26. "It all exploded later when I was 17. My parents started going through an eight-year divorce process. The only good thing I can say about it was that the proceedings went on long enough that custody of my younger brother, now 21, is no longer an issue. My parents' marriage broke down because my father never really got the hang of taking care of himself and my mother was depressed, with a tendency towards being emotionally abusive. She has all the earmarks of an adult child of alcoholics. When my father hit a point of feeling, 'I'm not happy. I haven't been happy for 20 years. I really need to be happy in my own life rather than living it for other people,' the marriage just started falling apart."

Mankind Project co-founder and workshop leader Rich Tosi, 60, comments, "The institution of marriage as it exists no longer seems to serve relationships as they now exist. Couples are looking for different things than couples in past generations. My parents who were born in 1918 and 1919 weren't really interested in being happy. I asked my mother after my dad died, 'Were you and dad happy?' She said, 'Didn't we feed you enough?' What that meant was her job as a mother was making sure her children were taken care of. That's all that really mattered. Giving us everything she could was her job. Being happy was sort of irrelevant."

"What's happened in our generation is we sort of assume some sort of material satisfaction. When we get married, we are now looking for spiritual partnership. Marriages aren't really set up to do that. The traditional marriage archetype is about raising children. As we've tried to add the spiritual partnership archetype on top of it, we've had problems. We haven't figured out how to do it. I believe one reason there are so many divorces today is that people are looking for spiritual partnership based on a model that is about raising children. The institution of marriage combined with the expectations of spiritual partnership drives divorce. This doesn't do any good for the gender wars."

THE DIVORCE HEART WOUND

Luke Entrup, 26, and founder of Beyond the Machine, an experiential gathering and training for young people ages 18 - 35, notes, "The divorce wound is pretty deep in my generation. I am one of the only people I know whose parents are still together." Characteristics of the divorce heart wound include fear of commitment, sticking to oneself, and finding it harder to be vulnerable or intimate.

"I can think of a friend who is 22," continues Luke. Her parents divorced when she was 11. The longest relationship she has had is four months. To me, that just doesn't seem right. She wants to have a friend that's a man. When they ask for more, she gets turned off. She is reluctant to get close to any man as a friend. She is frightened and doesn't want to be in a committed relationship. She draws the direct conclusion to her parents' divorce and she is very aware of it. There are many others having this same kind of experience. Just floating."

Rich Tosi is concerned about the impact of divorced families and single parents, be they mothers or fathers. "In divorced and single parent situations, often the child learns to favor one gender over the other. The possibility that the child will have to make some level of decision of who s/he thinks is right or wrong puts an enormous obligation on the child. My wife and I have been married for 34 years, but we have probably been spiritually divorced five times during that time. When a couple separates and they have been at war, is it healthier for the kids or not? I don't know. People have different experiences. It would be interesting if someone did a big study comparing what it would be like if the warring couple stayed together versus divorcing."

Another concern about broken families, and in particular fathers raising children without mothers and mothers raising children without fathers, is that the family structure will impact the child's view of the other gender. If a child has close, first-hand experience of both genders, at least they have some model to build from within themselves. Perhaps this raises the importance of the village it takes to raise a child and the need for an extended network of close friends and family, so a child can have caring adults of both genders directly involved in his/her life.

"Fractured families certainly won't give children an experience of a partnership model, and it is a partnership model we need to not have gender wars," reflects Tosi. "The best model for kids of the future would be parents who can fight and stay together and find a way to make it work. No statistics are going in that direction. The divorce rate of young people who have married in the 1990's is going to be extremely high. In addition to that, more people don't want to get married."

In my twenty years of being a therapist, I have seen that when couples separate and divorce as a result of what seems to be an irreconcilable war, separation or divorce often only fuels the war rather than ends it. Even if warring partners no longer see each other or speak to each other in their separate lives, the fires of the conflict burn strong at more subterranean levels. Children feel the impact of this undercurrent, which has a strong energetic charge. Living in the energetic force field of a silent, unspoken war can be heart wounding for children and partners alike.

I remember working with a 13-year-old girl in the wake of her parents' divorce. "They may be living separately," shared the girl, "but nothing has really changed. The tension is so thick you can cut it with a knife. Dad is getting remarried and mom is really hurt. She still feels betrayed and abandoned, even though their marriage is over. I love both my parents, but this tension tears me apart."

At times, the hidden conflict can erupt like a volcano and the war is visible on the surface again. Unless warring partners can understand the inescapable importance of doing the deep and often painful work of addressing the core issues that underlie the war, the war and its energy will fester and linger. I remember meeting a fortysomething man for dinner who had been divorced for ten years.

His wife and daughter lived in another state. His wife had remarried and even had a second child, but as he talked about his relationship with his ex and his daughter, the pain, the anger and the tension of the divorce were palpable and clear. He and his wife still got into battles over visitation and parenting questions. Legally they were divorced, but emotionally and spiritually, in ten years not much had changed.

Sometimes people are afraid of digging down to the roots of the war because the core issues are complex, push against acceptable social norms, or require deep soul searching and healing work. A fiftysomething man I knew, Steve, really loved his wife as the mother of his children, but did not feel a deeper connection with her as a spiritual partner. As they had both matured, they discovered sexual incompatibilities, which were a source of pain particularly to Steve. His libido and intimacy needs were significantly higher than his wife's. Their communication skills were lacking and virtually inaccessible for conversations as vulnerable, deep and complex as the ones they really needed to have to work things through.

While the stereotype is that women want to go to therapy and work out hard issues and men resist, in this case the opposite was true. "How many years do I live in what feels like an emotional and sexual prison?" he would ask. "I love my children and I want to have an intact family. But my soul is suffocating here. I have tried and tried to get my wife to work on the deeper issues, but she doesn't want to go there. She would rather just live at an emotional distance and not rock the boat."

Steve recognized he could be polyamorous, and that could help him meet his needs for love, intimacy and sexuality. Yet, his wife wasn't open to emotional or sexual bonds outside of the marriage. "What kind of model are we giving our children if the house is full of tension and mom and dad are obviously not getting along?" the man worried. "Is it better to get a divorce and focus on what works in our relationship — co-parenting our children, or to live in this never-ending tension?" For Steve, the thought of getting divorced was excruciating. To him, being divorced was a sign of failure. It was a social stigma, and something that would erode his already fragile self-esteem. "I stay in my marriage because I feel that it is better to suffer privately than show the world that I have failed, that I am broken by getting a divorce."

Creating a safe forum for Steve and his wife to work through the issues that unfolded in their marriage over time would have been the ideal solution. Being able to speak openly with their children about the difference between marriage as a way to raise children and marriage as a spiritual partnership would have eased tension for all involved. Being able to accept that growth and personal evolution is a lifelong process to be embraced rather than resisted, and that adult partnerships are living organisms — dynamic, continuously growing and changing — would also be important messages.

I trust there could have been a peaceful outcome, whether it was divorce or remaining married and reframing the definition of marriage, had Steve and his wife been able to dig deeper and address their core needs, concerns and differences. The model they would have given to their children about the complexities and challenges of partnership in our evolving world would have also been valuable in the long run. However, these subjects were just too scary and threatening for both Steve and his wife. So, they both suffered under the rubric of the gender wars. I felt both sadness and compassion for these two people and their children.We can only do what we are ready, willing and able to do. And in my heart of hearts, I wished they had been ready, willing and able to heal the conflicts and end the war. In the end, I had to just let them be where they were.

FORMS OF RELATIONSHIP AND THE NEXT GENERATION

As I interviewed twentysomethings about their experiences of relationship, two themes emerged. First, many twentysomethings are leery and skeptical about "marriage the way we have known it" as a form of relationship. Second, exploring gender identity, sexual orientation and relationship configuration is much more socially acceptable than it was in prior generations, and in some cases is even expected. I experienced the twentysomethings I interviewed working to find authentic relational pathways anchored in a soul-deep discovery process.

Darkhawk, 25, is one of the minority of her peers who has gotten married already. Yet she belongs to a growing number of young people, married and partnered, who consider themselves polyamorous. Many of the polyamorous twentysomethings I interviewed, including those who were married or otherwise committed to a primary partner, shared the belief that no one partner can have all the traits or characteristics that an individual person really likes or wants to have in their life. While it sounds romantic to hear singer Barry White crooning, "You're my everything," many young people have come to understand that none of us can be everything to another person.

"The more love and intimacy I have in my life, the happier I am," acknowledges Ruth, 26, also married and polyamorous. "Part of it is about fulfillment of needs. I really have more of a communal than an individual world view. No one can make it through this world alone. We are pack animals."

Justin, 29 and married for three years, is surprised to find himself one of the younger to marry amongst his peers. "When I went to my ten year high school reunion last year, most people weren't married yet. In high school I thought I was behind the times. I couldn't get a date to save my life. So, to be ahead of the game at this point in time is just strange."

Justin's sexuality, relationship and identity paths have unfolded over the past decade. "When I went to college, I had my own issues — depression and realizing I wasn't following the path in life that I wanted to be on. I didn't know how to handle that and women didn't seem to want anything to do with me because of that. I can't really blame them. In college I went through the biserious phase of my life. I fooled around with a couple guys. It was okay.

After college I got my first serious girl friend. I didn't go back. It just worked better that way for me. I consider myself straight, but the group I hung out with at college had permission to be bicurious. Most of them were gay, bi or at least open to different sexual expression."

Justin also discovered that he was polyamorous, that he could love multiple people at one time. "Everyone is different. You connect with some people in certain ways and other people in other ways. Between all of that it is possible to have complete fulfillment in your life. That is what is healthy and works for me. Poly doesn't work for many people. They can't imagine having more than one relationship. That isn't wrong any more than being poly is wrong. I encourage people to just consider the possibilities. That is what I have done in my life. I considered being bisexual and decided it wasn't my thing. What is important is to have the permission and freedom to find out who you are."

When Darkhawk looks amongst her peers, she sees a variety of relational pathways. Her college room-mate identified as gay in college. Then she met her current partner, and spent several months in disbelief. "She would say, 'He's male. I don't understand!'" recounts Darkhawk. Her college roommate and partner are now in a long-term relationship, bound together through a pagan commitment process called handfasting. "They are doing a sequence of one year handfastings renewable each summer," tells Darkhawk. "They recently bought a house together."

A significant number of Darkhawk's peers are, in her words, "Doing a lot of short-term relationships, figuring out stuff. I know of one case where the woman is figuring out bisexuality. In a different social group, I have a friend who identifies as lesbian with a Brad Pitt exception. Another friend identifies as gay without identifying as gendered — sort of gender queer as opposed to transgendered. I have a friend in another forum who is transgendered — female to male."

A whole new language of gender, relationship and even spirituality is emerging, as twentysomethings discuss commitment, handfasting, polyamory, gendered or not gendered, male-to-female and female-to-male transgendered, gender queer and more. Darkhawk feels that education about sexuality and relationships needs to include information about human variety. "I don't think a lot of people are aware there have been widely differing attitudes to aspects of sexuality and the like. In ancient Egypt, there was no regulation of sexuality before marriage. There is an American Indian tribe that recognizes there are three genders — two spirits. There are African and Carribean groups where if a woman wants to take on the man's role — get married and take on a wife — she can do so. When I took sex ed in high school, they didn't even mention that there are gay people!"

VARIATION AND CULTURE

It seems that each successive generation pushes the envelope forward a little bit more as collectively we re-examine what it means to be a man and a woman. For babyboomers, men with long hair and women wearing pants pushed the gender envelope. Today's young people have new and creative ways to play with the concept of gender, exploring the feminine and the masculine parts within themselves. Darkhawk comments, "I know one guy who is the femme-ist of us all, and most of the people I hang out with are female. One of our running jokes is he is the prettiest lady amongst us. It is fairly normal in some circles I know for a woman to go to a party in a tux, and a guy to wear sparkly nail polish. I get the impression that a lot of people are fairly comfortable picking up gendered bits and playing with them. Sometimes they keep them around. Sometimes they discard them."

"It is a lot more acceptable and in some cases expected for women to explore same-sex experiences," comments Luke Entrup. "With men, it's still very taboo. That's curious to me. The culture sees it as very attractive for women to have had bisexual experiences. It's a deeper level of freedom. It's another form of initiation, a rite of passage. I also think it's a natural part of human development around sexuality. I see more security around sexual identity evolving in my own peer group."

"I think it is natural to ask the question, 'am I attracted to my own gender?' From that, the individual is really able to establish their sexual identity. Right now it's okay for women to ask and explore, but not for men." Justin would second that, even though he was fortunate enough to find himself in a college environment that was safe enough for him to explore his attraction to his own gender. "With men there's still that whole macho thing — having to be manly. Fooling around with other guys doesn't fall into the manly stereotype."

Bill Kauth, a founder of the Mankind Project, and Luke's mentor in developing Beyond the Machine, feels that today's 18- to 35-year-olds don't need gender differentiation as much as the babyboom generation did. "Parents of the babyboom generation lacked the ability to love in a heartfull, present way," notes Kauth. "I believe the soul death that occurred during World War II was so profound it impacted our parents' ability to love. They were soul dead humans. This is part of why children of the 60's were so hungry to find spirit. We went around the world looking for spirit and soul. The carnage of World War II led to a lot of internalized shame — just being alive at a time of carnage. We suffered a planetary soul death."

"I learned that by finding my own Vietnam shame," continues Kauth. "It affected many people, whether they were in the war or a protester. It is no surprise that in places like Puna, where Rajneesh's spiritual community is, the people there are Germans, Americans and Japanese — the ones who were the big players in the war. Their kids are hanging out there trying to reclaim their souls."

Kauth feels that all the healing work babyboomers have done has helped them be more loving parents to their own children. "The young people I have been spending time with feel loved. Their ability to let love in is greater. When babyboomers were children, we could not feel our caregivers offer their full emotional presence. It's an energetic response loop. So, we started creating bogus identities early. We got into therapy. Some of us have reclaimed and taken back some consciousness, the ability to love. We have been able to love our kids enough so that they don't carry the same neurotic fears we did."

INTERNAL AND EXTERNAL MANIFESTATIONS OF THE GENDER WARS

Luke Entrup feels that gender issues are not as much in the shadows with the next generation as with the previous generation. What is most charged is what is in the shadows. "When we first started creating Beyond the Machine, we started with a group of young men with the help of elder men. We started sharing it with women who thought it was great and wanted to be involved too. We got a lot of advice that men needed to work with men and women needed to work with women — that this was the only way it could be safe. We listened, but it just didn't fit for us."

Entrup feels the external gender wars are not quite as intense or dynamic a situation as they were 20 or 30 years ago. "Today, men and women are coming together to do their soul work and look deep within. It's less about gender with my generation and it's more about who we are as people. When I am working with my elders, they are a lot quicker to point the finger at gender than my generation. At times it is important to point to the differences. Sometimes it comes from a fear base. Gender issues certainly come up in our work, because there is so much wounding around engendering our youth. It just doesn't seem quite as vocal as in previous generations."

While babyboomers have fought battles with each other in the external manifestations of the gender war, Darkhawk reflects that some of the gender battles in her generation are internal, within oneself. "I have my own internal battles with 'appropriate female behavior,' she notes. I realized a couple of years ago that I had gotten an image of appropriate female behavior that was doing professionalism — going out and getting a good job and working. I realized that I have more of a personal focus on home and family stuff. It's a throwback, betraying our feminist ideals. I found it sort of interesting and very annoying."

"The concept of gender conflict seems to have become an internal issue. Is it appropriate to be a sensitive new age guy or the hard working family provider? I wonder how many people have a conflict like that. At the moment, I am a housewife most often. I am a writer and I write. Every so often I have a conversation with my husband to make sure he thinks this is okay — that I am not out there holding down a job and contributing to family income. In the culture overall, I still see a lot of gender and sex stereotyping which I find amusing. Every time someone starts spewing off the stereotypes, I am clearly male."

Kevin, 23, observed that through the creation of magazines like Maxim and SHM, the media has "equalized" the genders, not necessarily for the better. "I went to Vassar, where people take feminism for granted. Maxim says to guys 'Here's how to get laid on Friday night.' Cosmo says to women, 'Here's how to please your man.' It's the same thing. It would be good if magazines made an effort to help men learn to communicate with women. A problem with magazines like Maxim and SHM is they present a very limited vision of what a man is. These magazines don't challenge cultural assumptions about what it is to be a man. It really isn't helping anything."

Jen, 28, reflects, "One of the biggest challenges in this age are the prejudices and systems that exclude alternate relationships. We're still fighting for basic civil liberties, much less rights for polyamorous families and others." Ruth, 26, comments, "Before rebels thought more. Now the rebels of our generation are the ones who think less. Nobody cares about the truth now. It used to be that forbidden knowledge was banned — chi gong in China...or weapons."

"Now you don't have to ban knowledge. People don't seek knowledge because they are distracted. If you look on the Internet you can find more information than you can imagine. But people aren't looking. The average child spends six hours a day in front of a screen — television, video games and the Internet combined. That is more time that I usually have for myself!"

THE POWER OF ROLE MODELS

Since actions speak louder than words, children often learn more from how we live our lives than from what we say. Psychologist and author Margaret Paul poses the question, "Are you being the person you want your child to be?"

"Many parents today really try to be better parents than their parents were," writes Paul in her article "Parents — What Kind of Role Model are You?" "They attempt to be there for their children — to listen to them, support them, spend time with them, as well as hold them and nurture them. Their children grow up feeling loved and valued by these loving parents, yet these same children struggle as adults in many areas of their lives. I have numerous clients who tell me that they had wonderful parents who truly loved and nurtured them, yet these clients are struggling in their work, their relationships and their lives in general."

"The common issue," continues Paul, "is that their parents did not role model for them personal responsibility for their own feelings, needs and physical health. They did not teach them through their own behavior how to take good care of themselves physically and emotionally." *She poses many good questions:*

❧ Do we follow our passions or spend our spare time watching TV?

- ❧ Do we take good care of our health or smoke cigarettes, eat badly and get little exercise?

- ❧ Do we have a meaningful spiritual practice that helps us connect with our hearts or do we stay mostly in our heads?

- ❧ Do we have a process for managing conflicts with others or do we tend to withdraw, get angry, resist or comply as a way to control or avoid the conflict?

- ❧ Do we avoid life's difficulties with alcohol, drugs, gambling, spending, TV or other addictive behavior or do we learn from life's challenges?

- ❧ Are we boring because we are just trying to be safe and maintain the status quo, or do we extend ourselves and take risks that result in aliveness and vitality?

Paul goes further, raising questions of emotional role modeling:

- ❧ Are you honest or do you let your children think it's okay to withhold the truth or even lie outright?

- ❧ Do you role model integrity or do you behave in other ways that you would not want announced in the newspaper?

- ❧ Do you stand up for yourself or do you let others walk all over you?

- ❧ Do you tolerate abusive situations or do your children see you take action on your own behalf.

Both Margaret Paul and Mankind Project co-founder and workshop leader Rick Tosi offer some important coaching tips on how to be a conscious, positive role model for your children.

Being there is important. Being there for yourself is the foundation.

Paul comments, "It's very important to realize that, while being there for your children is vital, it is only half of good parenting. The other half is being there for yourself with honesty, courage and integrity. It's not enough to treat your children with love. You need to treat yourself with love as well if you want your children to grow up knowing how to take loving care of themselves."

Children need models of how adults work through arguments.

A client of mine who recently turned 60 commented, "When I was a child, when my parents had an argument, there was never any discussion of it. They would have a fight. Then it was over. That was it. When I experienced anger at my wife, I never felt safe expressing it. I realized I never learned how to work through conflict in a productive way."

Tosi notes, "Sometimes a mom and a dad are going to fight and disagree. When you can discuss it with a child, it allows them to be part of the family again. Disagreements are part of what separates. When my wife and I were raising our children, when we disagreed or had a fight, we would have a discussion with our children. I would say something like, 'I got a little angry at mom and I overstated what I wanted.' It is important to be as honest as possible at the level the child is able to understand. I believe kids are getting it anyhow. Better when it is discussed consciously." When you model working through a disagreement and being emotionally accountable about your part in a conflict, you create a safe environment for your children to learn conflict management skills.

Respecting and honoring differences is more important than understanding.

To respect and honor another person and their point of view goes beyond the logical, rational head understanding to a heart understanding. If you just stop at the mind, you lose something critical. Tosi notes, "Some women want men to talk and act like women. They are missing a heart understanding of what it feels like to be a man."

Active listening is an important process to model.

Active listening is a powerful tool, which Tosi feels is underutilized. "Active listening can support understanding between the genders. In our trainings we use a form of it where we slow the process down and make sure that each person talks in short sentences. The listener listens and repeats back what they have heard. Of all the things we do, this creates the most understanding."

When parents model speaking and listening from the heart, they teach their children a deep respect.

"We invite couples to create simple rituals they do with each other on a daily basis. We hear back often that couples invite their children to witness their mother and father treating each other like sacred people during the ritual. Watching your parents respect each other goes a lot further than telling your kids to respect each other!" acknowledges Tosi.

CHILDREN NEED TO BE SEEN AND HEARD FOR WHO THEY ARE

When I was a child, a common motto was "children should be seen and not heard." Not hearing children is a way of wounding their hearts and denying them the nurturance it takes to develop a rooted sense of self. Storyteller and group leader Michael Meade notes, "If someone has never been heard deeply, they can't hear the deep speech of anyone else." Once the heart is wounded, "it's unlikely the correction or healing will occur unless the sympathy is equal to the wound."

Meade is involved in a project called "Voices of Youth," helping create a context where everyone can be seen for their uniqueness and respected collectively as well.

"We work with all kinds of youth, boys and girls, all ethnic traditions and cultural root stocks. In America, you don't have to go far to find tremendous diversity. The heart of America. Our culture tends to homogenize everything. White culture becomes an emptying of culture. The whiter it becomes, the less you can cultivate it. The more mainstream it gets, the further it gets from whatever roots it could have had or should have had. Our program is called Voices of Youth because we are trying to get that voice that has something to say that could only be said by that person."

As children are both seen and heard for who they are, they develop a solid, rooted sense of self. Really loving a child is to be able to see and hear him/her for who s/he is.

CHILDREN NEED MENTORS

Mentorship is part of the "it takes a village to raise a child" model. Boys need older male mentors to help them explore and develop their identity as men. Girls need older female mentors to help them explore and develop their identity as women. Both boys and girls need mentors of other genders, so they can develop a healthy, grounded sense of all genders.

Mentors can connect with children through a common interest, be it math, soccer, dogs or singing. A good mentor will appreciate the child for who s/he is as a unique person. Mentors have the wonderful opportunity to help nurture and steward a budding soul at many levels, including gender identity.

"One of the greatest challenges in coming to be a man or a woman is seeing through the illusions that are created by our current culture," acknowledges Luke Entrup. "We need to seek out mentors and guides who really do understand what it means to be an awake man or an awake woman. This is really hard because the defaults we are creating in our society are out of balance. Getting unplugged from the cultural illusion is the most difficult part. There's a constant barrage with no time to stop and digest the inundation. There is no silence. It's harder to sift through the barrage and find the inner voice, find out what works and what doesn't work about what we are being fed."

INITIATION

Marking significant passages in a man's or woman's life with personal and communal rituals can contribute to emotional, spiritual and cultural growth and development. A common criticism of today's society is that we lack initiation rituals that help boys become men and girls become women.

In cultures that do have initiation rituals, what is required of the young initiate may be more than is just challenging or reasonable. For example, some tribes have "initiation rituals" where masculinity is "achieved" through surviving the initiation. Child psychologist and author Larry Cohen asks, "Is masculinity not something that is inborn rather than something that has to be achieved?" Cohen talked about a Native

American tribe that referred to masculinity as "the big impossible," because the failure rate in the initiation ritual was so high.

"An important message is that maleness is inborn, not made. It doesn't have to be proven constantly. When we push boys to achieve, while wanting competence is a worthy goal, we need to make it clear that their masculinity is not at stake. You might win. You might lose. And there IS something at stake. It's just not your essence that's at stake."

Rich Tosi is involved in initiation work that helps men be deeply appreciated as men and women be deeply appreciated as women "Once that happens, the need to fight with the other gender isn't there," comments Tosi "If I am centered in who I am as a woman or a man, and confident about who I am, then I don't need to be in a gender war. Men who are not confident in themselves, who are not sure who they are as men, need to engage in some kind of war. The more authentic a man is, the less he needs to put a woman down. When a man can get in touch with who he is spiritually at a heart level, things just change. You don't necessarily need to have to say 'now go out and respect women or respect men.' It is about respecting anyone who is different than you are, gender being an important category. Difference is everywhere."

Emotional and spiritual maturation is itself an initiation process. Many adult men are still like boys and many adult women are still like girls. For men who are more like boys and women who are more like girls, war is more likely. Getting in touch with one's essence, with the sense of self that lives deep inside us, is a journey we need to take to mature. Helping our children develop a spiritual center within, and learn to listen to and live from their hearts will go a long way towards preventing the gender wars.

War on the inside creates war on the outside. Tosi believes, "We will have limited success stopping gender wars or any other kind of wars until the internal is changed. The external is a reflection of what is going on internally. In the New Warrior Training, one of the things we say is for a man to be a new warrior, his battle ground is no longer out there. It is in his heart. Until you can succeed in the battle in your own heart, the external wars will continue."

Women's body changes are part of an internal initiation process. For example, with menstruation, women's bodies change in a way our ancestors seemed to understand. Ceremonies have been created around these changes. People today demonstrate less understanding for the sacred role of natural bodily changes and the importance of marking passages with rituals.

Male initiations appear to be external, notes Tosi. There are no corresponding body changes for boys that are as profound as menstruation is for girls. "The male needs to be taken out of the home and go through a process of initiation. When a boy doesn't, he will go out and create something to do that. And if he doesn't know how to do that, he will do it in a dangerous way. I believe that's what's happened in our culture if you look at street gangs and college hazing."

Our society is missing respected elders who can guide boys along their journey of maturation. A father cannot do it for his own son. It needs to be someone else. The father is often too close to the son to do the process. When a father is too closely identified with a son, he will become defensive and overhelpful or get in the way of allowing his son to do what he needs to do. Tosi finds this is especially true when a man is going through a deep initiation process.

THE ELEPHANT STORY

Rich Tosi told me a story about elephants in South Africa that illustrates the importance of mentoring boys so they understand more about who they are. Adolescents have vast energy, and they need to learn how to channel it.

Somewhere in the late 1980's there were too many elephants in one part of South Africa. So, they were moved to another part of South Africa. In this place where the elephants were transplanted, after about 10 or 15 years a strange thing happened. Rhinoceroses were being killed by young male elephants. No one had ever heard of anything like this before. Young male elephants were not aggressive. But there was a pack of young male elephants going around killing. What was discovered was that when the elephants were moved, only the mothers and their young were moved. No older male elephants moved with them.

When male elephants develop, they go through must, like a teenage boy who is 14 or 15 years old. They become very aggressive. What controls the teenage energy of the boy elephants is the older male elephant. Without older male elephants in the pack, the young male elephants go nuts. Their sexual energy gets destructive. A relatively peaceful animal becomes a killer. The presence of older male elephants contains the eruptive energy of the young male bulls.

Tosi remarks, "There seems to be a similar dynamic that goes on in our culture with young boys who don't have male elders. While street gangs are an example, it can happen with white middle class kids too. It's not an ethnic or class thing. Without older males there, this energy goes wacko. I think part of creating gender peace is bringing boys through processes where they understand more about who they are, not so much controlling, but channeling the energy."

REFRAMING THE DEFINITION OF A GOOD DAD

Child psychologist and author Larry Cohen comments, "Fathers are both men and parents. We have had a lot more training to be men than parents. Most of our training to be men ill prepares us to be parents." Our culture puts a lot of pressure on men to work hard, succeed professionally and financially provide. As I discussed in Chapter 4, over the past handful of decades since feminism, this same pressure is now applied to women.

Social visionary and father Jerry Koch-Gonzalez would like to see our culture change its understanding of fatherhood "so that how good a dad I am in terms of loving my children becomes more important than how many dollars I produce for my family." Cohen adds, "There is a tendency to toughen boys up for the tough times when they'll have to be out in the world. From this you get an exaggerated masculinity. You prepare boys for the world by loving and respecting them. Boys need to see their fathers crying. They need to be cuddled and read to by their fathers."

Being valued for money and protection and not as nurturers leads to men being marginalized as parents. When Cohen's daughter Emma was a baby, and Emma's grandparents were around, if Cohen was holding Emma and she cried, her grandparents would take her from his arms and give her to her mom. "It was seen as the mother's job to comfort the crying child. I like to hold a crying baby. I see the communication in holding a crying baby until they fall asleep in your arms. Most men don't know or recognize this."

Another obstacle to healthy fathering is men's fear of attaching for fear of not being able to handle loss. Our culture's way of cutting men off at the heart also cuts off their ability to bond and nurture their children. Because men know they can't handle loss, they are reluctant to attach. "Just being a comfortable presence is the most nurturing thing men could do," acknowledges Cohen. "Most men have never experienced being nurtured in the presence of a man. So, they cannot offer it."

The feminine counterpart of helping men be good dads is allowing, valuing and reintegrating the feminine back into our families and our culture. Children need both maternal and paternal nurturing to grow. As I pointed out in Chapter 4, our culture has overmasculinized both genders and lost touch with feminine energy and its value, both at work and at home. Children need heart and home energy to feel safe and secure. To the degree we have buried the feminine in the shadows at this time in our evolution, we are undernourishing our young adults and children.

PREVENTING THE GENDER WARS: PARENTING GUIDELINES

H*ere are some guidelines we can follow to parent children in such a way that we help prevent the gender wars:*

1. **As a parent, come to know who you really are.** The more grounded, clear and authentic you are within, the more present you can be to your child. Grounded self-knowledge allows us both to see our children for who they really are and to role model a balanced, integrated, authentic and fulfilling life path.

2. **Create a community around yourself and your children.** It does take a village to raise a child and children need to feel their connection to the larger whole to learn that we are not all alone in this world. Community creates a catchment net to help all have what they need in both good times and bad. "A community-centered world view is something we had and lost," acknowledges Ruth, 26. "At 46, I hope I am living in a sustainable community with a group of people I care about

and who care about me. I hope we are living an active and sustainable lifestyle and teaching others you can do the same without sacrificing the comforts of modern life."

"By raising children in a world view that is much more friendly to the natural human psyche, we will find less conflict. We will find happier children and happier parents." Ruth points out that indigenous people don't have problems with their youth the way our culture has. They are not trying to box them into something they cannot be. The things they teach their children are practical skills for their lives — things they need to know and they know they need.

3. **Help your children develop both roots and wings.** "We do a better job giving roots to girls and wings to boys," reflects Larry Cohen. "Of course, there are always exceptions, but in general, a lot of what we have to do is catch up against the trend." Cohen cited two examples:

First, there were a a series of experiments in the 1970's called the Table Top Experiments. There was a baby and a group of young adults who didn't know the gender of the baby. An audiotape of the baby crying in another room was played. The question that was explored was how long did the adults wait to go in the other room to attend to the crying baby. What they found was that if the young adults thought the baby was a boy, they waited longer than if they thought it was a girl. The experiment illustrated that girls get comfort sooner than boys, but girls don't get to experiment and explore. Boys get to experiment and explore, but they don't get comfort.

Second, Sadker and Sadker wrote a book called **FAILING AT FAIRNESS**, which looks at what is harmful for girls in childrearing practices. One example given in the book was a 10th grade math class. In the example, a girl asks the teacher for help and the teacher solves the problem for the girl. A boys asks the teacher for help and the teacher tells him to go solve it for himself. Cohen comments, "Neither gender is really getting what they need here. The girl is not being helped to think for herself, but she is getting some nurturing. The boy is getting to think for himself, but he isn't getting any nurturing. Children need connection and relating with room to grow."

4. **Become emotionally literate and teach your children emotional literacy.** Emotional literacy includes knowing what our feelings are, being able to articulate them, and say them to one another, and being able to negotiate the dynamics that go on between people. Emotional literacy is a key skill for building intimacy with self and others. Jerry Koch-Gonzalez believes developing our capacity for emotional literacy is essential so we can be guided by feelings of love, compassion and caring in all our relationships. Luke Entrup comments,

"Our culture has a long way to go around emotional literacy. As men, emotional literacy is important, yet we don't have any clear roles models for it in our culture."

As parents, it is important we do the work to increase our emotional literacy. Our emotional literacy will improve our ability to parent our children. And emotionally literate parents can be better teachers of emotional literacy to their children, both through words and example.

5. **Provide an abundance of respectful, nurturing touch.** Respectful, nurturing touch is an emotional, spiritual and developmental need. Joseph Kramer, founder of the Body Electric School, expresses, "To develop an empathic connection, children need to learn to touch and be touched by others. How much touch has been in someone's life from the earliest age, how much the mother touches her baby, is essential. Children's sexuality doesn't look like adult sexuality. It's all the feelings in the body of being touched, being held, being bathed. There are ways of being with a child that gets his/her sense of self involved in feeling good. The experience of nurturing touch teaches the child that 'part of who I am is feeling these sensations of being touched, caressed and being held.'"

Bill Kauth adds that parents who can hug and embrace their children in an emotionally embodied way communicate energetically that their children are loved and safe in a very rooted way. "At a cosmic level, love is who we are. For our evolutionary learning, we need to learn to receive love. When we open up our heart chakras enough to feel another's vibrational field, we experience love as a pure feeling modality."

6. **Support your children in accepting their natural bodies.** When today's media tells both boys and girls their bodies aren't good enough, our children need messages that their bodies are natural and healthy as they are. Psychologist Dan Kindlon cited a study in which 16% of high school boys had used creatine in the past month to increase their muscle mass. Creatine is banned in professional sports, yet available at CVS and over the Internet. "Our culture is telling us we need to alter our appearance with plastic surgery, steroids for muscle sculpting, engineer our moods with psychopharmacology and our foods with genetic engineering," Kindlon reflects. Children need support to be the people they really are and to learn to care for and live in the bodies they were born with.

7. **Recognize that boys have an inner life.** A danger in the parenting of boys is that we apply female benchmarks to male ways of communication and language. "If boys don't talk," notes Larry Cohen, "If they don't share, they are seen as not having an inner life. Not to

be seen to have an inner life is not to be seen. This leads to getting used to not being seen, and wrestling with wanting to be seen and not wanting to be seen."

Girls and women are often more verbal than boys. "Just because a person isn't verbal doesn't mean something isn't going on," continues Cohen. "For teenage boys, the posters they have in their room and the music they listen to is symbolic language." The heart language of boys may not be words, but the symbolic language of posters, music and Pokemon cards.

8. **Teach children to respect their own gender and other genders**.
"One of the causes of the gender wars is that we don't respect each other," says Rich Tosi. Children need to learn not only to respect, but also honor one another. We need to teach children the differences between boys and girls and honor the differences. We can extend this attitude to gender fluid and transgendered people as well.

Creating safe, open spaces where boys and girls and young men and women can have dialogues about the nature of gender is important. Young people need the room to explore, learn and come to their own conclusions, rather than being brainwashed by the media. Luke Entrup advises young people to "speak out when you hear friends and associates speak from a place of ignorance around issues of gender." There is a lot of gender awareness and sensitivity training to do.

9. **Teach your children that sex is normal, healthy and human.**
More awareness, knowledge and experience are needed so people know they have a right to a rich, fulfilling sexual life. "We need to have knowledge and experience more accessible at age appropriate times," believes lawyer, longtime HAI community leader and mother, Lynn Thomas. "A person can only discover their sexual potential through knowledge and awareness."

I remember when I was 10 or 11 years old and I used to visit my friend Ann at her house. Ann, her friend Kirsten, and I would play strip poker. As pre-pubescent girls there was an innocent joy and education in taking off our clothes and seeing how our bodies compared to one another's. I am so glad Ann's parents didn't shame us or stop us for doing this experimentation. I wonder now if they knew what we were doing. Having the safety and freedom to explore our budding bodies with our close friends was innocent, harmless and growthful for all.

"As it stands, having sex is a way of manifesting profound teenage rebellion," acknowledges Darkhawk. "A lot of people have sex for just that reason. It screws up getting people to make good decisions." Kids need sex education that is more grounded in relationship skills, and exploration of differences to find an authentic personal sexuality. "When I was in high school and taking sex ed," Darkhawk continues, "they couldn't even mention that there were gay people."

Kevin adds, "I think it is important to foster an environment where children feel comfortable discussing their sexuality with you when they want to. Let them know that who they are is not something they need to be ashamed or afraid of. I recently read an article about a high school kid and his coming out to his family. It was great to read about how supportive they were. I became interested in gay rights when I read a sad article about a kid in Cleveland who committed suicide because he couldn't live with himself as a gay man. The article made it sound like his family was trying to be supportive of him, even though he never came out to them. The fact that he committed suicide over his sexual identity was very painful."

ESSENTIAL QUESTIONS:

1. When you were younger, what were your role models for sexuality and relationships?

2. What kinds of mentorship have you received about becoming a man or a woman over the course of your life?

3. What kinds of mentorship would you have wished to have at different life stages?

4. How have you come to define your sexual identity and your gender identity?

5. If you are a parent, what are ways you can help your child or children grow into an authentic sense of gender identity and sexual identity?

6. If you are not yet a parent, but want to be a parent one day, what experiences do you want to make sure you have to develop yourself so that you can be a mentor and role model for a male or female child?

Chapter 11

RESTORING ESSENTIAL CONNECTIONS:

NATURE, SOUL, RELATIONSHIPS, COMMUNITY AND GOD

*"We must remind people that the world is sacred,
and that we are part of the natural world;
a web of life that we cannot live without."*

— www.sacredlands.org

Our culture and many of us individually have developed a myopic vision of our lives, the problems and obstacles we face and the steps we need to take to confront and resolve them. This is understandable in light of the heart-woundedness that permeates our culture. A wounded heart often pulls inward, focusing its energies on mere survival. Interconnection and mutuality are far removed in this wounded state. Accordingly, in the face of the cultural heart wound, we have lost our sense of the collective, and our connection to the earth and the other living beings who cohabitate our planet alongside us. One of the most painful side effects of our cultural heart wound is the normalization of isolation — to realize how alone we truly are.

I believe human beings need to nourish and sustain five essential connections, both individually and collectively, to have balanced, grounded, healthy lives. These connections are with nature, soul, other people in one-on-one relationships, community and God. To lose sight of any one level diminishes the quality of our lives. To become disconnected from any or all of them leads to illness, lostness, despair and confusion.

Many of the individual and collective problems we face today cannot be solved by looking at life through the myopic lens of the individual. We need to recognize the interconnection of the many layers and levels of life, and recognize the interdependence of humans, the earth, and all living beings. We need to heal our relationship with the collective and the earth to have a context to know our own souls. We need to heal our relationship with our own souls to restore a sense of connection with other living beings, and our sense of the life force, or however we define what many people call God.

Gender reconciliation worker Will Keepins finds great meaning in the metaphor, "the leaves can heal the tree." Most simply, as a quote on the sacredlands.org website reads, "All things are connected. Whatever befalls the earth befalls the sons and daughters of the earth. Man did not weave the web of life; he is merely a strand in it. Whatever he does to the web, he does to himself." To come to this awakening collectively would be a major breakthrough for the human species. In this chapter, I hope to provide both tools and support to remind us of our place in the web of life and our part in helping the leaves heal the tree.

ROOTS AND ROOTLESSNESS

Several years ago, I was looking for a new housemate, to rent a room in my home. I had put an ad in a Boston paper that used to be "the" place to find housemates before the Internet became such a force. And I was amazed to receive calls from person after person who felt that the one year commitment I was asking a potential housemate to make was more than they could imagine.

"I could consider six months," sighed a thirtysomething woman, "But I don't know what will happen with my job, and in a year, I don't know where I will want to be." "A year!" exclaimed a fortysomething man, as though I was asking for the moon! "I can't possibly commit to THAT long a timeframe."There were over a dozen responses with a similar flavor before I stopped and decided not to continue the search for someone to live in that room.

As I thought about it, I realized just how rootless and unsettled people's lives have become in these chaotic and in many ways, dark times. The pace of our culture moves faster and faster. People uproot their lives and travel great distances in a globalized workplace, where no one commits to anyone and the pull is away from teams, community and the collective. Two decades ago, when I worked for the now extinct Digital Equipment Corporation, long-term rootedness in jobs, homes, and relationships seemed more important, or simply more available.

In the past two decades, our culture has undergone tremendous transformation and change. Just several decades earlier, people spoke of "lifetime employment," settling into a community to build deep roots and connections that would last them a lifetime. The very fact that companies like Digital and Polaroid, humanistic organizations with solid products, innovative capabilities and skilled management, have moved from success to oblivion, shows us just how dramatically times have changed.

I was deeply touched recently as I listened to the members of a group I lead talk about all the uncertainty in their lives and what they could not count on. One woman grieved that she just could not count on relationships to last over time. Several highly skilled people were struggling financially and professionally, trying to find stable work. Even if they found work, would their companies keep their jobs for long? Was it a better bet to move out of the area? I realized how this group, which had made a six month commitment to meet weekly, may have been one of the more stable forces in many of the members' lives.

Only one group member, a man who owned a house in Vermont in the farming town he grew up in, had a sense of rootedness and continuity. He worked weekdays in the Boston area, and went up to his rural home on the weekends. He could still count on being part of a world that had managed to stand still in time. The same people live there now as when he was a kid. The houses are old and still stand, free of strip malls and modern housing developments. There, you can walk in the woods, and find quiet places that remain natural and pure. The pace of life is slower and simpler there. Perhaps this town is a bit of an anachronism. But there is a kind of peace and rootedness in that anachronism.

THE WILLOW TREE AND THE MAPLE TREE

As we have become disconnected from the earth, we have become rootless and displaced. We find ourselves floating, emotionally, spiritually and often practically. Without roots to anchor us to the ground, we are battered by the winds of life. Nature gave me a very graphic illustration of this truth during a hurricane more than fifteen years ago.

I owned a small house in Shrewsbury, MA. My backyard featured a collection of trees of distinction. Two trees were particularly prominent: a large willow tree, and a smaller but compact maple tree. I had been told how quickly willow trees grew and that their wood was light, not dense. Their roots were far reaching, but shallow. I could see willow roots spreading across my lawn and into the adjacent property. The maple tree, on the other hand, grew more slowly. Accordingly, its wood was more dense with a strong taproot that went deep into the ground.

The evening the hurricane arrived, I remember being awakened from my sleep by the roaring sounds of the powerful wind shaking all the trees. The wailing winds and quaking trees frightened me. I looked out my window, and saw the willow tree swinging back and forth. Its shallow roots were no match for the power of the storm. As I saw the winds taking the willow, I ran for cover in my bed, as the giant tree began to fall over. I prayed to God it would fall down without crashing through the roof of my house. I closed my eyes and clutched my stuffed animal, feeling the house shake as the tree came crashing down, headed towards my house like a rocket ship.

When the crash was over, I hesitantly looked out my window, and saw that I had been very lucky. The willow tree had fallen right next to my house, but managed to spare the house in its fall. A huge constellation of roots was exposed, reaching all the way up to the roof from the ground. I thanked God my house and I escaped unharmed! I curled up and went back to sleep.

I awoke once again to a bolt of lightning, cracking and sizzling through my yard. I heard a great crash, but I did not look out the window this time. I waited til the morning when the storm had passed, and it was safe to go outside. I marvelled at the tumbled willow tree on the ground, with its huge, elaborate, hollow root system unveiled in the air. I realized the bolt of lightning had struck the maple tree. The maple tree had survived the winds that took the willow, held steady by its deep taproot. The bolt of lightning had claimed one of its biggest branches. My backyard was a battlefield, and my trees were its casualties. The willow had been lost in the battle, while the maple though injured, was still vital and alive.

What a metaphor the trees gave me for the human journey! While we have no control over the winds of life, we can learn from the maple about the importance of rootedness! I believe people, like trees, need a taproot, and a solid system of other connections anchoring them to the ground. Without a root system, how can we be nourished? How can we withstand the winds of life?

ROOTEDNESS AND SOUL SURVIVAL

In our ever changing transient world, where our connections with the earth, community and the collective are more distant or broken, our very survival becomes threatened. This is certainly true on emotional and spiritual levels. And I see how it can also be true physically. When people hit crises, they fall with no catchment net. They emerge hurt, wounded, homeless, penniless and alone.

Most species of animals are territorial in at least some ways. Our dog's crate is his safe space. My cats have established their own zones in my apartment. About a year ago, I took in a 7-month-old kitten whose primary human could no longer care for her. A solo animal, unable to integrate with the existing tribe of five felines, this new addition found herself searching desperately for a territory to call her own. As the alpha male and even the quietest elderly female cat proceeded to block her efforts to put down roots, the new kitten became increasingly anxious and skittish. I realized I needed to find a new home for Lila where she could be a solo pet. How much energy we waste when there is no home base to draw from! In a rootless state, we waste so much psychic energy just trying to survive!

I read a very poignant article in the Wall Street Journal about a sixty-two-year-old man with thirty-six years of experience in the insurance industry who had been out of work for a year. He had sent out 700 resumes looks for a middle management job. He and his wife were down to their last $2500. Unable to pay his bills, and on the verge of losing an essential part of his root system, his ability to remain in his home, he started standing by a highway at rush hour wearing a plaquard that read, "Insurance/management job wanted. 36 years experience" along with his phone number. As I shared this story with a group of friends, one man commented, "He's not going to find a job. He is used to supervising filing clerks and there aren't filing clerks anymore!"

We need to join together and address this growing pattern of rootlessness. We cannot do it alone. We need to restore essential connections with the earth, with our own spirits, with friends and loved ones, with the collective. We need to sustain these connections to establish a sense of rootedness, a sense of home. Like the wolves, we need packs to travel in, where everyone has an essential role in maintaining the social order, so the needs of both individual and collective are attended to. I hope the pendulum of change will soon show us that we have swung to one extreme of disconnection and rootlessness, and that it is time to swing back towards the center! Our soul survival depends on it!

COMMITMENT

One of the things that stood out for me in the housemate search I described earlier in this chapter was the number of people who are truly afraid to make commitments. We are afraid to put down roots, because so many forces in our lives seem out of our hands. It is hard to tell if this commitment phobia that permeates society today is a symptom of our rootlessness or if our fear of commitment has actually created the state of rootlessness. Which is the chicken and which is the egg?

While fear of commitment emerges in an environment of uncertainty, when we don't know what tomorrow will bring, and we are afraid of being trapped in an unworkable situation, commitment is necessary for almost anything to be sustainable. Commitment is like planting a seed in the earth. If the seed is not planted, nothing can germinate and grow. Commitment creates a foundation, a structure, a container. And the structure holds possibility, just like a rhythm, a heartbeat. Commitment is not a guarantee that things will go as we wish, but it is definitely a step we can take in a positive direction.

To live in a state of commitment phobia is a bit like being a deer in front of the headlights. As we remain afraid of whatever it is that we fear, we don't make any movement towards what we really desire. In our fear-ridden state, we are more likely to be hit metaphorically or literally, as we remain frozen in a path of danger.

For our energy to be used in positive, focused ways, we need to become clear where we want to direct it. This is true for our personal growth, for sustainable relationships with others, and for our collective well-being. I used to keep a Goethe quote about commitment on my refrigerator many years ago that reflected once we are committed, then God can do his/her magic in our lives. Once we are committed, the spiritual forces of life can support us. Without commitment, there is no container to hold the spiritual energy we have to channel and direct, and there is no direction to channel this energy towards.

Commitment provides a kind of rootedness, and from this rootedness comes a kind of connectedness, safety and sustainability. When the winds of life get rough, the power of commitment can give us both the emotional and practical space and support to weather whatever we need to, to work things out.

I. *THE EARTH AND THE NATURAL WORLD*

> *"Connecting with the earth is part of the process of transforming the inner. There is nothing to be done while opening up and truly experiencing connection with the earth, and the inseparability of it. Nothing needs to be done other than taking it all in and being a part of it. That is complete transformation for most and for myself. As I heal my psyche, my soul, my spirit, the earth heals. As the earth heals, I heal. As it transforms, I transform. And so works the interconnection of healing."*

—Luke Entrup

The earth is our home, our mother, and all the living beings that share our home and mother are our brothers and sisters. Human beings, having become individualistic and self-centered, seem to forget this. Amy Hughes is part of the founding circle of www.sacredlands.org, an organization founded to educate people both through programs and living example, about a more sustainable way of life. The sacredlands website offers information and face-to-face gatherings allow for community interaction and discussions. "We can't live without the planet. It would be absurd to think we can be exempt from the laws of nature. But that's exactly what our culture is trying to do," comments Amy.

"I was recently forwarded an article that the Shell corporation is soliciting writing samples on the question 'Do we need nature?' They are offering a $20K prize to the winner of this contest. This is an insane question to ask!" acknowledges Hughes. "We are an embedded part of the natural world. Our denial of this has caused so much damage to the planet."

"Sacredlands is a very macro project. Many people focus on individual issues such as the salmon who cannot swim upstream because of human-made dams, nuclear power plants, and forests which need to be protected. Sacredlands is about changing people's minds, not just changing what they are doing. We are working to bring more consciousness to what people are doing. Most people are not aware that in North America we are consuming 95% of the resources produced in the world, and we have 5% of the world's population."

"The vast majority of people are simply not aware of the damage we are doing culturally speaking. We are distracted by the pleasant things we are doing in life and our privilege. The mark I can make on the world is to make people aware of the damage humans are doing to the world and to convince people to care."

Hughes finds it amazing how edited the news we get is. "For example, a piece of a part of what could be linked to a nuclear weapons program that was buried under a rose bush for 12 years in Iraq behind a scientist's house made headlines all over the world. The message was, 'We found it! Weapons of mass destruction!'

In contrast, the fact that this amazing solar wing which was an experimental solar-only powered device — a major concept in how we might get around, was only a footnote in a Yahoo side page that I just happened to look at."

LEARNING TO CARE FOR THE EARTH

B oth Amy Hughes and Beyond the Machine Founder Luke Entrup offer some good suggestions about how we can learn to care for the earth.

1. **Examine where we are getting our information and how much thinking we are doing for ourselves.** Hughes notes, "We need to be conscious of how much we are doing our own thinking versus accepting what someone else might have to say. If we are taking someone else's ideas, we need to ask them what their motivations are in giving us the messages they do. In the case of the mainstream media, it is the profit motive.

2. **Unplug from the culture, even for a moment.** Entrup encourages us to unplug from the information, the technology culture, just for a moment, and take off our shoes and walk in the earth. "It's a wonderful first step, and for some, that is all that needs to happen to be more eco-friendly." Life in the mainstream culture breeds a fast-paced, myopic, disconnected experience that is often remedied by even a brief experience of connection with the earth. We need to slow down and re-experience our connection with the earth.

3. **Take the earth into our hearts**. Entrup recognizes that we miss many golden opportunities to see how beautiful the Earth, the living organism is. "I fall in love with the earth, and realize I am not separate from it. For me, it means slowing down, sometimes taking the hand of someone else and pointing out the beauty, finding silence." If we can take the earth into our hearts and fall in love with the earth, we can then offer this experience to others around us.

4. **Become more conscious of the choices we make in our everyday lives.** Hughes suggests, that as we go about our daily activities, we think about what our actions mean. "The choices we make should reflect how we view the world and how we want to affect the world. You can pursue a lifestyle that is in line with what you really believe." One person really does have an impact.

5. **Recognize the fundamental interconnection between the earth and our inner experience.** Connecting with the earth is part of the process of transforming the inner. There is nothing to be done while opening up

and truly experiencing connection with the earth, and feeling the inseparability of oneself and the earth. We can experience the interconnection of healing: As I heal my psyche, my soul, my spirit, the earth heals. As the earth heals, I heal. As the earth transforms, I transform. This can be the most complete healing and transformative experience.

OUR FOUR-LEGGED SOULMATES

I met my first soul-mate when I was less than one year old. I fell in love as soon as I saw him. He was steady, loving, and always glad to see me. His name was Mittens and he was a black cocker spaniel who lived next door. My mother has pictures of me sharing special times with Mittens: sitting on the steps at his house with my jacket and winter hat on, playing on the lawn with Mittens on a beautiful summer day, and exchanging loving glances when he and I were about the same size. Great love is sometimes cut short by the rhythms of life. Mittens died when I was two-and-a-half. My heart was broken, but I never forgot the depth of our connection or the warmth of his love.

The term "soul-mate" is most often used to describe a romantic partner, and certainly a human being. Yet, some of our deepest and longest lasting bonds are not with people, but with the cats, dogs, horses, rabbits and other animals we share our lives with — our four legged companions. As our world moves faster, as our lives get busier and more scheduled, and as we have less time to be with family and friends, our four-legged friends are often the most constant source of love and companionship in many people's lives. Our four-legged soul-mates provide emotional and spiritual connection and can serve as our teachers and healers if we are open to them.

In his book **THE SOULS OF ANIMALS**, Gary Kowalski writes, "To me, animals have all the traits indicative of soul. For soul is not something we can see or measure. We can only observe its outward manifestations: in tears and laughter, in courage and heroism, in generosity and forgiveness. Soul is what's behind the scenes in the tough and tender moments when we are most grippingly alive....Soul is the point at which our lives intersect the timeless, in our love of goodness, our zest for beauty, our passion for truth. Soul is what makes each of our lives a microcosm — not just a meaningless fragment of the universe, but at some level a reflection of the whole." It is no surprise movies like "Seabiscuit" and television shows like "Miracle Pets" capture the hearts and minds of so many people. Our relationships with our four-legged and other animal companions help us feel connected to our own souls.

Kowalski comments, "Without anthromorphizing our non-human relations we can acknowledge that animals share many human characteristics. They have emotional lives, experience love and fear and possess their own integrity which suffers when not respected. They play and are curious about their world. They develop loyalties and display altruism. They have 'animal faith,' a spontaneity and directness that can be most enlightening."

Our four-legged soulmates offer humans many essential gifts. They:

♘ Provide emotionally safe spaces for our vulnerability and pain

In my nearly twenty years of practice as a therapist, I have had countless clients tell me how they have turned to their four-legged friends for comfort, solace, safety and protection in the hardest of times. One man, who was brutally beaten by his father as a boy, found his lifeline in his pet dog. When the beating was over, the dog would always appear, ready to crawl into the boy's arms. This dog provided the only love, warmth and safety, this man, then boy, knew. The dog would snuggle up close and allow the boy the space to cry and express his pain. He would take his dog into his bed and curl up tight, with the dog's head next to his heart. It is no surprise that most children sleep with stuffed animals at some point in their early lives, a symbol of the safety our fellow creatures provide.

♘ Help us heal

More than 10 years ago as I was leading a workshop at a community center, the resident cat provided feline ministry. I was facilitating a woman who was experiencing body memories related to childhood sexual abuse. She felt a tightness in her throat and the strongest urge to throw up. She gagged and she gagged, but she could not throw up. She disconnected from her emotional experience as she felt the intensity of her inner urge.

As this woman was despairing that she just could not reach her deepest feelings, Persephone walked through the door. She proceeded to the corner of the room where the woman was standing, and proceeded to gag repeatedly and throw up. The group stood in awe, recognizing that Persephone had just expressed what the woman could not. She had taken on the healing work this woman was struggling with and worked on this woman's behalf.

♘ Attune to the energy of the soul

In **THE SEAT OF THE SOUL**, Gary Zukav writes, "Behind every aspect of the health or illness of the body is the energy of the soul. It is the health of the soul that is the true purpose of the human experience." Our four-legged friends attune to the energy of the soul, and sometimes manifest physical illnesses that reflect the healing we need to undertake. I have a friend who suffered from a congenital hip problem which caused chronic pain. His dog developed a similar hip problem, as though his empathy ran as deep as his own body and soul. In a culture so full of fear and unsafety, I find it no surprise that so many cats and dogs die of renal failure. In Chinese medicine, the kidneys are the organ where we process fear.

I was struck by the remarkable parallel between the birthing experience of my recently deceased 17-year-old soul-cat, Querida, and my own birthing experience. When Querida's own mother was in labor, she crawled into my bed between my legs and gave birth to Querida there, as though she was my baby. When Querida went into labor she had a long, difficult 48-hour labor, giving birth to only one kitten. When I went into labor with my son Alexander, now 7, I too had a long difficult 48-hour labor. And as fate had it, I too have just one child. Querida was particularly attentive to me when I was pregnant, sleeping on my heart at night, and always staying close by.

♋ Teach us to overcome our fears

Horses can be incredible teachers about fear and overcoming fear. Equine therapist and college professor John Dore acknowledges, "They are prey animals. Fear is their primary emotion. So they have a lot of fear about anything unusual happening in their environment unless they are trained and can trust a human to train them." Because horses have a lot of experience being with their own fears, they can provide an emotional space for humans to be with theirs.

"If you allow it, horses will provide a space for you to be with your feelings. I believe horses are flooded with feelings a lot of the time. Their feelings arise in the body and can flood the body. With humans, once there is a feeling, the mind comes in and starts to appropriate — to label, express and categorize what is felt. Horses tend to be in a feelingful state all the time without the interference of the mind. When a human is in the context of a horse, their opportunity and ability to go to their feeling state is heightened."

♋ Can be our partners in communion

In the movie "Seabiscuit," a deep sense of communion developed between boy and horse. Red and Seabiscuit lived the soul-mate experience. They had a lot of deep issues in common: the history of their traumas matched, their loneliness matched and their caring matched. Their deep connection led to a sense of synchrony when Red rode Seabiscuit. They experienced the best of relationship, coming together in oneness, a spiritual communion.

Each night when I am putting my son to bed, our three-year-old gray cat, Toss, comes into my son's room as soon as I begin to read Alexander his bedtime story. Toss seems to recognize the special ritual of putting Alexander to bed and wants to join us in this kind of communion.

II. *SOUL*

> *"The individual unit of evolution is the soul. This perception is new to us, because as a species, we have not before been aware of the existence of the soul. In our religious thoughts we acknowledge what we call the soul, but we have not, until now, taken it seriously enough to consider what the existence of soul means in terms of everyday experience, in terms of the joys and pains and sorrows and fulfillments that make a human life."*

— Gary Zukav
The Seat of the Soul

While I was a child and I used to speak of the soul, well-meaning adults would often pull me aside and caution me, "Don't use that word or people will think you are a religious fanatic." Somehow, the only visibility the word "soul" seemed to have was through the lens of organized religion. I found myself feeling sad and disconnected by this feedback. My experience of soul had nothing to do with organized religion at all. It was an energetic experience I sensed in my body.

Soul was something I felt deep down in the core of my being. I could find it in the depths of my heart and the center of my belly. I would often ask myself what is the difference between soul and spirit. I experienced soul as the life force residing in the body, and spirit as a current of life energy flowing through the body. I also felt that soul and God are interrelated. The soul is what embodies and defines who we are as individual beings. In this sense, soul is the piece of God in each and every one of us. Spirit is the pathway of connection from the universal oneness to the individual and from the individual back to the universal oneness. God speaks to us through the currents of the spirit and lives in us through the embodied experience of soul.

As I got older and studied psychology, I was greatly disappointed. I expected to be studying the soul, as I knew it. After all, psyche means soul. But what I encountered in my college psychology classes was a study of the personality, of cognition, of thought, or behavior. Even feelings were called "affect," which seemed to have nothing to do with heart. While this study was about human beings, it was not about soul.

In his book **THE SEAT OF THE SOUL**, Gary Zukav speaks to this very occurrence. "Psychology means soul knowledge. It means the study of the spirit, but it has never been that....Because psychology is based on the perceptions of the five-sensory personality, it is not able to recognize the soul. It is not able to understand the dynamics that underlie the values and behaviors of the personality. Just as medicine seeks to heal the body without recognizing the energy of the soul that lies behind the health or illness of the body, and, therefore, cannot heal the soul, psychology seeks to heal the personality without recognizing the force of the soul that lies behind the configuration and experiences of the personality, and therefore, also cannot heal at the level of the soul."

Head-heart and mind-body splits have contributed to our distance from direct experience of "soul." Zukav continues, "We have developed an extensive knowledge of the physical apparatus that the soul assumes when it incarnates. We know of amino acids, neurotransmitters, chromosomes and enzymes, but we don't know the soul. We do not know how these physical functions serve the soul or are affected by it...."

In our distance and disconnection from soul, we have neglected our soul-deep needs. "We have not turned our attention to the needs of the soul. We have not considered what is required for the soul to be healthy. We have not studied the soul, or sought to help it attain what is necessary to its evolution and health." That so many people live in a crisis of meaning, searching to discover who they really are, why they are here and what they should be doing reflects our cultural inattention to soul and needs of the soul.

SOUL AND RECOGNITION

In order for us to connect, to know self and other in a deep and authentic way, we need to share and receive the experience of soul. Peter Gabel reflects, "Each of us has a fundamental need to see and be seen by the other in one's humanity. It's a need that's as fundamental as food and shelter. Recognition is not just with the eyes, but with the body. That is why young children die from failure to thrive when they are not held even when they are in the presence of material sustenance. You can see this when you have a child — the awesomeness of the child's capacity to become present to you. The joy in the child's smile and the fact that the child has no need to look away from the other's gaze are awesome reminders of who we once were and who we could become. Our longing for recognition is the longing to emerge from a state of detachment and evasion of each other into a relationship of mutual presence. The experience of becoming present is an experience of vitalizing social connection. I first experienced it as an adult in the consciousness movements of the 1960's."

Soul yearns for recognition — both self-recognition and mutual recognition with others. While the soul needs solitary time for reflection, it also needs interactive time for connection. Perhaps recognition can be explained as an energetic phenomenon, one of resonance. When we connect with our own soul, we feel the vibration of connection and recognition. When one soul meets another soul and connects, there is also an energetic vibration.

I have found that we each have different soul frequencies, and when we meet another being whose frequency matches ours, there is a profound experience of energetic connection. This helps explain why we can meet perfectly nice people with whom we feel no connection, and others with whom organically we feel more resonance and connection. In his book **CARE OF THE SOUL**, Thomas Moore comments, "One of the strongest needs for the soul is for community, but community from the soul point of view is different from its social forms. Soul yearns for attachment, for variety in personality and particularity."

RESTORING OUR CAPACITY AS ORGANS OF PERCEPTION

When we live life from a soul-centered place, we become aware of the deep, rich and nourishing capacities of our senses. After the attempted rape and murder when I was sixteen, I found myself disconnected from my sensual fullness, and embarked on a healing pathway to restore my own sense of soul. The result of my journey was a body-centered, heart-centered psychospiritual therapy method called Emotional-Kinesthetic Psychotherapy. In 1990, I opened a school, the Institute for Emotional-Kinesthetic Psychotherapy to provide a three-year, apprenticeship-based training program in this method.

When the school was in full bloom, we held a meeting of our board of advisors. I often found myself at a loss for language when trying to describe my work to a stranger, because what transpired was soulful, energetic and at a level much deeper than words. A colleague at the meeting, Billie Jo Joy, in response to seeing a video of my work commented, "what you are doing is restoring the human capacity of being organs of perception." "Wow,!" I thought to myself. She had articulated an essential truth. We are indeed sensory beings, and through fully developing our sensory capacity, we do become organs of perception. In our sensory experience is the root of love, intimacy, sexuality and our soul's expression.

The way our world has evolved, we have lost touch with this essential capacity, and we suffer for it. To be able to develop soul-centered relationships with self and others, we need to restore our capacity as organs of perception. We need space, time and guidance to learn about our sensual capacity. We need to learn to be present to ourselves. We need this quality of self-presence to come to know the experience of our own soul. What does it take to create this? Here are some of the answers some of my students came up with:

"Allowing myself to live in the moment"

"Being safe in the moment"

"Giving space to my feelings, whatever they are"

"Trusting the larger whole of things"

"Honoring our feelings"

"Becoming aware of habitual and authentic ways of being"

"Being in the feeling without being the feeling"

"Knowing when your physical body needs something and honoring that need"
"Developing a place of self-love and self-acceptance."

CARING FOR OUR SOULS

To care for the soul is to honor the divine within each one of us. We need to learn to be like geishas to ourselves and each other, looking for the beauty and uniqueness that resides deep within. Some of the things the soul needs include:

1. **Beauty:** Thomas Moore comments, "In a world where soul is neglected, beauty is placed last on its list of priorities. In the intellect-oriented curricula of our schools, for instance, science and math are important studies because they allow further advances in technology. If there is a slash in funding, the arts are the first to go, even before athletics. The clear implication is that the arts are dispensable. We can't live with out technology, but we can live without beauty." Beauty nourishes the soul and often has a sensual dimension. Flowers, a sunset, the White Mountains in New Hampshire reflect beauty not only through their physical form, but also through color, smell, texture and energy.

2. **Ritual:** Ritual embraces both ordinary and special gestures, happenings and things and makes them sacred. Moore notes that ritual enriches life as it "makes the things around us more precious, more worthy of care and protection...In a life animated by ritual, there are no insignificant things." Ritual slows us down and makes us more mindful of the moment, of our actions, and the meaning of even the smallest details of our lives. Rituals can also give structure and attention to important parts of our daily lives.

3. **Peace:** War, conflict and violence are not qualities of soul. Soul offers a deep space of respect for being, for difference and for the interconnection of all living things. In a space of stillness where all parts have their place in the larger web of life, one finds acceptance and peace. Gary Zukav writes, "Brutality shatters the human spirit. The soul cannot tolerate brutality. It cannot tolerate abundances of pain and irrationality. It cannot tolerate being lied to. It cannot tolerate jealousies and hatreds. These are contaminants, poisons for it."

4. **Balance:** A soulful life is one of balance. This includes finding the space and time for both solitary time and relational time, for being and doing, for thinking and feeling, for reflecting and acting. In a soulful life time is savored, and we move at a slow, steady, grounded, organic pace. We can mobilize our resources when needed, without the hypervigilant energy drain of always being "ready."

5. *Heart:* Moore reflects, "Only when the world enters the heart can it be made into soul." I have long believed that if the body is the temple of the soul, the heart is the gateway to the soul. It is through the heart that we connect with our own soul, and the souls of others. Moore comments, "It may be useful to consider love less as an aspect of relationship and more as an event of the soul."

6. *Honoring the body:* Sacred spaces deserve loving attention and care. Since the body is the soul's temple, it deserves loving attention and care. How we eat, move, rest, replenish and cleanse ourselves impacts the soul. Moore reflects, "The body is the soul presented in its richest and most expressive form. In the body, we see the soul articulated in dress, gesture, movement, shape, physiognomy, temperature, skin eruptions, tics, diseases, in countless expressive forms."

7. *Honoring our interconnection:* Moore writes, "Our soul is part of a larger soul of the world, anima mundi. This world soul affects each individual thing whether natural or human-made. You have a soul, the tree in front of your house has a soul, but so too does the car parked under that tree." The soul replenishes itself through the energetic experience of feeling our interconnection with the larger world soul and all living things.

8. *Sensuality and the erotic:* In a soul-centered life, we experience the full receptive and expressive capabilities of our sensuality. We find the erotic in nature: in riding a horse, in tasting the nectar in a flower, in hugging a tree. With the sensual and the erotic comes an aliveness that runs through every cell of our bodies. This current of soul energy invigorates us and sustains us.

9. *Work as vocation:* Soulful work is work we are called to. It is not something we mentally choose, but instead something that finds us, if we allow it to, through the unfoldment of our lives. Soulful work may require effort and focus but it replenishes us as well. It is spiritually lucrative and emotionally fulfilling.

III. *RELATIONSHIPS*

> *"Friends should be permanent. It shouldn't be 'I'm going to move across the country with my wife.' Those messages create the superfluous nature of the other. We can't fully count on the other to be there."*
>
> — Peter Gabel

Human beings have a deep need for connection and relationality. Author Peter Gabel reflects, "Every moment of our lives we are motivated by the fact that we are social beings. We fundamentally long for the presence of mutual affirmation and connection." In our heartwounded state, however, our relational longing is often buried or forgotten.

"Most of our lives we spend in the conditioning of our artificial (socially proscribed) roles. The newscaster is an example, with glazed eyes, detached from the other, deeply withdrawn into the self, presenting an outer persona as if that persona were who he really is. The effect is to deny the other access to the withdrawn inner self who longs to be seen but is terrified to be seen. We become enveloped in a universe of isolation, and are not aware of it at the same time. We protect ourselves by making it unconscious, by denying the longing," comments Gabel.

DISEMBODIED RELATING

In our terror to be seen, it is no surprise that disembodied relating is often more prevalent than embodied relating in today's world. We focus on efficiency, and technology has become our efficiency toolbox. E-mail has taken the place of the handwritten letter, and often the phone call. It is expedient. We can do it quickly and at whatever time works for us. Real-time relating is more cumbersome. It requires that two people synchronize their schedules, even for a phone call.

Face-to-face meetings are the most difficult to arrange because we are so busy. We lose sight of the visceral value of seeing someone face-to-face, being with them. When we are face-to-face or side-by-side, we are in the other person's energy field and they are in ours. We can literally touch and be touched. We can use all of our senses for expression and perception.

As technologically-based relating replaces face-to-face communication, the sensory data available in our exchanges diminishes. The telephone relies primarily on our auditory and intuitive capacities. E-mail allows only an intuitive sensory response, lacking real-time sensory interchange. As we become too busy to sit down for daily face-to-face dinners with the same person or people, we lose both a ritual of communion and sensorily shared presence — from tasting the food to sharing its energy.

I have danced for many years in "partner-dance" communities, where people can dance together for many years and know no more about another person than their first name. My friend Helena once described the "three minutes of intimacy" that people come to receive — connecting on the dance floor for the duration of a song. During that time people meet in the body and touch. The relating ends when the music stops. We learn to live with a string of momentary interactions, like a string of crumbs from a collective loaf of bread. I found this kind of connecting felt like emotional and spiritual one-night stands. While for some, that is a valid way of life, a measured dose of intimacy they can tolerate and even enjoy, for me, "three minutes of intimacy encounters" became painfully empty. How difficult it can be to go deeper with others, and develop a more multidimensional, longer-standing bond.

Gabel notes, "We have a little hole inside of us like a balloon. The experience of mutual recognition, when it occurs, is a feeling of being present to the other and feeling the other in oneself — the completion of self through the other. When we misrecognize each other as we are thrown into false forms of conditioning and artificial roles, the desire for connection doesn't disappear. To the contrary, people become attached to imaginary communities. The right wing offers people fantasies of being part of the unity of the nation. The church and family values symbolize this. We create pseudocommunities that are not characterized by authentic relatedness of I and thou, of authentic presence."

Sometimes I wonder, are full sensory relationships going extinct? We become physically intimate with substances we can eat and drink, making sensual contact with these foods in compensation for the relational sensory contact we really need. It is no surprise that obesity is an epidemic. We turn to comfort foods, instead of the comfort of human sensual contact.

One day I noticed one of my clients talking about "nursing" her cup of coffee. Nursing evokes an image of closeness, the connection between mother and child. Nursing provides a primal sensory comfort. How sad that instead of nursing one another we have chosen socially acceptable durgs like coffee and white sugar to send us on an energetic and emotional/spiritual roller coaster of ups and downs — chemical highs. We have learned to crave the anonymous holding of a substance rather than the personal, relational holding of another human being.

Recently, the *Wall Street Journal* featured an article describing a language that has developed in the business world to allow people to appear as though they were interested in others and making social contact, when their real goal was to avoid any kind of contact. Reading the list of "effective phrases to avoid contact" turned my stomach. This kind of false language may be creative and effective in an impersonal environment, but it violates the deeper needs of soul and reinforces our disconnection from self and other.

Peter Gabel describes the state of contactlessness and disconnection we have normalized as "underneathness." "Many people go through their whole lives where the terror of humiliation dominates the desire to connect to other. People live underneath the world when they are like that, averting their eyes from the other, shrinking back and imagining they are underneath the world that is above them. We create the common experience of a world outside of us full of people peering out at one another. We become one of the others to the other without realizing what we are doing."

MAKING CONTACT

To feed our souls, we need to establish safe, workable ways to connect and make contact with one another. Men and women each have ways of making contact with their own gender and the other gender.

Author Dan Kindlon comments that we often look at male bonding from a female perspective and not a male perspective. This is problematic. "Why do men play cards together? To connect. To BE together. Women put down men playing cards. They don't see the whole inner culture that takes place between men. When guys are playing cards they might not need to raise the stakes so everyone will show up. It's more important to have everyone there than to win all the time. Women won't see this. The key is you are relating in a male way."

Kindlon continues, "Competition is a way of making contact for men. It is making contact on male terms. When male athletes slap each other's butts, they are making contact on male terms. The war bond is the tightest bond men can have. Top male athletes have a strong connection — a team bond. Musical bands have it too. What is important is both relationship and loving the game. The game is a goal we are trying to achieve together, a male version of love. It moves beyond individuality to a sense of the whole, a sense of we."

Carl Greisser, Executive Director of the Mankind Project feels one way men need contact from other men is to challenge each other. "Men need to speak to each other with honesty and really push each other to look at what's at the edge. Men can help each other ask, 'what are we hiding from?' and 'what am I hiding from?'"

Women need similar qualities from men in order to make meaningful contact. Greisser continues, "Men need to show up in their power, with integrity, having outgrown their neediness to the extent they are able to. I think there's safety that men can bring to women when they do that. This is really crucial to women in our culture. Men need to do emotional work with other men to help make this happen."

Likewise, women need to bring empathy, support, challenge and the honesty of their feelings and reactions to men. "This contributes," acknowledges Greisser. "It gives men a sense of safety. When I get the combination of those things from my partner, it makes it easier for me to drop into the truth of my feelings, which is the most difficult thing for me to do, especially with grief and sadness."

Therapist Karen Engebretsen-Larash comments, "Women and men process information differently. Feelings are the same, but men and women think differently. Feelings need to be experienced internally. How they get expressed is another process. There is a lot more latitude for women to display a myriad of feelings and express them. Because socioculturally in American society men aren't supposed to reveal what's really going on inside, they stuff the process down. They don't allow themselves to emote. Unfortunately, this often turns into anger because there is nowhere for that energy to go."

As a woman opens her heart and uses the power of her heart, she creates the safety for others to do the same. It is particularly powerful when men are able to express their true feelings, given the cultural barriers towards authentic emotional expression for men. Engebretsen-Larash notes, "In the men's group I have been running for the past 2-1/2 years, when one of the group members experiences really intense feelings it gives permission for the others to be honest about what is going on inside of them as well." Emotional safety promotes heart opening and sharing, which creates more emotional safety, which promotes more heart opening and sharing. As we open our hearts and share, we connect, making authentic, soul-centered contact.

IV. *COMMUNITY*

> *"We have a spiritual longing for community and relatedness and for a cosmic vision, but we go after them with literal hardware instead of with sensitivity of the heart(e.g. we want to know all about people from far away places, but we don't want to feel emotionally connected to them."*
>
> — Thomas Moore

Community is a basic human need, yet it is so hard to create and sustain in the current state of our culture. We suffer emotionally and spiritually for this. Community is where the collective spirit resides. When we gather together in community, a collective energy comes into being. Because our modern society is characterized and enamored with progress, production, growth and expansion, our eye is on the prize of movement, change, and more, more, more. We become mentally and physically entranced on the gerbil wheel of producing, without realizing either how much energy we are expending or how our lives are monodirectional. Once entranced, we forget there is any other way to live.

Gender reconciliation worker Will Keepins, notes that sadly, "western culture by its very nature destroys community." He cited the work of Helena Norberg-Hodge, a Norwegian woman who did extensive service and activist work in Northern India, and author of the book **ANCIENT FUTURES**. Norberg-Hodge witnessed a deconstruction of a sustainable society due to the impact of western civilization coming in.

Three things tore the culture apart:

1. **Separation of worship and spiritual life from secular life.** Keepins comments, "Suddenly church became something you do on Sundays rather than having spirit integrated into daily life."

2. **Loss of time.** Prior to the infiltration of western culture, people worked 3 - 5 hours each day doing what we call "work." They

spent the rest of their time cultivating community and relationships. Keepins reflects, "They lived in a psychological and cultural wealth available only to the absolute rich in the western world today."

3. **Stratification of relationships by age**. Prior to western culture, everyone related with people of all age groups from infants to elders. People had close personal friends in all age groups. After the arrival of western culture, people only hung out with people in their own age groups.

Keepins notes, "Now middle agers were striving to get ahead and elders were ignored. There was no concept of poverty before western culture arrived. There was no word for it. The whole western culture infected the Northern Indian culture in ways that weren't visible. Western economists said we increased GNP. But social structures that allowed for sustainable relating were systematically deconstructed."

I have watched how it has become increasingly more difficult over the past twenty years to establish and sustain community and on-going relationships. This past weekend my son and I were invited to a pancake breakfast at a friend's house. My friend's son and daughter were there along with friends their ages, as well as two other adult friends. It was fun to be sitting in the kitchen while Chuck was making pancakes and Elisabeth was graciously helping host the breakfast as the kids socialized and a stream of people moved in and out of the kitchen. Even though my son felt a bit shy when we were at the gathering, as we were leaving he told me he had enjoyed himself.

I saw Chuck last night at a choral rehearsal, and thanked him for such a lovely event. He reflected back, "You know, it was really nice having people over to my house. I don't get to do that often anymore." I found myself nodding in agreement. The same was true for me. There was a time where I got together with friends and colleagues for lunch regularly, had dinner guests and more frequent parties. Now, my son's birthday party is the big social event of the year. Everyone is busy, so coordinating schedules is an advanced mathematical equation. And having the time and space just to prepare, cook and entertain seems like more of a luxury. I accept this reality, yet it saddens me.

I watch how I struggle to balance all my different roles and responsibilities, as I attempt to live a simpler life than many Americans. I have great empathy for the juggling my peers and colleagues undertake. If we are to increase our engagement in community, we need to rethink our priorities, goals, values and the institutions we have created that drive our lives. How do we live economically sustainable lives while also investing in relationships and the collective? Is it possible to create a "parallel universe" as described by Peter Gabel, where we step outside the mainstream structures and build models that embody our deeper values? The intentional communities and co-housing movements are two attempts to create new models of community. Both models are attempts to address the issue of sustainable living with social structures that support individuals, families and the collective.

CREATING COMMUNITY: WHERE DO WE BEGIN?

Here are some starting points to build community:

1. **Create emotionally safe, spiritually safe forums where people can speak and listen from the heart.** Speaking and listening from the heart creates a sense of emotional and spiritual community, as people feel safe to tell their truth and let go of the cultural baggage. Will Keepins reflects, "In all the gatherings we do, no matter how juicy the information is, the groups don't want to get back together unless a heart opening happens." When we open our hearts, connect and bond, the impetus is created to continue and develop a collective relationship. At the Institute for Emotional-Kinesthetic Psychotherapy we used the term "community of the heart" to describe what Keepins speaks about.

2. **Experience community in an intentional on-going way.** For people to come together by choice to experience and build community is very powerful. Just as it takes time to establish an intimate relationship, developing a mutually held sense of community also takes time. If a group of people make the commitment to gather together again and again over time, and really get to know and invest in one another, then it is possible to experience intentional community in an on-going way. Churches and other houses of worship used to provide this function, and some still do.

   I am grateful that I am part of several communities that provide a sense of emotional and spiritual continuity. I sing in a choral group called the Mystic Chorale, where members both share a love of music and singing, and have a desire to connect through music. In the Northeast community of the Human Awareness Institute, community members share a commitment to love, intimacy and creating win-win relationships.

3. **Become aware and re-educate ourselves about our responsibility to the collective as well as to ourselves.** Our culture has indeed been individual-oriented, almost to the point of forgetting that the collective exists and that our well-being depends on it. Gender reconciliation worker Molly Dwyer expresses, "Western culture has been enamored with individuality and the rights of the individual. We fear anything with a community base to it. We need to get to a

point where we recognize the interdependence of our phenomena. This education and awareness needs to be integrated into our grade schools, as well as teaching adults how to come together and be with each other in community."

4. **Recognize we need a vision and understanding of community to take care of our loved ones**. Molly Dwyer notes that one of the reasons family structures are so weak is that they don't get our attention. Most of attention gets focused on "work" and earning money. Individuals are just beginning to learn how to stay grounded in self-care as they live their lives on a daily basis. "Community is eroded by everything we are taught to value by the mainstream culture. Possessions and status are what we are told will make us happy. We must separate from the mainstream. This requires a real commitment to pull ourselves out of the mainstream," says Dwyer. This is not easy. Like the frogs in the pot of water where the temperature has slowly risen to the boiling point, human beings are drowning in the mainstream and don't even know it.

CREATING A NEW CULTURE

Many good people are leading projects to help us create a more sustainable culture. I interviewed many such people whose work and words I have included in this book. Jerry Koch-Gonzalez, founder of Spirit in Action is one such person.

When I asked Koch-Gonzalez how to describe Spirit in Action he answered, "We define it as a movement-building organization. That means everything we do is in the context of supporting the social change process to be more effective, more powerful and more meaningful." Spirit in Action's main project is called Circles of Change — a combination training program, dialogue and grassroots think tank. Circles of Change are small groups that meet with each other and explore the connection between spirituality and social change. Koch-Gonzalez explains, "We define spirituality as connection to the whole, not institutionally or religiously based, though it can be for any particular participant. The process in the group is community building, getting to know one another, and exploration of people's activist history, and spiritual understanding or misunderstanding as the case may be."

Koch-Gonzalez feels we rewire society by connecting to other human beings. "You have to have a support group," he reflects. "Part of my inspiration comes from feminist stories of consciousness raising groups. Women came together and asked 'what is going in ourselves and our lives?' 'Why do we feel the way we feel?' They turned what seemed to be personal issues into political issues, reclaiming power in the context of personal support. They integrated the personal and the political in a collaborative way."

What people need to connect is sometimes really small. "Whenever I am involved with giving lectures, when the lecture is done, people need to turn to each other and have a conversation about what happened." That connection with a neighbor or neighbors is a simple, yet profound gesture. "Don't just ask questions of the authority," coaches Koch-Gonzalez. "Think through what you have heard. Reflect it back. Make connections with people around the topic."

Koch-Gonzalez encourages us to form personal alliances at work, at school, and in whatever contexts we are living and working. Support groups provide us with allies. When we innovate, step out of the mainstream, work for positive change or even just speak our truth, it often feels like being a salmon swimming upstream. "An ally will not think you are crazy. They will find your concerns and projects refreshing," comments Koch-Gonzalez.

Peter Gabel recognizes our legal system is one of the major structures underpinning our culture. Peter Gabel served for twenty years as president of New College of California, whose public-interest law school educates lawyers in a socially conscious model where other people are seen as the source of our completion rather than as a threat to our existence that we need to protect our rights against.

Gabel reflects, "Law is considered to be the binding viewpoint that gets articulated through a language of rules and when the culture can use force to intervene in people's lives. So, people come to understand it as binding values, even though the values are submerged in the rules. Contract law is the central structure of economic markets. It defines freedom and equality in terms of arm's length stranger interactions among people who seek to make a profit from each other, instead of a community of people longing to connect and affirm one another, and to open the channel of empathy, compassion and mutual understanding to connect with each other."

"There's nothing in the constitution about heart values. The constitution was a heroic victory of the human spirit, the achievement of individual liberty, the sanctity of the individual mind and body, the right to think your own thoughts and be your own person. That was 200 years ago and was well and good. The challenge now is different — to connect the self with other and not to separate the self from the group."

"What we have created through the achievement of individual liberty as the most binding western value is a world of separation and control, a democracy of strangers, which because of their estrangement, and because the idea of being an individual means separated and at arm's-length from, at odds with another is the essence of the structure of the American law."

As our culture evolves into the era of the soul-centered relationship, our models for law, economics, education, health care and all other social institutions need to evolve from what we have known and what exists today. Gabel describes social movements as a "spiritual movement of being, the spiritual analog of physical movement." As we feel the pull of the evolutionary currents, and experience the tension that comes when our existing structures no longer serve our unfolding needs, individually and collectively we are drawn forth towards what needs to be created next.

V. *GOD*

> *"Until very, very recently, the idea of having a direct, personal relationship with God, complete with two-way communication, was assumed to be fanciful at best — and blasphemous at worst."*

> — Neale Donald Walsch

Earlier in this chapter I described my confusion at the response I received as a little girl when I tried to talk about my experience of soul. I was equally confused when I listened to people talk about the meaning of the word "God." I used to joke that God was Dog spelled backwards, and it was only partially a joke. I experienced God in the beauty of nature, in the energetic connection I felt with dogs, humans and other living beings who could give and receive love, and in the magic of what I learned to call "the spiritual dimension" of life.

Deep down inside I knew that life was a God-given gift, and that having been given that gift, my job was to use it to help people, to make a difference, to make the world a better place, to contribute to the highest good of all. I did not participate in organized religion when I was young, since my family did not have a strong religious orientation, but was curious what it was that the rest of the world did on Saturdays and Sundays.

I went through a time when I visited different houses of worship to see what people did when they were there. I grew up in a town that had ethnic and religious diversity, so I had my chance to explore Greek, Jewish and Catholic religious services just by accompanying my friends to their houses of worship. My high school best friend was Catholic, so I decided to see what it would feel like to go to church with her family every Sunday. In my twenties, I was engaged to a Jewish man who wanted me to take Hebrew lessons to learn about his culture. Being a good sport, I took a semester of lessons, and tried to learn what I could.

What I discovered about organized religions, regardless of the denomination, was that they were based on some fundamental beliefs about how life is and how people are supposed to behave, and that they had rules for good and bad behavior. While I could find value in some of the underlying principles which were common to most belief systems, I was saddened by the separation, judgment and prejudice that permeated individual religions. I watched people make bigoted comments about "Catholics," "Protestants," "Jews," "Muslims," as though there was a competition for which belief system was "right."

Very early, I concluded that organized religion as practiced in our culture often has very little to do with God. I learned to separate "spirituality" from "religion." Many organized religions as I experienced them were rooted in the very dualism that I feel our culture is needing to heal from in its next evolutionary stage. The mind-body, sex-spirit, human-God and good-evil splits felt wrong to me and did not support the oneness and wholeness that I believed was the authentic expression of life. I experienced life as following more of a spiral path than a black and white continuum. I found God in the center of continuums and not at the extremes.

As I experienced both trauma and healing from trauma, I began to believe that a pathway to God is through fully inhabiting our bodies. Embodiment is a spiritual path. Sexuality is a spiritual path. Coming to our senses and feeling our interconnection with the natural world is a spiritual path. Healing the mind-body, sex-spirit, head-heart, human-nature and human-God splits are all parts of our healing path at this next stage of human evolution.

In preparing for a presentation on Sexuality, Spirituality and Gender for a conference last year, I came to realize that one way of looking at our evolutionary task from a spiritual perspective is to look at the place where healing masculine and feminine energies integrates with the place of healing the sex-spirit split. The following diagram illustrates this concept:

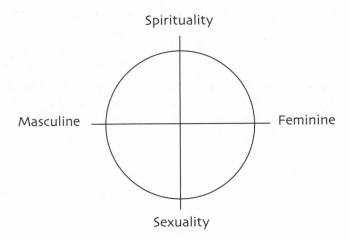

The place in the center of these two continuums is a leverage point for the next phase of human evolution. Evolution follows a spiral path, and at the very top of a spiral is a point of unity, where all the different threads along the way find a place of integration. To restore our spiritual essence and our sense of soul, we need to heal both the sex-spirit split and the masculine-feminine split and find a place of integration. A full relationship with God is a passionate, embodied, sexually expressive, energetically integrated relationship.

In her book **DO I HAVE TO GIVE UP ME TO BE LOVED BY GOD**, Margaret Paul answers the question "what is God?" very thoughtfully: "God is love, and all that love encompasses. God is the source of compassion and truth, peace and serenity, freedom and joy, creativity and beauty, healing and transformation. God is Spirit, consciousness, wisdom and power. God is the learning, evolving and loving force that creates and sustains all of life."

God is the energy inside the spiral path that evolution follows. Life unfolds as God does his/her/our common work along the spiral path. Paul writes, "You can know God only when you can experience God and you experience God when you literally feel within your own physical being the beauty, love and truth that is God." Knowing God is an emotional, energetic, embodied experience. Knowing God is very different than believing in God. Belief is abstract and theoretical. Experience is tangible and palpable, and makes an imprint on our neurological and emotional circuitry.

Earlier in the book I described Jean Liedloff's experience with indigenous people that led her to write **THE CONTINUUM CONCEPT**. She saw, sensed and felt the power of a society where people truly lived in community, and offered collective presence and holding for each child born into the community. The loss of this collective connection, and our subsequent disconnection from the continuum that is life has provided a deep heartwound that has wounded our spirits and obscured our innate right to a sense of connection with God. Paul acknowledges that in our Western culture, from birth, many of us are treated in ways that disconnect us from a direct experience of God. We are abandoned, alone, abused, neglected.. and we translate our experience as being abandoned by God.

Paul tenets we can develop direct knowledge of God either because our parents were able to love us as children in the way we needed to be loved or because we have found ways to heal our spiritual wounding and re-establish a connection with God. She describes characteristics of people who have one way or another come to a place of living with God in their lives:

> ℧ They know that we are all spiritual beings, that our lives are eternal and that our present choices affect our souls. They do not fear death because death transcends the body.

> ℧ They see life on this planet as a gift from God. They have a sense of purpose.

> ℧ They recognize that all of us have the Spirit of God within,...regardless of race, religion, gender or sexual orientation.

> ℧ They see their bodies as temples for their souls. They accept the sacred privilege of caring for them.

🐦 They see our planet as a gift and accept the privilege of keeping it healthy.

🐦 They have faith that God is leading their souls towards the highest good.

🐦 They take personal responsibility for their own pain and joy.

🐦 They set appropriate boundaries against being disrespected, used and abused by others.

🐦 They create balance in their lives, giving themselves time to be alone, time to pray and meditate, time to work, time to play with others, and time to express their creativity, passion, aliveness, joy, laughter and love.

🐦 They operate primarily in the moment, with love, rather than obsessing about the past and projecting it onto the future.

ESTABLISHING AN EMBODIED MODEL FOR LIVING WITH GOD

I realize the model I have presented for knowing and understanding God, an embodied model, is radically different from what many people have learned in religious education of many denominations. We need to evolve a new vocabulary to build a bridge from where we are in our spiritual understanding to where we need to go. The new vocabulary is an evocative vocabulary — one that rings true or resonates deep within, one that touches and moves the listener. What resonates or rings true can be felt in the body, and therefore, can be felt at the soul level. The new vocabulary is one of energy, which is really at the heart of an embodied model of God and at the root of our experience of being alive.

Peter Gabel speaks of this new language. "The nature of how one elicits our common longing has to be evocative, expressive and carry the resonance of metaphor. The body is direct. It is kinesthetic, in the energy field. To speak of the energy field is very difficult without being seen as a flake today. This is an intuitive language. Its capacity for truth depends on its revealing something the other recognizes. It's not making an argument but evoking an essential aspect of existence."

"In the best elements of the religious world this language is understood, like a call and response in churches. We are trying to evoke an inner reality. We rely on the experience of revelation. It is not normal language to talk about the space between us and the denial of desire. These are abstract when seen as concepts. You are trying to convey an experience of recognition, not teach a new set of concepts that people are supposed to memorize as the truth."

Over the years as I struggled to find ways to communicate what Emotional-Kinesthetic Psychotherapy, the heart-centered, body-centered, psychospiritual soul therapy I developed was to the world at large, I discovered I needed to reach people at an emotional, energetic level, just as Gabel describes. I learned to give examples rich in energetic language. I needed to evoke something in them so they could understand from a soul point of view, not a head point of view. To embrace an embodied model for living with God, we need a language that is anchored in the heart, a language of energy and embodiment, not only the head language we are fluent in today.

In closing, the pathway we must follow to steward evolutionary energy is a healing path. Gabel notes, "It cannot be an instantaneous revolution. It has to be a new development of self-awareness that helps us thaw out the fear that separates us." Our evolutionary task is to restore "the magic of seeing the uniqueness and commonness of the human core." The embodied dimension is important in this healing process. The embodied realm is where people are inherently connected at the ground of their existence. Restoring the essential place of the embodied world allows a whole, integrated and vital spirituality.

The www.sacredlands.org has a very poignant and powerful quote, that seems like a fitting way to end this book. "The people of the Earth who are engaged in civilization are lost, and it is our goal to help them find their way home....Imagine a world where community is more important than being a good consumer. Imagine that when you wake up in the morning, you KNOW that you are secure, and that no matter what happens there is an entire community around you that will take care of you....This immanent world view offers cradle to grave security, community and caring." May we find a way both on our own and together, to create a world where we have healed our wounded hearts and reclaimed our core power. This is a world where we live, breathe, work and rest from the soul level up. May we embrace the evolutionary current that is inviting us to bring forth soul-centered relationships, a soul-centered society and a soul-centered way of life.

ESSENTIAL QUESTIONS: *Appreciation*

Appreciation, both giving it and receiving it, nourishes heart, soul and relationships. Too often our energies are focused on what is next rather than what is already with us. As you reflect on these questions, I invite you to take a little quiet time and reflect on what there is to appreciate in yourself and your life. Writing your answers in a journal and sharing them with a friend, partner or group of others is a way to deepen the experience of appreciation.

❦ What do you appreciate about yourself? What do you appreciate about the qualities of soul within you?

- ❧ What do you appreciate about your relationships with friends and loved ones?
- ❧ What do you appreciate about the earth and the natural world?

- ❧ What do you appreciate about community? Are there any communities you are part of right now? What do you appreciate about each community?
- ❧ What do you appreciate about the Great Spirit, the life force or God, however you define it?
- ❧ What do you most appreciate about the gift of life?

MEDITATION AND EXERCISE: *Making Contact*

Take a moment to get comfortable, closing your eyes as long as that is comfortable...taking whatever time and space you need to breathe....letting your chest and belly fill with air as you inhale....and allowing your chest and belly to relax as you exhale....Allowing yourself to be comfortable, and adjusting your position any way you need to be more comfortable...allowing your focus to be with your heart, noticing where you feel your heart when you hear the word "heart."...Take a moment to notice how your heart is feeling physically and emotionally right now...Is it full? Is it empty? Is it heavy? Is it light? Is it separate? Connected? Take a moment to let yourself become a little more familiar with whatever is happening in your heart right now.

And whenever you feel ready keeping your focus with your heart, take a moment to ask yourself the following questions:

- ❧ How do you make contact with your own soul?
- ❧ How do you make contact with others?
- ❧ How do you make contact with the earth and the natural world?
- ❧ How do you make contact with a sense of the collective?
- ❧ How do you make contact with the Great Spirit, life force or God?

Take a moment to let yourself just be with whatever you are sensing thinking, feeling....And whenever you feel ready, allow yourself to very slowly and gently bring your focus back into the room and make some notes about what you experienced during the meditation. You may want to write the meditation questions down on a piece of paper or in your journal, and write answers to each question.

You may also want to consider the following ways of making contact:

❦   making contact through silence

❦   making contact through the senses
     (touching, tasting, smelling, seeing, hearing)

❦   making contact through being receptive and receiving

❦   making contact through being generative and putting forth

❦   making mutual contact

Which of these ways of making contact do you consciously engage in? Which of these ways of making contact feel more comfortable or natural to you? Which ones feels more challenging or difficult? You may want to make notes on these questions, and share them with a friend, a partner or a discussion group.

HeartPower Press
Resources for Personal and Cultural Evolution

Mission Statement

*H*eartPower Press is committed to offering resources to support personal and cultural evolution. We provide tools that invite introspection, dialogue, authentic relationship and community, and contribute towards soul-centered living in a sustainable world. We provide books and materials written from the heart to the heart, addressing the needs of the growing population of Cultural Creatives for a healthy, meaningful, integrated life in these quickening times. We have a special interest in spiritual perspectives on gender, relationship, sexuality, social transformation, self-care and the Earth that serve to guide our journey into new paradigms. ♥

*F*or more information on Heartpower Press

❦ please visit our website at

www.heartpowerpress.com

❦ or send us email at

LSMHEART@aol.com

Resources for the Reader

Books

Anand, Margo, **The Art of Sexual Ecstacy**, Tarcher, 1991.

Anapol, Deborah Taj, **Polyamory**, 1997.

Boylan, Kristi Meisenbach, **The Seven Sacred Rites of Menarche**, Santa Monica Press, 2001.

Boylan, Kristi Meisenbach, **The Seven Sacred Rites of Menopause**, Santa Monica Press, 2000.

Bonheim, Jalaja, **Aphrodite's Daughter**, Fireside, 1997.

Buss, David, **The Evolution of Desire**, Basic Books, 1994.

Carnes, Patrick, **Out of the Shadows**, Hazeldon, 2001.

Carnes, Patrick, **Sexual Anorexia**, Hazeldon, 1997.

Deak, Joanne, **Girls Will Be Girls**, Hyperion, 2002.

Deida, David, **Finding God Through Sex**, Plexus, 2000.

Easton, Dossie and Catherine A. Liszt, **The Ethical Slut**, Greenery Press, 1997.

Eisler, Riane, **The Chalice and the Blade**, Harper, 1988.

Eisler, Riane, **Sacred Pleasure**, Harper, 1996.

Gabel, Peter, **The Bank Teller**, Acada Books, 2000.

Gersh, Aron, **Deeply Touched Inside: Metaphors of Sex and Love**, Human Potential Press, 1990.

Gilmore, David, **Manhood in the Making**, Yale University Press, 1990.

Glendinning, Chellis, **My Name Is Chellis and I'm In Recovery From Western Civilization**, Shambhala, 1994.

Golomb, Elan, **Trapped In the Mirror**, Quill, 1992.

Greenspan, Miriam, **Healing Dark Emotions**, Shambhala, 2003.

Haddon, Genia Pauli, **Uniting Sex, Self and Spirit**, Plus Publications, 1993.

Haidl, Crystal Syben, **Three**, UnConventional Books, 2003.

Heitmiller, David and Jacqueline Blix, **Getting a Life**, Penguin, 1997.

Henderson, Hazel, **Building a Win-Win World: Life Beyond Economic Warfare**, Berrett-Koehler, 1997.

Kaldera, Raven, **Hermaphrodeities**, Xlibris, 2002.

Kindlon, Dan and Michael Thompson, **Raising Cain**, Ballantine Books, 1999.

Kingma, Daphne, **The Men We Never Knew**, Conari, 1993.

Kingma, Daphne, **The Future of Love**, Broadway Books, 1998.

Kipnis, Aaron, **Knights Without Armor**, Tarcher, 1991.

Kowalski, Gary, **Souls of the Animals**, Stillpoint, 1999.

Lerner, Gerda, **The Creation of Patriarchy**, Oxford University Press, 1986.

Levine, Judith, **Harmful to Minors**, University of Minnesota Press, 2002.

Liedloff, Jean, **The Continuum Concept**, Addison-Wesley, 1977.

Marks, Linda, **Living With Vision: Reclaiming the Power of the Heart**, Knowledge Systems, 1989.

Marks, Linda, **The EKP Study Guide**, Institute for EKP, 1990.

Miller, Niela, **Counseling in Genderland**, DIfferent Path Press, 1996.

Montagu, Ashley, **Touching: The Human Significance of the Skin**, Harper and Row, 1986.

Moore, Thomas, **Care of the Soul**, Perennial, 1994.

Ogden, Gina, **Women Who Love Sex**, Womanspirit, 1999.

Paul, Margaret, **Do I Have to Give Up Me to Be Loved by God**, Health Communications, 1999.

Paul, Margaret, **Inner Bonding**, Harper-Collins, 1992.

Pearsall, Paul, **The Heart's Code**, Broadway Books, 1998.

Picucci, Michael, **The Journey Toward Complete Recovery**, North Atlantic Books, 1998.

Real, Terry, **I Don't Want to Talk About It**, Fireside, 1997.

Real, Terry, **How Can I Get Through to You**, Scribner, 2002.

Resnick, Stella, **The Pleasure Zone**, Conari, 1997.

Russek, Linda and Gary Schwartz, **The Living Energy Universe**, Hampton Roads, 1999.

Sadker, Myra and David Sadker, **Failing at Fairness**, Touchstone, 1995.

Sheehy, Gail, **Passages**, Bantam, 1977.

Small, Jacquelyn, **Awakening in Time**, Eupsychia, 2001.

Surrey, Janet, and Samuel Shem, **We Have to Talk**, Basic Books, 1999.

Walsch, Neale Donald, **Conversations With God**, Putnam, 1999.

Welwood, John, **Journey of the Heart**, Perennial, 1996.

Zukav, Gary, **The Seat of the Soul**, Fireside, 1989.

Journals

Spirituality and Sexuality
Publisher: Ani Colt
3 Central Avenue, Newton, MA 02460
www.spiritualityandsexuality.com
anicolt@aol.com

Gaian Voices
Publisher: Susan Meeker-Lowry
RR1 Box 84, Fryeburg, ME 04037
smlowry@pivot.net

Organizations and Trainings

Beyond the Machine www.beyondthemachine.org
Getting a Life www.gettingalife.com
HeartPower Press www.heartpowerpress.com
Heart Science Foundation www.heartsciencefoundation.com
Inner Bonding www.innerbonding.com
Insight Seminars wwwinsightnewengland.org
Institute for Emotional-Kinesthetic Psychotherapy www.healingheartpower.com
The Body Electric www.bodyelectric.org
The Human Awareness Institute www.hai.org
The Mankind Project www.mkp.org
Sacredlands www.sacredlands.org
Shalom Mountain www.shalommountain.com

Index

Diagrams and Charts

Meditations and Exercises

People

Key Ideas